Harry Kelsey is the author of *Sir Francis Drake: The Queen's Pirate* and *Sir John Hawkins: Queen Elizabeth's Slave Trader*.

'Philip as King of England has hitherto been a rather overlooked figure in English history. This book is a timely attempt to place him centre stage.' – *Anna Whitelock, author of* **Mary Tudor: England's First Queen.**

Philip of Spain King of England

THE FORGOTTEN SOVEREIGN

HARRY KELSEY

I.B. TAURIS

LONDON · NEW YORK

Published in 2012 by I.B.Tauris & Co Ltd
6 Salem Road, London W2 4BU
175 Fifth Avenue, New York NY 10010
www.ibtauris.com

Distributed in the United States and Canada Exclusively by Palgrave Macmillan
175 Fifth Avenue, New York NY 10010

ISBN: 978 1 84885 716 2

A full CIP record for this book is available from the British Library
A full CIP record is available from the Library of Congress

Library of Congress Catalog Card Number: available

Designed and typeset by 4word Ltd, Bristol
Printed and bound in Sweden by ScandBook AB

Contents

Illustrations and Maps

Illustrations

Maps

Illustration Credits

All of the outline maps were made by the author. Other illustrations are from the collections of the Huntington Library, except as noted below:

Abbreviations

AGS	Archivo General de Simancas
AGI	Archivo General de Indias
BL	British Library
CDIE	*Colección de documentos inéditos para la historia de España*
HMC	Historical Manuscripts Commission (National Archives)
ODNB	*Oxford Dictionary of National Biography*
PRO	Public Record Office (National Archives)

Preface

When Mary Tudor came to the English throne in 1553, she was a spinster, somewhat elderly (late thirties) for the time, and anxious to restore the practice of the Catholic faith that had been her one consolation during a bitterly conflicted youth. Much earlier, while she was still a child, Mary had been promised in marriage to her cousin Charles, who was both King of Spain and Holy Roman Emperor. Now facing old age, Charles suggested that she instead marry his son. Philip was a widower, more than ten years Mary's junior, and currently serving as regent during his father's absence from Spain. Mary accepted, an agreement was signed, and in the course of time Philip and Mary were married. Thus began a curious period when a Spanish king shared the throne of England.

This study began during research for biographies of Sir Francis Drake and his cousin Sir John Hawkins. Both sailed in English ships when Philip was King of England. Drake later gained fame as Philip's archenemy. Hawkins, somewhat older than his cousin, claimed to have served Philip and later became deeply involved in curious negotiations with Philip over men in his fleet who languished in Spanish prisons. If all this arouses your curiosity, it certainly did the same for me, and I resolved to find out more.

The research was made possible through generous grants from the Giles W. and Elise G. Mead Foundation and the support of my own institution, the Huntington Library. Much of the material comes from the superb rare book and manuscript collections of the Huntington, as well as the British Library, and various other institutions. Other materials were consulted in Spanish archives, most notably the Archivo General de Simancas, whose staff do everything possible to make historical research a pleasure.

Several scholars have made helpful suggestions, including Robert T. Smith and Robert Keane. Robert Ritchie read the entire manuscript, as did Joanna Godfrey; both of them offered corrections and otherwise kept me from embarrassing errors.

Introduction

The maestre de campo *ordered the firing of muskets and arcabuces. When the enemy saw this, they fired back. Our own men called them cowards and said ugly things about their lack of spirit, calling them Lutheran chickens.*

Pedro Coco Calderón

On the morning of 20 July 1588 English lookouts standing on the cliffs near Plymouth spotted a great Spanish armada sailing up the coast. There were perhaps 130 ships, the largest fleet assembled in the Channel in more than thirty years. The Great Armada was a message of war sent by King Philip of Spain.

As the Spanish fleet made its way up the coast there were running fights and losses on both sides, including Francis Drake's capture of a Spanish pay ship. But the first real battle came on the twenty-ninth in the roadstead off Calais, with gunners on both sides firing at such close range that cannoneers could shout and curse at their enemies while reloading for another shot. For nine hours the battle raged, while the fleets drifted east between Gravelines and Ostend.[1]

In the course of the battle both the Spanish and the English ships felt for the first time the real effect of the enemy artillery. The Spanish flagship took more than a hundred hits in her hull, masts, and sails, with several shots below the waterline that caused serious leaks. Two Spanish galleons, hoping to grapple with the enemy, worked their way past the battle line and into a nest of English ships. In the melee one galleon had five guns put out of action, decks very nearly destroyed, pumps broken, and rigging in shreds. Nevertheless, her captain broke out the grappling hooks and challenged the English sailors to come alongside for a fair fight. When they would not, his crew shouted out that they were "cowards" and "Lutheran chickens" and drove the English ships away with musket fire.[2] There was serious damage on the English side as well, but luck was on the English side.

At the end of the fight most of the Spanish ships were in reasonably sound condition, but the invasion army that was to meet the fleet on the coast was not ready. Consequently the Spanish commander had to abandon the plan to invade England. During the next week the Spanish Armada was caught in the fierce Channel winds and driven into the North Sea where the real destruction began. Battered by storms, the ships made their way northward around Scotland. About half of the Armada was lost on the long voyage home, many driven ashore on the coasts of Scotland and Ireland. Thus, by hard fighting and good luck an English fleet managed to end the threat of invasion by the Spanish king who had once been King of England.

Exactly thirty-four years earlier Philip of Spain had brought an armada of similar size to England, where he received a lavish welcome. The difference was that he came as a bridegroom, ready to meet his royal bride. In a proxy marriage just a few months before, this Spanish prince had become the husband of Queen Mary Tudor and, by treaty, King of England. How could that have happened? Philip was a foreigner; could England have welcomed a foreign ruler? Beyond that, Philip was staunchly Catholic, and Mary's father, Henry VIII, had assumed the role of head of the church in England.

There were other problems. Philip was young, fair-haired, a father, and a widower. Mary was much older and though once considered pretty, she was no longer thought to be terribly attractive. From childhood Mary had been betrothed to a succession of royal suitors, but now she was in her late thirties, still a virgin, and thought to be past marriageable age. Still, she was Catholic, a pious girl who hoped to bring England back into the Catholic fold.

When Philip began his formal education, humanism was transforming the intellectual life of Europe. Philip studied under some of the outstanding humanistic scholars of Spain. He read widely in two or three languages, though he never developed the linguistic ability of the father whose empire he hoped to inherit. Introduced to government Councils at an early age, Philip acquired administrative skills that were probably unmatched in European rulers of his day. He also traveled across Europe and developed a familiarity with diplomatic relations among the ruling families.

Mary, for her part, also studied under humanist scholars and developed a respectable skill in languages. However, she was never close to her father, nor was she trained in government and administration. In an age of religious upheaval Mary was a religious traditionalist, and Philip was as well. Both had keen minds and were quick to learn. Both expected to be married as part of an arrangement meant to promote national and dynastic interests.

Love was not supposed to be part of the relationship between royal husbands and wives. If love developed during the course of a royal marriage, it might be an asset, or it might not. If one party was in love, while the other was not, problems could occur. This seems to have been the case when Philip was King of England and Mary was Queen.

Three questions capture our attention. How did a Spanish prince become King of England? Once there, why did he leave? And how did things go so badly awry afterwards that his next fleet came in full battle array? The answers are not simple, but they are interesting. A good place to start might be the education of the two royal lovers, Philip and Mary.

Chapter 1

A Spanish Prince and an English Princess

> *It has pleased Our Lord to deliver the Empress, my very dear and very beloved wife. Today, Tuesday the twenty-first of the present month, she gave birth to a son. I hope in God that he will prove to be of service for you and for the great good of these kingdoms.*
>
> Charles V

At a little after four in the afternoon, while the rain came down in torrents, the bells of the church of San Pablo de Valladolid started ringing wildly. At the signal other bells in the city joined one by one. Across the narrow street in the great house of Bernardino Pimentel, the young Empress Isabel had just given birth to a son. The new father, Emperor Charles V, waited just long enough to hold the baby in his arms, then handed him back to the nurse. With his whole court Charles then marched through a temporary wooden passageway connecting the house to the church of San Pablo, where the choir monks sang a *Te Deum*. Once the service ended, the emperor signed a proclamation addressed to each of the cities of Castile, announcing the royal birth: "It has pleased Our Lord to deliver the Empress, my very dear and very beloved wife. Today, Tuesday the twenty-first of the present month, she gave birth to a son. I hope in God that he will prove to be of service for you and for the great good of these kingdoms. I pray to Him that

1

it may be so and that I may better serve you, as this is what I have longed for."[1]

The date was 21 May 1527. Just ten years earlier, when Charles first arrived in Valladolid, he was a stranger, speaking little and understanding less of the Castilian tongue. Born and raised in the Netherlands, Charles was an outsider in Spain, unwelcome in the country he had come to rule. Though scarcely seventeen years of age, he was already ruler of the Netherlands, Duke of Burgundy, and Archduke of Austria, all titles inherited from his father, Philip the Handsome. The thrones of Spain were his by inheritance from his grandfather, Ferdinand of Aragon; but he was a foreigner, and the Spanish nobility was reluctant to welcome him. In fact, they preferred his younger brother Ferdinand, who had been born and raised in Spain, knew the language, and understood all the local ways. Perhaps worst of all, Charles brought with him a full complement of Flemish supporters, who proceeded to grab the most lucrative offices in church and government. Spanish discontent became so severe that the *Cortes de Castilla* finally presented Charles with a list of eighty-eight demands, including these: get married and produce a Castilian heir to the throne; stop appointing foreigners to office; and learn the Castillian language in order to speak to people and understand what they have to say. To this last Charles replied: "We will try very hard to do it."[2]

Discontent grew during the next year, and reached a peak when Charles left the country to take up the imperial crown. Then a general revolt swept the towns of Castile, not finally suppressed for another two years. When Charles returned, he imprisoned some of the remaining offenders, executed the worst, and pardoned the rest.[3]

Midst all the turmoil of ruling the Netherlands and the Holy Roman Empire, Charles worked very hard to keep his promise to the cortes. He learned the language of Castile, gave key appointments to local people, married, and produced an heir. It took a decade, but Charles finally became undisputed ruler, and Philip was his heir. There were grand celebrations in Valladolid and elsewhere, when the little prince was baptized on 5 June 1527 in a wonderful ceremony at the church of San Pablo.[4]

Fig. 1   Charles, King of Spain, in 1521

A story, passed through the Dormer family of England, gives some insight into the religious rivalries in Valladolid, as well as the Spanish royal baptismal protocol. The royal rooms were in the house of Bernardino Pimentel. This grand structure lay next to the plaza that fronted the great church of San Pablo. The main gate of this dwelling faced toward a Dominican convent, a smaller church in a less prestigious parish. However, a tall window in the royal suite faced the plaza of San Pablo, and it became the door of a special passageway built to connect the house and the church. Suitably decorated for the occasion, the temporary hallway brought the baptismal procession to the church, without the need to enter the confines of the other parish. The little prince was carried in the arms of Don Iñigo de Velasco, *condestable* de Castilla and duque de Béjar, who was godfather. He was accompanied by the emperor's sister, Leonora, widowed Queen of Portugal and Queen of France, who was godmother. At the door of the church the entourage was met by Alonso de Fonseca, archbishop of Toledo, along with other bishops and dignitaries. Following an ancient formula, these worthies asked the godparents what they wanted. Answering for the prince, they replied that they wanted baptism. The archbishop then proceeded with the ceremony, during which the infant cried, as infants are wont to do. Afterwards the King of Arms introduced the new heir by three times proclaiming him: "*Don Felipe por la gracia de Dios, Príncipe de Spaña.*" After a solemn *Te Deum* the royal entourage returned to the house of Bernardino Pimentel, and the infant prince went back to bed.[5]

Meanwhile in England a young princess, a distant relation of the Spanish heir, suddenly found court life much less congenial than it had been. Born on 18 February 1516, Mary was the child of Henry VIII of England and his wife Katherine of Aragon.

Henry expected his wife to produce a male child to inherit his throne. During the first decade of their marriage Katherine was pregnant at least six times, producing both boys and girls, but Mary was the only one who survived infancy. Thus Mary was heir to the throne of England. She was a pretty little girl, and Henry loved her. But she was not the son that Henry wanted as his heir, so Mary often suffered from her father's cold indifference.

While Mary was still a child Henry began to use her as pawn in international diplomacy. At the age of two she was promised to the heir to the throne of France, at the age of six to Charles himself, who was her cousin, and at the age of nine to a younger son of the French king.[6]

When they were first married, Katherine was certainly a pretty girl, but her beauty faded as time passed. In any case, Henry was never inclined to be a faithful husband, and his ever-roving eye lit upon a succession of mistresses and temporary lovers. One of the young ladies actually produced a son, who was christened Henry and supplied with the honorific Fitzroy. When it became more and more likely that Katherine would not bear a son, Henry began to treat the boy as though he might possibly inherit the throne, leaving Katherine and Mary to brood in isolation. On the other hand, the mother of young Henry Fitzroy found herself abandoned for a new prospect who had caught the king's fancy. This young woman, Anne Boleyn, keeping in mind the fate of her predecessors, made it plain to the king that she wanted a husband and not just a lover. Henry, for his part, began to think that if he married Anne, she might be able to give him a legitimate son. Therefore, he determined to end his marriage to Katherine.[7]

As a Catholic, Henry could not divorce his wife, but if their marriage were invalid, he was free to marry Anne. Henry began to think the marriage to Katherine was invalid. As a young girl Katherine had been married to Henry's older brother Arthur. However, Arthur died at the age of fifteen, and Katherine then married Henry. So there was his solution: if Katherine's earlier marriage to her husband's brother had been consummated, then by canon law there was a relationship of affinity between them, and they could not marry. At the time their marriage was arranged the problem did not seem to be insurmountable, for Katherine swore that she was still a virgin (and Henry later boasted that this was indeed true). But just to be on the safe side, Henry's negotiators secured a papal dispensation for affinity before the wedding took place. It was a small point, but there was another, less serious and equally obscure: the canonical impediment of "public honesty," arising from the fact that a previous marriage had been contracted.

Fig. 2   Katherine of Aragon

This was not considered a problem at the time, and the marriage negotiators seemingly considered that it was unnecessary for the dispensation to cover that point.[8]

Eighteen years later, increasingly anxious to take Anne Boleyn to his bed, Henry said that these and other matters made him doubt the validity of the papal dispensation. Gathering his expert theologians and canon lawyers Henry began to say that Katherine had not come to him as a virgin and that in any case the papal dispensation was insufficient to overcome the various difficulties. Then Henry introduced a novel argument. He claimed that a verse in Leviticus forbade him to marry his brother's wife: "And if a man shall take his brother's wife, it is an unclean thing: he hath uncovered his brother's nakedness; they shall be childless."[9] On its face, this was a weak argument, based on a verse of scripture that was ambiguous at best,[10] for Katherine was not a wife but a widow. And other verses in scripture, cited in the annulment of Katherine's marriage to Arthur, seemed to encourage marriage with a brother's widow.[11] It is not clear why Henry chose this verse as the basis for his appeal.

In the end, the pope refused to annul the marriage between Henry and Katherine. Thereupon, in some haste, Henry married Anne, and got a new archbishop to annul his marriage to Katherine. In the course of events Katherine was deprived of her royal status, and Mary was declared illegitimate, no longer eligible for succession to the throne.[12] Within a few months the new queen gave birth to a girl, Elizabeth. Though disappointed again in trying to produce a son, Henry had little choice but to welcome Elizabeth as the new heir to the throne.

The pope responded to all this with a bull of excommunication against the English king. Henry then had Parliament declare that the king was supreme head of the Church of England. Thus, with a few rash moves Henry managed to reject and humiliate both Mary and her mother, in the process alienating himself from most of Catholic Europe and plunging England into more than a century of turmoil.

It was a period of agony for Mary, who was barely in her teens when Henry began living openly with Anne.[13] Childhood for a royal heir was never uninterrupted bliss, but Mary's youth was more troubled than most. Separated from the loving care of her mother, and denied the attention of her father, she became morose and disillusioned. Kept away from the court, she was never able to observe how the country was governed. Instead, she learned that courts were places of favoritism and intrigue, a useful lesson, but not sufficient training for a future queen.

In fact, Mary was not educated to become a ruling queen. Rather, she was taught to develop her mind in such a way as to strengthen her practice of the virtues of chastity and charity, the chief marks of a good woman. Governing was best left in the hands of men. Mary was trained only to be a good wife for a king and a good mother for a prince.[14] From time to time there was talk that she might inherit the throne, perhaps allowing her husband to do the work of governing, but by the time she was twenty this seemed to her like a distant possibility. She had sufficient grace and charm that various lesser princes sought her hand. But nothing came of these negotiations, and Mary began to realize that Henry would never allow her to marry. The reasons were not hard to find: a foreign match would bring with it the threat of invasion and foreign rule, while a marriage at home might well split the kingdom between rival claimants to the throne.[15]

When the time came to begin Mary's formal education, the choice of a tutor was left in Katherine's hands. Even though there were scholars of great stature in England, Katherine looked abroad for help. With some prompting from Sir Thomas More she became the friend and patroness of Juan Luis Vives, a Spanish humanist teaching at the University of Louvain. In 1521 Vives had completed a study of Augustine's *City of God* and dedicated it to Henry VIII. Very soon thereafter, with some prompting from More, Henry made a small annual grant to Vives. The new pension arrived just in the nick of time for Vives, who had lost his patron at Bruges.[16] A little later Vives completed a new book, *De institutione fœminæ Christianæ*, and dedicated the work to Katherine, suggesting that it be used in directing the study of the young princess.[17] This was not just gratitude on the part of Vives. He hoped that the dedication would move the queen to increase his stipend and invite him to stay in England.

LVDOVICVS VIVES VALENTINVS
Splenduit in terra gelidam quæ respicit Arcton
Natum fœlici sydus in Hesperia:
filius ac totum radij effulsere per Orbem
Viues doctrina & quos tulit & pietas.

B s

Fig. 3   Juan Luis Vives, Mary's tutor

England, 1523, Mary's education

By this time Mary was seven years old. Vives wrote in his book that a child should start reading somewhere between the ages of four and seven. If his words were framed to fit the little princess, as they probably were, then Mary may already have begun to read. At the same time, her mother was very likely showing Mary how to spin and sew and to perform other domestic duties. Katherine herself had learned these skills from her own mother, Isabel, and Vives said that such work was as fit for "a pri[n]cesse or a quene" as for any other woman.[18]

So what was the point of learning for a woman? In the mind of Vives, Mary could have no better example than the three daughters of Thomas More. Their father had considered learning as the foundation of goodness and chastity. Mary should not just learn "uoyd uerses, nor wanton or triflynge songes, but some sad sentence, prudent and chaste, taken out of holy scripture, or the sayenges of philosophers." Beyond this, given Mary's lively mind, she might properly be encouraged to study Latin and to read the works of the church fathers and Aristotle and Plato as well.[19]

In 1523, with no new grant forthcoming, unable to support himself at Louvain, and under some pressure from his family, Vives decided to return to Spain. Making one last try for a subvention from the English crown, Vives stopped in London on his way home. There he was welcomed by Cardinal Thomas Wolsey, who arranged forthwith that he should have a teaching post at Oxford. Later in the year Henry and Katherine went to Oxford for an unprecedented visit with the Spanish scholar. On this occasion Vives gave the queen a copy, perhaps in manuscript, of his new treatise on the education of children, *De ratione studii puerilis*. In the introduction to the work Vives recalled that the queen had asked for a brief program of study that Mary's tutor might follow in instructing the young princess. This was his response. Katherine must have been pleased, because she invited the scholar to spend the Christmas holidays with the royal family, which he did.[20]

In the summer of 1524 Vives completed a list of maxims entitled *Satellitium siue symbola*.[21] He dedicated this to Princess Mary

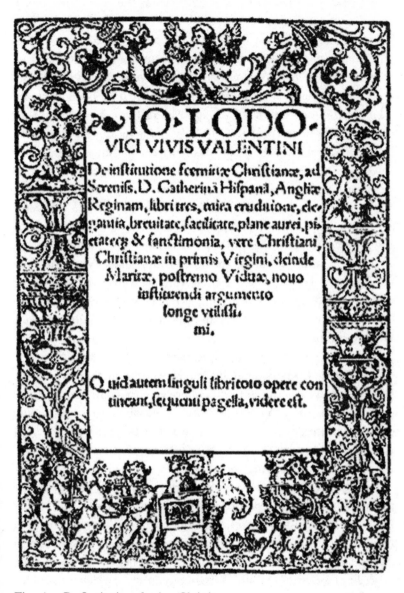

IO·LODO·
VICI VIVIS VALENTINI

De inftitutione fœminæ Chriftianæ, ad
Sereniff. D. Catherinā Hifpanā, Angliæ
Reginam, libri tres, mira eruditione, elegantia, breuitate, facilitate, plane aurei, pi-
etatecꝗ & fanctimonia, vere Chriftiani,
Chriftianæ in primis Virgini, deinde
Mariæ, poftremo Viduæ, nouo
inftituendi argumento
longe vtiliffi-
mi.

Quid autem finguli libri toto opere con
tineant, fequenti pagella, videre eft.

Fig. 4   *De Institutione fœminæ Christianæ*

and admonished her to make these maxims the rule of her life. It seems pretty clear that Mary did this – as her maids-in-waiting later attested – especially the first and the last: *Scopus vitae Christus*; and *Mente deo defixus*. When she became queen, Mary ordered that number 91, *Veritas, temporis filia*, be placed on her seal and her coins.[22]

Largely because of these books dedicated to Katherine and Mary, it is often said that Vives was Mary's tutor. If so, it was only for a brief period. From the time of his arrival in England to his final departure in 1528, there were only six or eight months when Vives could possibly have been in Mary's company. On several occasions Katherine seems to have asked Vives to become Mary's tutor, but he apparently did not do so until November 1527, when he returned to England and perhaps then began to teach Latin to the young princess. This brief period came to an abrupt halt in February 1528, when Cardinal Wolsey had Vives put in confinement because of his friendship with Katherine and his opposition to the divorce. Upon his release, Katherine advised Vives to leave England, and he did so without delay. A few months later Katherine wrote to ask Vives to represent her interests in the divorce proceedings before Cardinals Wolsey and Campeggio. Vives declined, saying that he felt Mary should not dignify the proceedings with her presence. Katherine considered this a betrayal and never forgave him for it. Thus, in trying to take a middle position on the divorce question, Vives lost the friendship of both royal patrons. In short order he was deprived of his pension, and he never returned to England.[23]

Rather than himself serving as tutor to the princess, Vives recommended the Oxford scholar and humanist, Richard Fetherston, who was schoolmaster to the princess from about 1525 to 1533 or thereabouts. Fetherston also served as chaplain to Katherine and was one of two who did represent her in the divorce proceedings. Because of his public opposition to the divorce and his later refusal to take the oath of supremacy Fetherston was imprisoned in 1534. After a long imprisonment he was taken in 1540 to Smithfield, where he was hanged, drawn, and quartered.[24]

One instructor who did not oppose the divorce was Giles Du Wes. At Henry's request he served Mary as French tutor, just as he had Henry himself and his brother Arthur as well. Mary was so taken with the French lessons devised by Du Wes that in about 1540 she ordered them to be published. That she was still studying with Du Wes seems clear from his introductory remark that "I have her so so [sic] taught and do teache dayly."[25]

Mary's skill with languages is well documented. By 1527, when she was only eleven years old, Mary could converse readily in French, Italian, and Latin.[26] Her skill in Latin improved so much that in the early 1540s, when Henry's current queen, Katherine Parr, decided to commission a translation of the Paraphrases of Erasmus, she asked Mary to do the English rendering of St. John's gospel. Mary agreed to do so, but ultimately regretted the decision. Nicolas Udall was chosen as editor of the English version, and as copies of the various gospels became available, the anti-Catholic diatribes in his introductions caused great offense to faithful Catholics. Apparently not wishing to cause offense herself, Princess Mary refused to deliver her manuscript, telling the queen that it was not sufficiently polished for publication. In reply the queen suggested that the chaplain, Francis Malet, could put it into shape. Finally, Mary said that she did not want the work to appear under her name.[27] Seemingly for this reason the first printing contained her translation of John's gospel, but it was unattributed and lacked an introduction. In later printings Mary's translation was introduced by Udall, with lavish praise for Queen Katherine, for Mary, and for scholarly women in general, but without Udall's usual caustic references to the pope and the Catholic Church.[28]

Chapter 2

Training a Prince to Rule an Empire

*Defend the faith; never allow heresy to enter your
kingdom; support the Holy Inquisition; and
insist that your officials perform their duties
well and administer justice fairly.*

Charles V

While the English queen struggled to educate her daughter in
the court of a philandering king, Isabel, the wife of the emperor,
met an equally daunting challenge in the Spanish court. When
Charles left in 1529 on imperial business, the empress and young
Prince Philip stayed behind, along with little Princess Maria, born
just thirteen months after her brother.[1] For several years the
court was composed mainly of women whose husbands, fathers,
and brothers had gone with the emperor. If we can believe the
account of a gossipy bishop, neither the ladies nor the gentlemen
lacked for company. Antonio Guevara reported that young men
flocked to the court and found a friendly reception. Apparently
the court ladies expected their absent husbands to misbehave,
and they seemed determined to even the score. As the good
prelate noted, the ladies of the Spanish court were like the
daughters of Israel, when "seven women threw themselves at a
single man." Philip was only five at the time, but the bishop's
remarks indicate the sort of court in which the boy and his

younger sister grew up, with young men and women laughing and flirting all around.[2]

But the bishop exaggerated. While the temper of the Spanish court was not exactly monastic in those days, most of the people behaved themselves. The most serious offense seems to have been committed by two young lovers who married without royal permission. When the news broke, the young man fled the country, and the girl went to a convent, at least for a time. The marriage was later nullified, not because the pair lacked royal permission, but because the girl was too young to marry.[3]

The Spanish royal family was reunited in Barcelona on 22 April 1533, when Charles and his entourage returned to Spain. During his absence Isabel had taught Philip to be courteous and obedient, but she did nothing to begin his formal education. So Philip had reached his seventh birthday before Charles signed a proclamation on 1 July 1534, ordering Juan Martínez Silíceo to take charge of the boy's education.[4] Silíceo was soon joined by a cadre of additional tutors: the great mathematician Honorato Juan de Valencia; the famous humanist Juan Ginés de Sepúlveda; the instructor of the pages Bernabé de Busto; Cristóbal Calvete de Estrella, who taught the prince in Silíceo's absence; and several others.[5] The prince was also given a separate household, under the direction of Juan de Zúñiga and his wife Estefanía de Requeséns. Lest the boy lack for suitable company, their son Luis de Requeséns became his constant companion.[6] The two boys were never lonely, for several dozen other pages were attached to the household, at least some of the boys attending classes with the prince.[7]

There is an interesting story about the proliferation of pages in Philip's household. One day, as he was riding through town with his tutor, a woman approached and asked him to accept her son as a page. The little prince replied that he could not, because he already had too many pages. When the woman kept insisting, the boy said in annoyance: "Look for another prince; the streets are full of them." This sort of behavior often annoyed the queen, and at times she lost her temper, spanking the little boy, and causing her ladies to weep in sympathy.[8]

Fig. 5   Philip's mother, Isabel of Portugal

Philip liked boyish games – jousting (at least once with burning candles), wrestling, and riding. He hunted with falcon and with crossbow, bagging rabbit, hare, deer, wild boar, and any other animal he could find roaming his father's forests.[9] He could sit in the saddle for hours at a time returning at the end of the day still fresh, while his instructor was exhausted. "While he went out and returned in a litter, he rode horseback on the mountain for a good six hours," said Zúñiga. "To him it seemed like two hours; to me like twelve."[10]

Philip especially depended on the companionship of his friend Luis. One day when Luisito did not appear as early as Philip thought he should, the little boy threw a rock at his window, hitting his friend in the face. Luisito was more surprised than hurt, but Philip immediately dropped the stones he had left in his hand and consoled his friend saying he would not throw rocks at him any more.[11] On another occasion Philip himself was injured while trying to separate two boys who were fighting with sticks and daggers. In the process he received a little cut on the cheek, just below the eye. Wounding a prince was serious business. There was talk of severe

17

consequences for the combatants, who were both imprisoned for a time. But Philip insisted that he was not hurt, and it appeared that his injury did not actually come from a dagger. Even so, the pages learned that the prince was to be treated somewhat differently from the other boys at court.[12]

As the royal court moved frequently about the kingdom, Philip managed to catch and recover from an array of childhood diseases. It is not possible to be certain just what all of them were, but none seem to have been terribly serious. At the age of nine he had a mild case of *viruelas*. This was probably chickenpox, which was prevalent among children of Madrid, where the royal family was then staying.[13] At various other times he suffered from scabies, recurrent fevers, dysentery, and constipation.[14] It is difficult to say much with certainty about these childhood diseases, which were reported frequently to Charles. Menéndez Pidal thinks they were "more important than Silíceo would admit." Some authors tend to believe that Philip was a sickly child. Others do not. In any case, his illnesses do not appear to have been more frequent or serious than those of the other pages at court.[15]

The royal physician, Villalobos, treated the diseases with the usual remedies of the sixteenth century, including purges and bleeding,[16] but he also prescribed a diet that he thought would help ward off the worst ailments. For the most part, this consisted of meat: chicken, fried and roasted; partridge, beef, and venison; along with soup, salad, bread, and the occasional bit of fish, as well as fruits and vegetables.[17] In particular, he advised moderation at meals, and young Philip seems to have complained at times about not being able to eat as much as he would have liked.[18] In any case, the diet was not so different from that served at his mother's table: salt beef, menudo, soup, and various game and domestic fowl (doves, geese, capons, ducks, partridges, and pheasants), plus winter melons, blancmange, pastry, cake, and "various other delicacies."[19]

Though his father had given him a separate household in 1535, Philip did not really live apart from his mother and his two sisters, with whom he was always very close. For this reason, he was devastated when the queen died, on the first of May 1539. Charles determined that her burial should be in the tomb of the Catholic

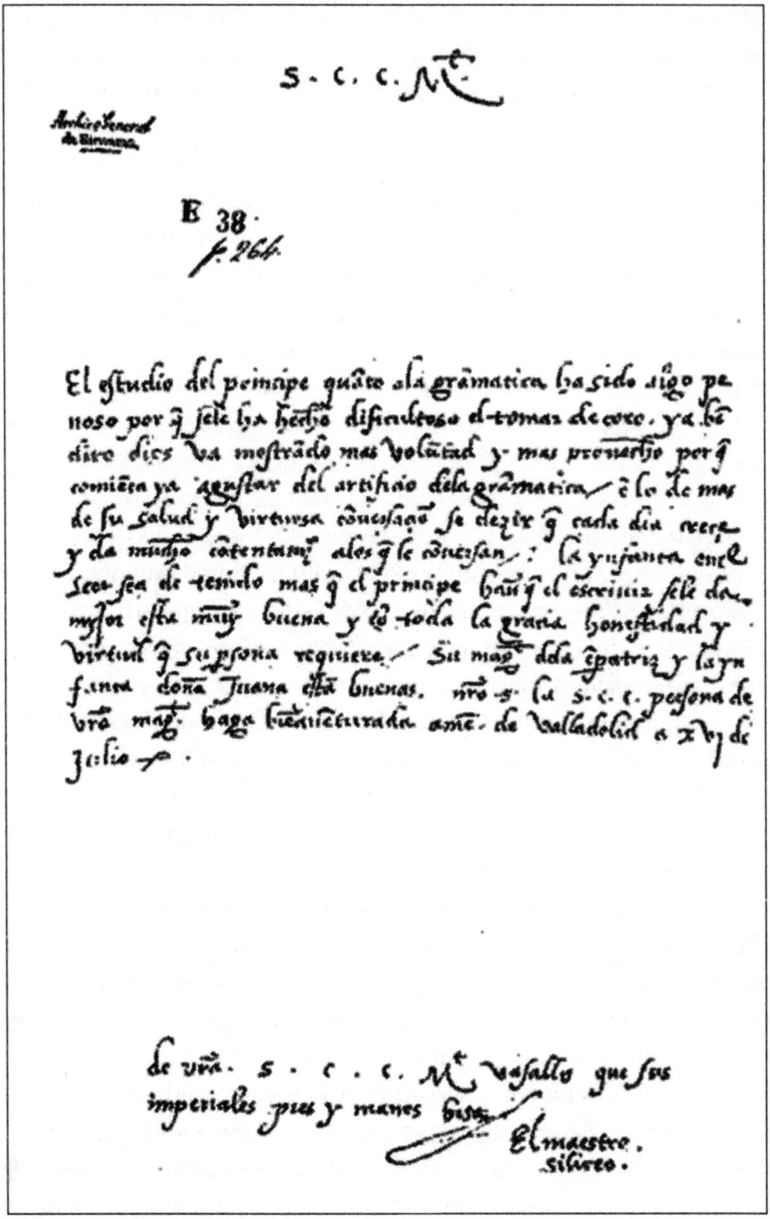

S · C · C · Mt

El estudio del prínçipe quãto a la grãmatica, ha sido algo pe-
noso por q sele ha hecho dificultoso el-tomar decoro. ya he
dicho dias va mostrãdo mas voluntad y mas provecho por q
comiẽça ya a gustar del artifiçio dela grãmatica, e lo de mas
de su salud y virtuosa cõuersaçõ se dexir q cada dia crece
y da mucho cõtentamẽ alos q le cõuersan : la ynfanta en el
leer sea de tenido mas q el prinçipe haũ q el escriuir sele da
mejor esta muy buena y cõ toda la graçia honestidad y
virtud q su psona requiere. Su magt dela emperatriz y la ynfanta doña Juana esta buenas. nro s la s.c.c. persona de
vra magt haga bienaventurada anṫ de valladolid a xvj de
julio

de vra. s. c. c. Mt vasallo que sus
imperiales pies y manos besa
El maestro.
sileceo.

Fig. 6   Letter from Juan Martínez Silíceo

Monarchs in Granada, agreeing also to her final request to be buried without embalming. He organized a grand procession to take the coffin from Toledo to Granada. Following royal protocol, the twelve-year-old boy led the procession, riding immediately behind his mother's coffin. Through most of that melancholy journey Philip maintained the stolid composure that was to mark him throughout life. Even so, at the beginning in Toledo he fled the procession and rushed into a nearby church to weep bitter tears. In Granada further protocol demanded that the queen's body be inspected a final time before the coffin could be placed in the tomb. It was a ghastly experience for everyone. The Marquis of Lombay, official guardian of the body, was so thoroughly appalled by the stench and the sight of the decaying corpse that he eventually renounced court life and joined the new Company of Jesus.[20]

After the death of the empress Charles began to take a more direct interest in the education of his son. For a time Philip attended Council meetings, read correspondence, and listened when his father explained the reasons for his decisions. But Charles was eventually called away. There was a revolt in the Netherlands; there was religious unrest in Germany; and there were continuing problems with the Turks. Philip was left once more with his tutors and his fellow students.[21]

On his return in 1541 Charles once more took his son's education in hand. Dissatisfied with the boy's progress in languages, he appointed Cristóbal Calvete de Estrella to teach him Latin and Greek. The prince already understood Portuguese, his mother's native language, and he eventually acquired a working knowledge of French. But he did not study English or German, and he was not really at ease with any language but Spanish.[22] Because Philip was becoming more directly involved in governmental matters, Charles also added a secretary, Gonzalo Pérez, to the prince's household.[23]

Philip's real love was administration, and in this he was an apt pupil to his imperial father. A good bit of paternal advice is on record in a series of instructions Charles composed for his son. Signed at Palamós in early May 1543, the two documents gave Philip detailed directions for conducting both his personal life and the affairs of government. First and foremost, he told Philip to see that the church and the government worked closely together. "Keep your eyes on God and offer Him your work and your cares." Beyond that, Philip should, "Defend the faith; never allow heresy to enter your kingdom; support the Holy Inquisition; and insist that your officials perform their duties well and administer justice fairly."[24] In his relations with the papacy Philip should show due respect to the Holy Father, but not allow him to meddle or contravene the laws of the realm. He was to consult the members of the Council before taking any action, making sure not to sign anything without first seeking their advice. He was to allow Zúñiga to read all of these instructions.[25]

A second letter was intended for Philip's eyes alone. In this document Charles warned his son to be very careful about his associates and his advisors, beginning with the members of his Council. Tavera, while honest and dependable, would favor the interests of the Consejo de Castilla. Zúñiga had a wife and sons who tended to take advantage of the man's official position. Silíceo was too indulgent toward Philip, who should look for a less lenient confessor. Cobos was honest and faithful, but might bear watching because he had a grasping wife. Alba was ambitious and overbearing and ought to be kept in his place.[26]

Philip was also to watch his conduct around the women of the house. His sisters were growing up; Philip should act the gentleman around them and treat them as ladies. After Philip married, his wife should be treated in the same way, but with added care in the marital relationship. Too much exercise in the marriage bed could be dangerous to Philip's health. He should consider the example of his uncle Juan, who died at the age of nineteen, simply because of sexual excess.[27]

Though young, Philip had watched his mother rule during his father's earlier absence. With more direct instruction from Charles, he quickly acquired a good grasp of the intricacies of government. Beyond this, he was popular with the people who counted in Spain. In May 1542, when Charles summoned the *Cortes of Aragon* to meet in Monzón and asked them to swear allegiance to Philip, they proceeded to do it. The process was repeated in Zaragoza, Barcelona, and Valencia, with only minor difficulty about earlier oaths of allegiance to Philip's grandmother, Juana, called la Loca because she was mentally unstable. With these and other matters concluded, Charles appointed Philip to act as regent in Spain and told him to sign documents as "El Principe."[28] Charles was about to leave on another tour of the empire, but before leaving, he named a special Council to advise his son on matters of government. The members were Juan Tavera, cardinal and archbishop of Toledo; García de Loaísa, cardinal and archbishop of Sevilla; Fernando de Toledo, duque de Alba; García Fernández Manríque, conde de Osorno; Francisco de los Cobos, secretary of state; and his previous advisers, Juan de Zúñiga, Silíceo, Honorato Juan, and Ginés de Sepúlveda.[29]

In noble families it was understood that children would be married to spouses who could enhance the standing of their illustrious parents and ensure the continuation of the dynasty. This was surely the case with Philip. He was only ten when his father began negotiating for a marriage partner. Among the early choices were Margaret of Valois, daughter of the French king; and Juana de Albret, heiress of Bearne. Philip's sisters, even younger, were the subjects of similar negotiations. When Margaret and Juana proved to be unavailable, Charles decided that Maria of Portugal would be a suitable bride for his son. It scarcely mattered that the girl was twice a cousin to the prince; that, seemingly, is what papal dispensations were for. Nor did it matter that the boy was only fifteen when the negotiations started, barely sixteen when the marriage took place. His bride was even younger, by a few months.[30]

With the arrangements well in hand, Charles departed for Germany, leaving the details of the wedding to Philip and his Council. As the date drew closer, Philip began to hear that the princess might not be very pretty. He asked for a description and received a diplomatic reply: "She is as tall or more so than her mother, quite well formed, more stout than thin, but not in such a way as to be unpleasant. . . . Everyone says she is an angel."[31] When these assurances did not satisfy the prince, Silíceo wrote to say, "Her Highness is so much better than I could describe in writing . . . the most illustrious and most Christian and most beautiful lady in the

Fig. 7   Philip's first wife, Maria of Portugal

world."[32] Naturally, Philip was anxious to see her for himself, just as Maria was eager for a glimpse of her future husband. When he heard that her cavalcade was approaching Salamanca, he rode out to try to see her on the road. At a point near Aldeanueva, as he wrote to Charles, "I saw the princess without her seeing me."[33] At least that is what Philip thought. Maria, however, saw the prince leaning out a window just as she was riding by. The girl immediately cast her eyes down, as though she had not noticed him, then rode on to the place she was staying in Aldeanueva. The next day both arrived in Salamanca, and they were married in the cathedral that same night.[34]

It is not possible to know whether the two were pleased with what they saw. Maria was plump and plain, but pleasant and perfectly groomed. Philip was of moderate stature, but fair skinned with blonde, almost white, hair, and blue eyes. He had the lantern jaw of his father and grandfather, with big lips to adorn the face. Even so, most people thought both Maria and Philip were attractive. A decade later John Elder described Philip as possessing "a brod forhead, and grey iyes, streight nosed, and manly countenance. From the forhead to the point of hys chynne, hys face groweth smal. His pace is pri[n]cely, and gate so straight and upright, as he leseth no inche of his higthe, with a yeallowe head and a yeallowe berde . . . nature cannot work a more parfite paterne."[35] Even so, the pictures of Philip do not now conform to standards of masculine beauty.

According to one early writer, the thick protruding lips characteristic of the Hapsburgs were actually inherited from a Polish princess, Cymburga. She married Ernest the Iron and gave birth to a child, Frederic, who became the third Hapsburg emperor to have that name. The pouting lips that enhanced Cymburga's fabled beauty were not so attractive on Philip. Nor did he inherit Cymburga's strength. He was small and rather frail, while she supposedly could pound nails with her bare hands and crack walnuts with her fingers.[36] Philip's prognathous jaw was something else. Long presumed to be a Hapsburg inheritance, it may very well have come from the house of Burgundy, or so says a Hapsburg family story. For this story we may thank a French court gossip, Abbé de Brantôme. In his account, Queen Eleanor, sister of Charles V, had long suspected that the Hapsburg jaw was really of

Burgundian origin. Passing one day through Dijon, she paused to have several ancestral tombs opened, and was pleased to note both the protruding lips and the jutting jaw on the better-preserved remains of her ducal forebears.[37]

Once married, Philip took his father's advice to heart, though perhaps not in the way it was intended. Far from being uxorious, he was so neglectful of Maria as to cause gossip in the court. Charles thought Philip's problem might just be the bashfulness of an inexperienced teenager, but Philip's mother-in-law felt the boy was cold and thoughtless.[38]

Years later Prince William of Orange, involved in open revolt against Philip, said this was certainly not the case. He claimed it was a fact that as a youth Philip had slept with his own sister. As if that were not bad enough, he charged that before marrying Maria of Portugal, Philip had secretly married Isabel de Osorio, by whom he had at least two children. These accusations are almost certainly untrue, ridiculous, in fact, given the boy's age; but they have circulated for so many centuries that they are now established in Philip's biography.[39]

Neglectful he might have been, nevertheless, Maria was soon pregnant, and on 5 July 1545 she gave birth to a son, who was named Charles. It was a difficult birth, the infant suffering a deformed cranium in the procedure, and the princess suffering even more. The infant lived, but the mother died within a few days, aged eighteen. Though Philip may have appeared indifferent to his bride, he was heartbroken when she died. Pausing for the funeral, he took himself to the Monasterio del Abrojo, where he spent a month of mourning, even missing the baptism of his son. He returned to Valladolid only when the members of the Council insisted that his presence was necessary for the orderly process of government.[40]

In the months that followed Philip seems to have shaken off the pall of guilt and sadness that enveloped him after Maria's death. He got on with the business of government, aided perhaps by a new love interest. There is no certain proof of the matter, but two mysterious pieces of correspondence between Cobos and Charles V point to some serious dereliction on Philip's part. In the first Cobos reported his inability to speak to Charles about a matter that seemed to involve one or more of the ladies-in-waiting to Philip's sister Juana. In the second Charles asked Cobos to try once more to solve the problem, but to compose his report in carefully disguised language. Almost certainly Philip had an affair with one of the women in Juana's household.[41]

Whatever the case, Philip did not let personal matters interfere with his duties as regent. From the time he was a boy Philip stood in awe of the accomplishments of his illustrious father. As a young man he tried very hard to follow his father's advice, both in his personal life and in directing the affairs of the kingdom, which was precisely what Charles wanted him to do. In governing Philip always sought the opinions of members of his Council, just as Charles had directed. On routine matters considered in Council, Philip listened carefully to each member. Even when he already knew the answers, he often asked questions, just to draw out information for the others to consider. On more serious matters he consulted each councilor privately, but he always made up his own mind.

Despite his role as regent, Philip was still a student, studying languages and other subjects under the tutelage of his elders. His knowledge of Greek was always rudimentary, but with Latin he gained a proficiency that allowed him to read with ease and to maintain an extended conversation. Philip also had a decent understanding of the Portuguese of his mother. With a background in these languages it was possible for him to understand Italian and perhaps to converse in that tongue. French was another matter. He could read most things, but he never felt at ease in speaking French. He did not study English, since that language was not necessary for dealing with people in his father's empire.[42]

While continuing his studies, Philip began a systematic search for books through Estrella, as his principal agent for book purchases. His first acquisition was a large group of books on the classics and theology, followed by others on geometry, astronomy, architecture, history, warfare, and various occult topics. The authors he read included Aesop, Agricola, Aquinas, Boccaccio, Copernicus, Dante, Dürer, Erasmus, Petrarch, Pliny, Machiavelli, Savonarola, and Vitruvio. Many of the most important works coming out of the European presses found their way into Philip's library, and he tried to read them all. Such was his range of interest, that one biographer credited him with an "encyclopedic knowledge"[43] far beyond the norm for rulers of his time.

During the first years of his regency Philip relied greatly on the members of his Council. Things changed rapidly after 1545, when the three senior members, Tavera, Zúñiga, and Cobos, died. Only Alba remained on the Council, but he was out of the country. To replace the others Philip began to depend on the services of Fernando de Valdés and a new councilor, Luis Hurtado de Mendoza. Taking this opportunity to assert his authority as regent, Philip treated the new men as advisers only. His role and his prestige were further strengthened in September 1546, when his father named him Duke of Milan.[44]

As he grew in experience, Philip began to take and defend positions opposed to those of his father. For example, Charles, hard pressed by wartime expenditures, directed Philip to secure a sizable loan from the *cortes*. Philip responded that there was simply no more money to be had.[45] Strapped for cash, Charles was also pressing the pope for money, asking His Holiness for an outright grant of 500,000 ducados to help pay the debts he had incurred in wars against the Turks and the Protestants. When the full amount was not forthcoming, Charles suggested that Philip could secure the remainder by seizing church property in Spain. After a protracted discussion in Council, Philip wrote to remind his father that this was exactly what Henry VIII had done in England, with disastrous results both for the church and for Henry's reputation "throughout Christendom."[46]

Both Philip and Mary were children of kings, well educated, speaking and reading several languages, but there the similarities stopped. Philip was trained in the theory and practice of government, and he understood how to rule. Mary, on the other hand, was never allowed to participate in government or to learn the intricacies of court politics. At thirty she considered herself beyond marriageable age and was resigned to the idea that she would remain single. Philip, aged nineteen, was a widower with a royal son. No matchmaker would ever suppose that Philip and Mary were made for each other.

Chapter 3

Training a Princess
to be a Wife

I do recognise, accept, take, repute, and knowledge
the King's Highness to be supream head in earth
under Christ of the church of England, and do
utterly refuse the Bishop of Rome's pretended
authority, power, and jurisdiction within this Realm.

Mary Tudor

The early education of Mary and Philip could scarcely have been
more similar in approach and yet more different in outcome. While
Philip was trained to rule, Mary was taught to be a pious and
submissive wife. At the very time that Charles began to take the
education of his son in hand and introduce him to the operation
of the government, Henry completely separated himself from his
daughter, Princess Mary. And when his new wife produced a baby
– christened Elizabeth – Henry made the little girl Princess of
Wales, reducing Mary to the status of lady-in-waiting. Despairing
of a future in England, Mary began to listen to the blandishments
of Eustace Chapuys, the agent of Charles V, who talked of plans
for her escape to the continent.[1]

These plans had not proceeded very far when everything
changed. First, Katherine died. Then, victim once more of a roving
eye, Henry began looking for another queen. His current queen,
Anne, was imprisoned on trumped-up charges of witchcraft, incest,

and adultery. The marriage was quickly nullified, and she was speedily executed.[2] Parliament promptly declared Elizabeth to be illegitimate, leading Cromwell to call her "the late princesse the Lady Elisabethe." Suddenly both Mary and Elizabeth were equal before the law: both were illegitimate.[3]

With the death of Katherine and the impending execution of Anne, Charles saw a new opportunity to restore Mary to her position as heir to the throne of England. At his instructions Chapuys dropped his escape plans and began to urge the king to restore Mary to the status of a royal princess. In an extended personal conversation through Chapuys, Henry replied that he would certainly treat her as a father should, but he did not welcome this interference from the emperor.[4] The truth was that Henry still hoped for a son, though he realized that both Mary and Elizabeth could be useful, as marriage material if nothing else. So Mary was told that she could be restored to the king's favor, if she would only agree to accept two statutes, the first nullifying his marriage to Katherine of Aragon, and the second recognizing his authority over the English church. If she refused, she could expect to go to prison. While the emperor, through Chapuys, had always supported Mary in her adamant refusal to accept the king's terms, he now told her to sign the documents and hope for the best.[5] On 22 June, acting largely on the emperor's advice, Mary put her hand to a document prepared by Henry's advisers, allegedly without reading it. Here is what the paper said:[6]

> First, I confess and knowledge the king's majestie to be my Soveraign Lord and King in the imperial crown of this realme of England, and to submit myself to his Highness, and to all and singular lawes and statuites of this realm as becometh a true and faithfull Subject to do, which I shall also obey, keep, observe, advance, and maintain, according to my bounden duty, with all the power, force, and qualities, that God hath indued me, during my life.

This much Mary had always been willing to do, but it was not enough to suit her father. He insisted on total acceptance of the laws making himself head of the church and annulling the marriage with Katherine. Deserted by the emperor, but plagued by a nagging conscience, Mary agreed now to accept Henry as head of the church.

> *Item*, I do recognise, accept, take, repute, and knowledge the King's Highness to be supream head in earth under Christ of the church of England, and do utterly refuse the Bishop of Rome's pretended authority, power, and jurisdiction within this Realm heretofore usurped, according to the laws and statutes made in that behalf, and of all the King's true Subjects humbly received, admitted, obeyed, kept, and observed. And also do utterly renounce and forsake all manner of remedy, interest and advantage, which I may by any meanes claim by the Bishop of Rome's laws, process, jurisdiction, or sentence, at this present time or in any wise hereafter, by any manner, title, colour, mean, or case that is, shall, or can be devised for that purpose.

Even this was not quite enough. Henry demanded that Mary accept the nullification of the marriage between Henry and Katherine. Motivated by love for her mother, Mary had always refused such a compromise. But with Katherine in her grave, Mary could not resist, even though the final, humiliating provision implied nearly total rejection of her mother.

> *Item*, I do freely, frankly, and for the discharge of my duty towards God, the King's Highness, and his laws, without other respect, recognise and acknowledge that the marriage heretofore had between his Majesty and my mother, the late Princess Dowager, was by God's law and Man's law incestuous and unlawfull.

If Mary actually read the last two paragraphs, it is difficult to understand how she could have signed them. Still, her "Mary" appears at the end of each one. Chapuys says that Mary did not read them, though she knew in general what they said. Mary was devastated by the whole affair and regretted signing the document. But Chapuys reassured her: since she did it under duress, her conscience could rest easy.[7]

After all, the realm was still Catholic. If shrines and images and pilgrimage were abolished, and the king pretended to be head of the church, most of the liturgy and many practices of personal piety were widely observed. But not for long.[8]

Mary found herself once more restored to favor but at great cost to her conscience. She was to have her own servants, if not her own household, and everyone began once more to treat her as the king's daughter.[9] Moreover, Henry's agents began say that Mary would soon be acknowledged as heir to the throne, a matter that was always raised when there were negotiations about a possible marriage. Among Mary's prospective bridegrooms were Duke Philip of Bavaria; Charles, Duke of Orleans, who was second in line to the throne of France; and Dom Luis, brother to the King of Portugal. Other names surfaced as well, including, at Henry's suggestion, the emperor himself, though Henry can hardly have wanted the throne of England to fall into Hapsburg hands.[10] The throne, of course, was the great problem. Whoever took Mary as his wife could also become King of England, for it was universally agreed that a woman could not rule effectively and in fact should not rule at all, so long as her husband was able to do so. English negotiators worked long and hard to minimize this inconvenient fact. In the event they were unsuccessful, so Mary remained unwed.

In October 1537 the long-awaited son was born to Henry and his latest wife, Jane. On October 15 Mary was godmother at Edward's christening, perhaps the surest sign of her rehabilitation. As so often happened in those days, the queen died a few days later from complications of childbirth. In fairly quick succession Henry acquired an additional three wives, disposing of two along the way, just as he had done to their predecessors. None of this affected Mary's position, and she continued to enjoy her father's favor.

Though her legitimacy and that of her half-sister Elizabeth were never recognized in law during Henry's lifetime, their status was tacitly acknowledged by everyone. In 1536, while negotiating with Francis I, Henry instructed his ambassadors to say that Henry really wanted to reaffirm Mary's legitimacy, but "many things" kept him from doing so, most particularly a signed marriage contract. "We mynd not as yet openly to declare o^r mynd therein," is the way Henry put it. Despite all the evasion, when a new Act of Succession was passed in 1543, Mary was next in line following Edward. Of course, Mary's right to the throne depended on both Henry and Edward dying without further issue. Should a child be born to Edward or another child to Henry, Mary would follow them in the line of succession, provided of course, that she "kepe and performe suche conditions, which the kinges majestie shall hereafter . . . declare." Furthermore, Parliament specifically recognized that Henry could place a clause in his last will, altering the succession as he pleased.[11]

While Mary was not an active participant in any of the marriage negotiations, she was kept informed of their general tenor.[12] For the most part it is impossible to know what she thought of the prospective bridegrooms, for she was circumspect, both in her conversation and in her letters. Still, one romance stands out. In the fall of 1536 Philip of Bavaria appeared at court and began an intensive campaign for Mary's hand, working hard to convince both the girl herself and her father that he was an acceptable suitor. On Christmas Eve of that year they went strolling in the garden at Westminster Abbey. There, supposing they were hidden from view, the lovers kissed, something that had not been seen with any other suitor.[13] It was probably on this occasion that Philip gave Mary a cross of diamonds set with four pearls and a large pearl pendant.[14] As the romance progressed, Philip signed a letter to the king, written for him in Latin by a secretary. The letter described Philip's noble family and outlined his prospects for rule. He ended by saying: "These are the things that the most serene and prudent prince wishes to say. What remains is for your majesty to declare your intention to give your daughter in marriage."[15] While Philip was a Lutheran, Mary did not see that as a great drawback, and she sent word to her father saying so.[16] Perhaps Henry did see it as a problem, since the marriage treaty failed when negotiators could not agree on a declaration about the relationship between Henry and the pope.[17] Henry made no public decision in the matter, but both Mary and Philip eventually understood that he would never approve the marriage. As though to confirm his decision Henry ordered Mary to surrender the diamond cross to Cromwell.[18] Mary was disappointed, perhaps greatly so, if a later remark refers to this romance. In a touching conversation with one of her ladies-in-waiting Mary said she should be addressed as "Lady Mary, the most miserable woman in Christendom." It would be "most foolish to think that they would want her to marry outside of England," she continued, "or even in England, so long as the king her father should live."[19]

It was not just that Henry was offering his daughter as a possible marriage partner. Mary had been trained from childhood to be the wife of a king and had all the qualities that a royal suitor could desire: a willing disposition, a pretty face, and an agile mind. The emperor realized this and made numerous advances on her behalf. At various times he talked of spiriting her away from England; or of invading England, placing Mary on the throne, and matching her with an appropriately Catholic husband. And there were recurring rumors that Charles himself might claim her or that she would marry Reginald Pole. Though a cardinal, Pole had not been admitted to Holy Orders. The emperor's ambassador in Rome reported, on Pole's authority, that Pope Paul had refused to ordain him precisely because he wanted to keep him as a possible marriage partner for Mary. "Things might proceed in such a way that [Pole] could marry the princess," said the royal ambassador, "and for this reason His Holiness has not wanted him to accept any dignity except a crown."[20]

Henry's final attempt at marriage brokering came in the fall of 1546, just after the death of Maria, the wife of Philip of Spain. He proposed that the emperor should take Mary as his wife. As part of the arrangement Edward would marry the emperor's daughter, and the emperor's son Philip would marry Elizabeth. Probably Henry was no more serious about this proposal than he was about any of the others. As it turned out, Charles was not at all interested, flatly refusing, both for himself and for his children.[21]

Fig. 8 Princess Mary

As it turned out, Mary was correct in thinking she would never be allowed to marry, but the reasons for this changed after Henry's death in early 1547. By an act of Parliament and by Henry's will, Edward became king. Since the boy was only nine years of age, the government was entrusted to a council of sixteen advisers. Perhaps unfortunately, the young king's uncle, Edward Seymour, managed to take control of the Council and by his close relationship to the king, had himself appointed Lord Protector and Duke of Somerset. Within a short time Somerset and his Protestant allies in the Council put an Act of Uniformity through Parliament. This novel legislation replaced the Latin Mass with an English liturgy called "holy Communion."[22] The new ritual was established in a Book of Common Prayer that specifically rejected the Catholic belief that the Mass was a sacrifice and that, by the action of the priest at Mass, bread and wine were transformed into the body and blood of Christ.[23] Earlier changes had concentrated on the elimination of images, relics, and pilgrimages. The new ritual completed the transformation of the church and the sacraments, doing away with altars and rood screens, eliminating the distribution of Holy Bread, and substituting a general public confession for the Sacrament of Penance. The remaining popular devotions involving candles, rosaries, and prayers before images, already condemned as superstitious, were forbidden.[24]

For Mary, as for other English Catholics, the Mass was the central act of faith. She heard Mass every day, sometimes more than once, so she understood the Communion service to be the ultimate breach with the old religion. Somehow Mary had been able to rationalize acceptance of her father as "supream head . . . of the church of England." She also managed to suppress most of her annoyance with Henry's various attacks on traditional religion. As the imperial ambassador to England noted, "She remains firm and constant in her good attachment to our ancient faith."[25] Because of this she considered the Communion service an attack on fundamental Catholic doctrine.[26] She was not alone. All over the country ordinary people, still ardently Catholic, joined in rejecting Cranmer's new religion. Suddenly popular with the common people, Mary became a symbol of resistance to a new and largely unpopular church.

Chapter 4

The Grand Tour

*He left the impression of being severe and intractable;
so he was just acceptable to the Italians, greatly
disliked by the Flemings, and hated by the Germans.*

Michele Soriano

As the year 1548 dawned and Mary Tudor fretted about her
brother's religious novelties, Charles began the last phase of a
program intended to prepare Philip to become the ruler of his huge
and vastly complex empire. At age twenty-one Philip was already
an experienced executive, having governed the disparate elements
of his father's Spanish kingdom for the past five years. In this final
stage Charles directed Philip to undertake a grand tour of the
imperial capitals, where he could meet all the people who made up
the Holy Roman Empire. As a preliminary step, Charles told Philip
to reorganize the Spanish court in the Burgundian fashion,
instituting pomp and ceremony that would impress other rulers
with the grandeur of the Spanish monarchy. This meant a greatly
enlarged household: a corps of bodyguards, chaplains, servants, and
retainers, estimated by one visitor at 1,500 persons in all![1] The
estimate is no doubt an exaggeration, and Philip hated the new
ceremonies, but he endured them all in order to please his father
and the people he would meet on tour. For Charles it was a chance
to introduce his son to the imperial electors, hoping they would be

so favorably impressed that they would accept Philip as the next emperor. For Philip it was an opportunity to see the various territories in Italy, Burgundy, and the Netherlands that he would inherit.

The imperial inheritance was a major problem. Faced with the impossibility of governing such a far-flung empire alone, Charles had installed his brother Ferdinand as king of the Romans, ruling the German states and other dependencies. Even though the king of the Romans usually succeeded to the imperial title, Charles planned to have Philip as his successor. Ferdinand, of course, had other ideas. He not only wanted to be the next emperor, he wanted his son Maximilian to follow, and both of them managed to draw support from the imperial electors.

Looking for a way around the problem, Charles arranged for Maximilian to go to Spain and marry his daughter Maria. Together they would be left as regents during Philip's absence. This was no favor to Maria, if court gossip can be believed. Maximilian had grown up on the German courts, where scandalous behavior was commonplace. On his way to Spain, for example, Maximilian and his friends acquired a succession of female companions, keeping them for a few days of carousal, then abandoning them with small gifts or a few coins to pay for their services.[2]

While Philip and Maria might have objected to the marriage, they said nothing about it, as befit royal children. Instead, Philip arranged a grand reception for his cousin, and watched while he wed Maria in the palace at Valladolid, where Philip himself was born. The cortes were reluctant to see Philip go, for he had proven himself to be an intelligent and reasonable sovereign. More than that, he resided in Spain, while Charles was absent, living in a succession of his European capitals. Even so, Philip looked forward to the journey, and with Maximilian and Maria installed as joint regents, he set out for Italy.[3]

From Valladolid Philip and his party traveled eastward, reaching the shrine of Montserrat on 10 October 1548. There the prince confessed his sins, received Holy Communion, and commended himself to the protection of the Virgin of Montserrat. Two days later he was in Barcelona, where he dined in the lovely

Map 1   Sixteenth Century Europe

palace of Estefanía de Requeséns, widow of his former governor Juan de Zúñiga. The next leg of the trip was the responsibility of Prince Andrea Doria, who awaited Philip at Rosas, some miles to the north. It was no small undertaking. Doria had a fleet of fifty-eight galleys, plus other ships to the number of a hundred or so. Reaching Rosas, Philip insisted on crossing immediately, although the seas were very rough. Because of the foul weather, Doria chose to follow the coast to Genoa. The fleet reached Leucate on 10 November, the harbor of Marseilles a week later, and the Iles d'Hyères a few days after that. The anchorage at Port Cros was so small that the entire fleet could not enter the harbor at one time. As a result several galleys remained outside and were nearly swamped in the treacherous currents running between the islands. Looking for a better anchorage, the fleet sailed on, intending to stop again in the port of Villefranche near Nice. However, the weather improved, allowing the fleet to sail on to Porto Maurizio near Cape Mele. On the following day the ships arrived in Savona, where Philip remained for a few more days, awaiting word that the royal apartments in the palace of Andrea Doria were ready for his arrival. When he entered Genoa on 25 November, Philip was met by an honor guard who took him through the streets under a canopy to the door of his lodgings. Similar receptions happened elsewhere, with delegations from the Counts of Villars and Tende meeting Philip and offering him whatever assistance he might require. The young prince was greatly impressed by the elaborate preparations and cordial welcome, and he said so at appropriate times.[4]

In Genoa the Spanish prince and his entourage were entertained for more than two weeks, while diplomats arrived from all over Italy to greet him. During one night of festivities some of his soldiers had had a little too much to drink and began to scuffle; in the melee a local citizen was killed. In retaliation, a band of armed Genoese attacked a house where fifty Spanish soldiers were quartered, and the resultant fighting lasted for several days before it was all over. With peace restored, the ringleaders went to jail, and the celebration continued; thus the royals were only slightly inconvenienced.

When Philip and his party left on 11 December in a furious snowstorm, he was richer by 13,000 ducats, a gift from the city.[5] A few days later he reached Milan, where he was met by Ferrante Gonzaga, commander of all the Spanish forces in Italy, and Fernando Gonzaga, governor of Milan. Among those lined up to greet him were Duke Carlos of Savoy, Cardinal Madruzzi of Trent, the Duke of Ferrara, the marques of Pescara, and the Duke of Alba, along with ambassadors from Venice, Florence, and Sienna. A series of dinners, dances, and tournaments followed in dizzying succession. In the Royal Tourney Philip conducted himself with such gallantry as to excite the admiration of all the ladies, or so said his chronicler. Here and elsewhere Philip and his followers staged a *juego de cañas*, a typically Spanish game in which horsemen fought with spears and batons. It was a showy display, with armored knights clad in colorful tunics, but onlookers seemed unimpressed by the feats of equestrian skill and the mock combat.[6]

One part of the entertainment at Milan consisted of a *comedia*, an ingenious diorama of the city of Venice, with buildings and streets and canals, men and women, workmen and shopkeepers, some moving and some standing still. In the heavens above, a clockwork mechanism caused the sun to rise and set; at night the moon and stars appeared to move in their usual orbits, except when the sky was obscured by clouds.[7] To the Spanish visitors this was a great wonder. However, they soon became accustomed to extravagant productions of this sort, as each new city tried to outdo its predecessors.

Before Philip left Milan, the governor presented him with a gift of 20,000 ducats in the name of the city, plus another 100,000 in the name of the state. Philip responded with a diamond for the duchess and another for their daughter. Counting additional gifts for the shrine to Our Lady of Montserrat, Philip's donations at Milan amounted altogether to about 48,000 ducats.[8]

The celebrations continued everywhere Philip and his court appeared. In the duchy of Mantua, the cardinal, and his nephew the duke built "a great house" along the road, filled with food and drink and resting places for the passing cavalcade.[9] According to an English traveler Philip's entourage included 1,000 mounted horsemen and thirty or forty liveried footmen. Once in the city, the party proceeded past arches, columns, statues, and pyramids, covered with Latin inscriptions and complimentary verses. Sufficient tables were provided so that everyone, from the humblest to the greatest, was able to join the festivities. After weeks on the journey, and no doubt exhausted by continuous travel, Philip was a bit brusque when the Duke of Ferrara and ambassadors from Venice and Florence welcomed him to Mantua. As a result, said a hostile observer, "he obtayned throwghe all Italye a name of insolencye." The observation was partly true, a consequence of Philip's natural reserve, and the problem pursued him across Europe.[10]

At Villafranca the Spanish prince was greeted by Octavio Farnese, Duke of Parma and husband of Margaret, the natural daughter of Charles V. At Trent, where the church council had been meeting, Philip was received in the palace of Cardinal Madruzzi, who had gone ahead of the party to make certain that everything was ready for his arrival. Unfortunately, most of the delegates were elsewhere, and Philip was able to meet only a few of the bishops. Even so, he did not lack for company, for there were the usual feasts, and one masked ball lasted till dawn. He was especially popular with all the ladies, who wanted to dance with the handsome young prince, the heir apparent to the great empire of Spain. Everyone who met Philip in Italy was impressed by his consummate courtesy, his serious demeanor, and his remarkably mature judgement. If it had not been for his excessive reserve, his trip would have been a resounding success.[11]

From this point onward Philip was in Hapsburg land, where some of his finer traits of character were less highly regarded than in Italy. Even so, Philip was greeted everywhere by noble members of his family, accompanied by imperial electors, government dignitaries, and church officials. In Munich Duke Albert was his host for a day of hunting and nights of dining and dancing. Philip was especially taken with the dazzling daughter of the Duke of Bavaria. He was even more taken with her sister-in-law Anna, Philip's cousin, and "one of the most beautiful and charming Princesses you can imagine." He danced all night with both of the women, and when he departed, he gave each of them lavish presents.[12]

EL FELICISSIMO

VIAIE D'EL MVY ALTO Y MVY
Poderofo Principe Don Phelippe, Hijo d'el Emperador Don Carlos Quinto Maximo, defde Efpaña à
fus tierras dela baxa Alemaña: con la defcrip-
cion de todos los Eftados de Braban-
te y Flandes. Efcrito en qua-
tro libros,
por Iuan Chriftoual Caluete
de
Eftrella.

Con Gracia y Priuilegio de la Imperial Majeftad,
para todos fus Reynos, Eftados y Seño-
rios, por quinze Años.

En Anuers, en cafa de Martin Nucio
Año de
M. D. LII.

Fig. 9 *El Felicissimo Viaie*, title page of a book written by Philip's tutor, describing the Grand Tour.

In Augsburg he was entertained by Antonio Fugger, good family friend and banker to the emperor. It was Lutheran country, but Philip followed his father's policy of tolerance, and was well received by everyone. The gift to Philip by the city of Augsburg was 1,000 florins, sealed in two cups of silver. Similar gifts there and elsewhere helped to defray the huge costs of the royal entourage. The celebration at Ulm on the banks of the Danube included a mock naval battle. There were only a few Catholics here, and their fourteenth century church was badly furnished. To show his concern, Philip donated chalices and ornaments for a new chapel, which he ordered to be built for the Blessed Sacrament. Later, at the Rhine, the royal party crossed on a bridge of boats.[13]

An escort from Brussels met the Spanish cavalcade at Speyer, and at this point the archers who accompanied Philip began to mount a night guard on the prince's lodgings, perhaps because they thought the area was less friendly than those traversed earlier. Just before arriving at Brussels, Philip stopped to greet his aunt Maria, widow of the King of Bohemia and regent of the Netherlands. She of course gave another splendid banquet, followed by more entertainment. This included a mock battle between "the whites" and "the greens" with cavalry, infantry, and artillery locked in furious combat for several hours.[14]

Finally the trip was over. After six months of constant travel Philip reached Brussels where he was reunited with his father, whom he had not seen for six years. Charles was only forty-nine, but he looked like seventy. He had been sick with gout for months, almost at the point of death, and he felt every year of his age. Charles desperately wanted to retire, but would not do so until he had made certain that Philip would inherit all his domain. This could only happen if his son made a favorable impression on everyone.

Charles first took his son to each of the seventeen provinces of the Netherlands, where Philip was solemnly received as the legitimate ruler after his father.[15] Determined to make everyone like him, Philip threw himself into the parties and celebrations with what seemed to him like unfettered enthusiasm, though he was never able to drink as much or play as hard as the Netherlanders and Germans.

While he liked the Dutch, Philip could not bring himself to like the Germans, and both were unimpressed with him. In fact, Maximilian was much more popular throughout the empire than Philip. In a report home the English ambassador remarked on "the great estimation in which Maximilian is held both in the High and Low Countries."[16] Philip, on the other hand was almost universally unpopular, at least in the opinion of the Venetian ambassador: "He left the impression of being severe and intractable; so he was just acceptable to the Italians, greatly disliked by the Flemings, and hated by the Germans."[17] Even so, Philip went through the motions. He tried to please the German princes, speaking to them in Latin or French. They were not impressed. "They take his taciturnity and retiring manners for ignorance," said one of his father's diplomats.[18] Ferdinand, who could have helped, worked instead to advance his own claim to the imperial crown. In an attempt to reach a compromise, Maximilian was summoned from Spain to Augsburg for a family conference, but there was no agreement, and Charles had to bring in his sister as mediator. Finally, after months of haggling, Charles was able to negotiate a complicated arrangement whereby Ferdinand would succeed him as emperor. In the course of time Ferdinand would abdicate in favor of Philip, who would promptly name Maximilian as king of the Romans and successor to the empire. Thus the imperial dignity would alternate between the two branches of the family. It was a compromise that pleased no one, including the electors, who preferred Maximilian and his German son to the young Spanish prince.[19]

With the family agreement concluded, everyone returned home. Philip went by way of Trent, where the Council was in session once more. Arriving there on 6 April 1551, he was welcomed by the papal legate as well as all the cardinals and bishops. Everything had been arranged by his old tutor, Archbishop Juan Martínez Silíceo. At a banquet on a pretty island in the middle of the River Adigo, Philip assured the worried delegates of his support along with that of his father the emperor. When his party left on 9 June, all of the delegates assembled once more to see him off. Interestingly enough, when Maximilian passed through Trent two weeks later, he was very nearly ignored.[20]

PROXIMVS·A·SVMMO·FERDNANDVS·CAESARE·CARLO
REX·ROMANORVM·SIC·TVLIT·ORA·GENAS
AET·SVAE·XXIX
ANN·M·D·XXXI

Fig. 10   Ferdinand, King of the Romans

On 12 July 1551 Philip arrived in Spain, relieved to be once more in familiar surroundings, but confronted immediately by new challenges at home. His son Don Carlos, six years old, was beginning to show some of the same emotional frailty that kept Philip's grandmother in confinement. Still under the care of Juana, Philip's younger sister, Carlos was old enough to have his own household. He ought soon to begin his formal education, just as his father had done. Juana could not continue to care for the boy, since she herself was about to marry Prince John, the heir to the throne of Portugal.[21] When Carlos heard this, he could not be consoled. After Juana actually departed for Portugal, the little prince wept for three days, complaining bitterly and creating a great disturbance. One writer told Charles V, "I am not a good enough chronicler to describe in detail everything the Infante said and did during this time."[22] It was just a sample of things to come. There was madness on both sides of the family, and Carlos had inherited a generous dose.

Almost as soon as Philip left Augsburg, the family compact fell apart. Even worse, the German princes began to ally themselves with Henry II of France, and forced Charles to flee for his own safety. Retreating with his army, Charles managed to mass his forces at Metz in the fall of 1552 and lay siege to the French army occupying the city. But the siege failed, and Charles withdrew to Brussels, where he sank into a deep depression.

In Spain Philip had been gathering troops and funds to support his father. For a time he planned to lead his own army to Metz and reinforce his father, but Charles vetoed the idea, not wanting a possible defeat to blacken Philip's reputation. Instead, the emperor began to put his own affairs in order. Philip would definitely take over the hereditary titles, but the imperial crown was no longer certain. Charles advised his sister to tell Philip that he should not count on becoming emperor.[23]

The main thing, said Charles, was for Philip to marry again and produce sufficient heirs to insure the succession. Before Philip had departed on his tour of the empire, Charles had suggested that he marry Jeanne d'Albret, daughter of the King of Navarre. Such a marriage would help to settle land disputes on the north-east border of Spain, but for that very reason Henry II of France could be counted on to oppose it. As an alternative Charles thought Philip might marry Marguerite, sister of the King of France and Philip's cousin. The other possibility was another cousin, one of Ferdinand's daughters. As it turned out, Jeanne married the Duke of Vendôme, and neither of the cousins appealed to Philip. His choice was to marry still another cousin, Maria of Portugal, thus strengthening the already close alliance with that family. As his father pointed out, marriage with a close relative would not create a problem for the children. "There is nothing in such talk that withstands serious examination."[24]

The proposed marriage would not be a love match. Charles wanted him to marry his cousin because she was rich. Maria's father, King Emanuel of Portugal, had left her a dowry of 400,000 ducados. Philip told Charles that he thought this would be a good marriage, because they could use the money in the war with France. Charles was ecstatic. He talked to the girl's mother, Eleanor, who by this time was married to the King of France. She told him that the Portuguese royal family was so pleased with the idea of a marriage between Philip and Maria that they would probably add another 200,000 ducats to the dowry. "I did not believe it, once I saw how things were going," said Charles. "Still, she insists and is persuaded that it is so (but I do not think it will happen): that they will add another 200,000 cruzados, just to show themselves to be our good and generous brothers."[25]

Philip sent his negotiators to Lisbon, but by the time they reached the city, King John III was having second thoughts. The additional 200,000 cruzados could not be paid after all. Moreover, the whole dowry would not be paid at once, but in annual installments, as cash became available. Finally, it seemed, the sum of 80,000 ducados still owed on Spanish Princess Juana's dowry would be deducted from Maria's dowry. This was too much for Philip, who found all the haggling distasteful in the extreme. He decided to call his negotiators home. Before doing this, however, he wrote to tell Charles what he had in mind.[26] The response could not have been more surprising. Edward VI of England had died at the age of sixteen. By Henry's will, the English throne now belonged to Princess Mary, who would require a husband to help her rule.

As usual, there was a slight difficulty. With considerable intervention by his chief minister the Duke of Northumberland, Edward had seemingly signed a will, naming Jane Grey as his successor, instead of his sister Mary. Jane was the daughter of the Duke of Suffolk and the wife of Northumberland's youngest son. Her claim to the throne was rather distant, but she was a firm Protestant, and therefore acceptable to the Protestant minority that controlled the Privy Council. Jane was a pretty girl in her mid-teens and was said to possess a brilliant mind, but she was a pawn for the ambitions of her parents and her father-in-law. No doubt reluctant to marry Northumberland's son, Jane was equally hesitant to claim the crown. Mary on the other hand refused to accept Jane as queen and began gathering her own supporters. Northumberland marched out to meet her troops, and while he was absent, everything began to change.[27]

Although the privy councilors originally had supported Jane, they gradually abandoned her. After nine days it was over. The Council proclaimed Mary queen and sent the Earl of Arundel and Lord William Paget to give her the news. Following an ancient tradition, the two approached Mary on their knees, with daggers turned toward their stomachs, making abject apologies for their behavior. Mary forgave them immediately and accepted them into her new council.[28] "At the present time," said Charles, "nothing could happen that would work out better."[29]

Chapter 5

Mary the Queen

The said Most Serene Prince Philip will enjoy the style, honor, and kingly name of the realms and dominions pertaining to the said Most Serene Queen, along with the Most Serene Queen his consort, and assist her in the happy administration of her realms and dominions.

The emperor's ambassadors hurried to meet with Mary. Simon Renard in particular relished the opportunity to advise the new monarch. In a private meeting in Mary's oratory Renard said that Mary should establish her own authority "by winning the hearts of her vassals and subjects." The proper course, in the emperor's mind was that Mary should delay making any changes in government. Instead, she should summon Parliament, then try to "win the favor of those who attend, and with the participation of Parliament do whatever the state of the realm might allow." She should follow the same course with religion. Mary might continue to hear Mass in her own private chapel, but she should wait for Parliament to make changes in the law before she allowed the Mass in other places.

Filtered through the mind of the ambassador, the imperial advice came out this way: "The labour of government can [only] with difficulty be undertaken by a woman." Mary needed a husband to assist her with the work of ruling, something "not within a woman's province." Always eager to have the emperor's opinion, Mary replied that she was not at all inclined to marry, "but preferred to end her days in chastity." Still, she could see that a royal marriage might be important for the country. She would be guided by the advice of the emperor, "whom she regarded as a father."[1]

When Charles read Renard's report, he could scarcely contain his enthusiasm. Writing to his son Philip, he said: "I am well pleased to see our cousin in the place and station that belongs to her, and I hope as well that with her prudence she can settle the religious question." But the possibility of joining England and Spain in marriage was almost too good to be true. Charles knew that the English would not be pleased to have their queen marry a foreigner. Still, he thought they might accept him once more as a suitor, just as they had in the treaty of 1522. "They have always shown that they like me," he told Philip. Then he added: "If they were to make a proposal to me, I could delay so as to put them onto you." Charles understood that Philip would not be thrilled with the idea of marriage to a somewhat elderly relative. "I only wish to put this before you," said Charles. "You can think it over and let me know your opinion. Then we will do whatever seems most acceptable to you."[2]

For European royalty, the purpose of marriage was diplomacy, and Philip understood this. In 1522, when she was just six, Mary had been betrothed to Charles by treaty. Now Charles was too old to marry again, but Philip was young and available. What Charles had in mind was nothing less than uniting the government of England with that of the Low Countries and bringing them both into an alliance against his enemy, France. This would give him ports and bases in England that would help to defend his possessions in the Netherlands. The sea route to the Netherlands had been in danger for the past several years. In 1548 the Scots Parliament had agreed that the child-queen Mary Stuart would go to France, eventually to wed Francis, son of Henry II. In return Henry was to help garrison the Scottish border. For France the advantages were great: a claim on Scotland, and a base from which to menace both England and the Netherlands.[3] Now this French threat could be neutralized. As Charles told Philip, "The advantages and benefits that would accrue are so obvious and grand that it is unnecessary to explain further."[4]

As Charles expected, Philip was not enthusiastic about the idea of an English marriage, and he said so, though with proper deference to his father.

> Regarding the matter of England, I am glad to know things have worked out well, and that my aunt has succeeded to the throne in that kingdom, first because it is due her and then because of the point made by your Majesty concerning France and the others. If she should decide on a marriage with your Highness and should find you so inclined, that would be most appropriate. But in case your Majesty decides on me, and if you wish to arrange things for me, your Highness knows that, since I am such an obedient son, I have no will but yours, even more so in a matter of such obvious import and moment.[5]

Willing though reluctant, Philip wanted the marriage proposal to come from Mary, rather than the other way around. But this was not going to happen. Mary preferred that someone else begin the conversation. For this reason Charles told Renard to meet with the queen once more for a frank discussion with her about marriage. Renard did so, and Mary told him that the Bishop of Winchester had already urged her to marry. But the bishop wanted her consort to be an Englishman, either Edward Courtenay or Cardinal Pole. Both were unacceptable to her. The reasons quickly became obvious. Pole, after delaying for many years, had recently received Holy Orders and was therefore no longer available. Courtenay was simply a rogue, and Mary refused to consider him. There were other reasons, of course, largely involving family and politics. In fact, Mary did not find any English candidate acceptable. She preferred to take a foreign husband. The emperor should make a proposal in writing, either with members of the Privy Council or directly with her. Meanwhile, she would willingly continue to speak privately with his ambassadors.[6] And so she did. The emperor did not put his proposal in writing, but Mary continued to consult frequently with his ambassadors, seeking their advice on every aspect of government.

The emperor was not the only one trying to arrange a marriage with the Queen of England. Several other noble families made offers, including Emmanuel Philibert, Duke of Savoy; Prince Luis of Portugal; and Archduke Ferdinand, Philip's cousin.[7] All three had their supporters in the Council and elsewhere, but their proposals got nowhere with Mary. In fact, the question of marriage was not at the top of Mary's calendar during the next few weeks. Instead, she worked to restore the Catholic religion, to assemble a loyal Privy Council, and to arrange a fitting time and place for her coronation. Records of these proceedings are sparse. Much of what is known of the negotiations comes from the reports sent home by the imperial ambassadors and other foreign dignitaries resident in London.

In early August 1553 the queen met once more with Renard. She received the ambassador in her chamber where an altar stood with the Blessed Sacrament displayed in a monstrance. There Mary told Renard that she intended to restore the Mass throughout the kingdom so that "those who wished to hear it would be allowed to do so."[8] Most people in London were pleased with the news, though not everyone welcomed the changes. Within weeks there were Masses in all the principal churches of London.[9]

Some Protestants were infuriated. On Sunday, 13 August a priest at Paul's Cross prayed for the souls of the departed and spoke glowingly of the fortitude of Bishop Bonner who had been sent to prison for refusing to renounce the Catholic faith. A group of protesters, apparently forewarned about the subject of the sermon, started shouting at the priest. When another priest came forward to help restore order, a man threw a dagger at the lectern, and finally the church had to be cleared.[10]

Despite a few such incidents, the transition was surprisingly peaceful. Protestants were a distinct minority in most of England.

With Mary's accession to the throne, statues and crucifixes were brought out of hiding; altars were reinstalled in the churches; and Mass was said once more – in Latin – to widespread approval.[11]

In assembling her Council, Mary continued to depend on the guidance of the emperor, as relayed through his ambassador, Simon Renard. Almost as soon as she heard of Edward's death, Mary began gathering a group of trusted advisors. The first members, entirely unofficial, were loyal servants of her household. By 10 July, when she felt confident enough to proclaim herself queen, Mary made the appointments formal. By the end of the month the Council numbered nearly two dozen members, and by the end of October there were twenty more. There were a few seasoned politicians, but the best of them were of doubtful loyalty. The men closest to Mary had little or no administrative experience. After some early uncertainty, they soon managed to sort themselves out, and a working group of half a dozen experienced men assumed general control of the government. These included Lord William Paget, the Earl of Arundel (Henry Fitzalan), Stephen Gardiner (Bishop of Winchester), Thomas Thirlby (Bishop of Norwich), Sir Robert Rochester, and Sir William Petre.[12] Arundel and Paget had supported Jane as queen; Gardiner was irascible and overbearing; Thirlby was untried. With no experience in governing and little reason to trust most of these veterans, Mary preferred to check everything with Renard. This annoyed the Council members, but Mary thought she had no real alternatives.

With some semblance of orderly government established, Mary proceeded with plans for her coronation, which took place on 1 October 1553. Princess Elizabeth, who had been brought up as a Protestant, "changed and recanted her error," after which Mary received her at court. Though Elizabeth almost immediately showed her insincerity, Mary allowed her to remain at court,[13] and Elizabeth rode in the coronation procession immediately behind the queen.[14]

On 7 October, just a week after the coronation, Renard told Mary that the emperor very much wanted her to marry his son Philip. This announcement was no surprise to the queen, for she could see clear advantages in such a marriage. After all, Philip was

Catholic, heir to the Spanish throne, and a likely successor to the imperial title. On the other hand, he was considerably younger than Mary (twenty-seven to her thirty-seven), and perhaps "inclined to be playful," which "was not her desire." More than that, said Mary, she was determined to rule on her own, without interference from a husband. Except for this, she would "completely love and obey the one to whom she gave herself, according to the divine commandment."[15]

There was one other problem. Philip already had a son, and this might complicate the succession to the English throne. In fact, there were rumors that Philip had fathered other children. According to one story, a girl in Brussels had given birth "very secretly" to his daughter. And Eufrasia de Guzmán, lady-in-waiting to his sister, had produced another daughter, or so it was said. Whether Philip's or not, Eufrasia's child was not a problem, for Philip arranged that she should marry the Prince of Ascoli, thus giving the little girl a father. Of course, this was all rumor, but the gossipy Venetian ambassador clearly believed it, and others did as well.[16] There may also have been a little boy, as reported by another Venetian ambassador, but this case is even less clear.[17] At any rate, Mary would not be getting a "chaste" husband. Even so, she felt certain he was "not in love with any other woman," and that perhaps was enough.[18]

Mary told Renard that she was interested in his proposal but said there were problems that needed to be discussed. In a list of responses to her objections, Renard said that Philip would only "restore and defend the true liberties of the land, without interfering or allowing his servants to interfere with its administration unless with the consent and at the wish of your Majesty and the council." Furthermore, he said, "not only would the kingdom's defense be safe" with Philip, "but the crown would be able to advance and follow up its just claims." And since the interests of both Scotland and France were hostile to those of England, a Spanish marriage would not involve the country in additional foreign conflict.[19]

Determined not to allow the Council to become involved in the preliminary marriage negotiations, Mary let it be known that she would make her own decision, and then tell the Council who

Fig. 11　Mary the Queen

she was going to marry. Once they learned that she had decided to marry Philip, a few members of the Council tried to change her mind. Sir Robert Rochester, Stephen Gardiner, and several others urged her to consider Courtenay once more, but she simply refused to do so.[20] At the same time others, in and out of England, continued to press their own candidates. The emperor's brother urged Mary to consider his son, the Archduke Ferdinand, and Anne of Cleves spoke to Mary in support of this proposal.[21] If the common people had any opinion in the matter, they probably favored a marriage with Courtenay, largely because he was an Englishman.[22]

The discussion did not last long, and before the end of the month the matter was settled. Mary called Renard to her chambers and again in the presence of the Blessed Sacrament told him that she had conferred with three members of her Council, Arundel, Paget, and Petre; she had spent several nights of weeping and prayer; finally, she had made up her mind. "God had inspired her," she told Renard, "to promise before the Blessed Sacrament to marry His Highness Prince Philip". "Her mind, once made up, would never change," said Renard, "but she would love him perfectly and never give him cause to be jealous."[23] With Mary's firm commitment in hand, Renard wrote immediately to Philip. "Your Highness should practice speaking French or Latin," he said, for these were the only languages Philip and Mary had in common.[24]

The royal wooing thus concluded, diplomatic maneuvers could begin. Surprisingly, Charles and his ambassadors carried out all the negotiations on their own, without consulting Philip. When Mary first began to talk about marriage, she said she would not choose a husband without seeing his picture. In the event, she did decide before seeing what Philip looked like. But the emperor's sister knew that Mary would want to see a likeness of her betrothed, so she wasted no time in sending her a recent portrait of Philip painted by Titian. The portrait, painted in 1550, showed Philip "in a short coat trimmed with white wolf skin." Bishop Granvelle thought it was no longer a good likeness, since Philip "would have grown in size and beard." Maria of Hungary, Philip's aunt, thought it was a good likeness "at the time it was made." Francisco de Eraso told Philip the portrait was "very good and like you."[25] Whether a good likeness or not, it pleased Mary almost as much "as if it had been His Highness in person."[26]

The announcement did not end the pressure on Mary to wed someone else. Ferdinand, king of the Romans, sent a diplomat to London to press his son's suit, and the ambassador of Portugal arrived on a similar mission. The speaker of the House of Commons, with support from Bishop Gardiner, came to court to speak at great length in favor of Courtenay, managing only to annoy Mary and strengthen her resolve not to marry anyone in her kingdom.[27] Paget, on the other hand, seeing that Mary had her mind made up, supported her decision to marry Philip.

With the various objections pushed out of the way, it was possible to begin drawing up a marriage treaty. Charles wanted the first draft to come from England; Mary insisted that Charles draw up the articles. Fearing that Bishop Gardiner still intended to scuttle the treaty, Paget also favored this approach. Paget's plan was that the emperor's terms would appear so reasonable that no member of the Council could logically oppose them. With this in mind, Renard and Paget worked out the general terms, anticipating all the objections the bishop and his friends might raise, and devising answers to them. When Charles saw what the two had concocted, he agreed to everything, insisting only that there should be two treaties.

His main objective was to unite England and the Low Countries as a buffer against his perpetual enemy, France. As a result, the first treaty concentrated on the marriage, succession to the thrones of England and the Low Countries, and a suitable dowry for Mary, who was very nearly penniless. The second treaty was designed to address all the English fears of a foreign marriage. By its terms Philip would promise on oath not to appoint Spanish subjects to office in England, not to take jewels or treasure out of the country, and not to remove Mary or any of their children out of the country.[28]

When Charles sent the drafts to London, he wrote to tell Philip about the state of negotiations. Then he seems to have had

Fig. 12   Philip in 1550

GARDINER BISHOP of WINCHESTER.

From an original Picture in the Possession of
EDMUND TURNOR ESQ.ʳ FR. & A.S.S.

HENRY VIII.

London Pub. July 2 1790. by E Harding N.º 132. Fleet Street.

Fig. 13   Bishop Gardiner

second thoughts and kept Philip's letter in Brussels until the middle of December. Thus, before Philip received his copies, all the other parties had agreed to the terms, and it was too late for Philip to object.[29]

On 16 December Charles finally sent the drafts to Philip, informing him that the queen and Council were in perfect agreement on the proposals. "Although two or three difficulties emerged," Charles said, "they are of such slight importance that we conceded." Charles immediately dispatched two royal representatives, members of the Order of the Golden Fleece, to London for the ceremonial signing, and he directed Philip to do the same. Charles even enclosed drafts of two documents that Philip was to have copied, empowering his own representatives to sign the treaty. "The two powers are in Latin," he reminded Philip. "Whoever copies them must be careful."[30]

Philip was furious. Through all the weeks of negotiation, while Charles and his diplomats worked with Mary and her agents on the exact terms of the marriage treaty, Philip had received only general reports on the progress of negotiations.[31] Charles obviously suspected the treaty terms would not please his son, and in this he was correct. The terms were demeaning and humiliating to the Spanish prince, and he mulled them over for days before finally agreeing to accept them.

The treaties were strange documents.[32] The aging emperor was the chief negotiator for his adult son.[33] The contracting parties were Charles, Roman Emperor and Spanish king, along with his son and heir Prince Philip, as the first party; and Mary, the Queen of England, as the other party. There was only one saving feature: the introductory paragraph, depending on interpretation, could give Philip reasonably wide authority in the government of the country.

> By virtue of the marriage so contracted, celebrated, and consummated, the said Most Serene Prince Philip will enjoy the style, honor, and kingly name of the realms and dominions pertaining to the said Most Serene Queen, along with the Most Serene Queen his consort, and assist her in the happy

administration of her realms and dominions, while
preserving the rights, laws, privileges, and customs of
the same realms and dominions.[34]

The rest of the document gave away much that Philip had come
to consider part of the Spanish patrimony. The Low Countries
would be part of the inheritance of any children Philip and Mary
might have. Even a female heir to the throne of England might
claim the territories. And if Philip's son and heir, Don Carlos,
should die without issue, the English sovereign might claim that
throne as well. The treaty also provided a dowry for Mary in case
of Philip's death, an annual payment of £60,000, levied on the
Spanish kingdoms and the Low Countries.

These were bad enough, but the most humiliating terms came
in the second document. This one contained a list of prohibitions
that Philip was required to accept on oath.

> The prince shall swear he will not promote to any
> office in England any foreigner. He will admit to his
> household English gentlemen and yeomen in
> convenient number and bring none in his retinue
> that will do any displeasure or wrong to the subjects
> of the realm; if they do he shall punish and expel
> them. He shall make no innovation in the laws and
> customs of England. He shall not lead away the
> queen from her realm unless she desires it, nor carry
> children of the marriage out of England, but let
> them be brought up there, unless agreed otherwise
> by the English nobility. If no children are left and
> the queen dies before him he shall not challenge any
> right in the kingdom, but permit the succession to
> come to them to whom it shall belong by right and
> law. He shall not carry out of the realm jewels or
> precious goods, nor alienate any appurtenances of
> the realm, or allow any part of them to be usurped
> by his subjects or others, but shall see all places of
> the realm, especially forts and frontiers, faithfully

> kept and by natives; nor allow the removal of any
> ships, guns or other munitions, but see them
> diligently kept and renewed. England shall not be
> entangled with the war between the emperor and
> the French king. Philip, as much as he can, shall see
> peace observed between France and England, and
> give no cause of breach, but may assist his father in
> defense of his lands and revenge of his injuries.

Although the second treaty seemed to assume that Philip would be joint ruler with Mary, the terms limited his authority in ways that he considered totally demeaning. The terms were totally unacceptable to Philip, but he realized that it was too late to make any changes. Instead, Philip had his notary prepare a formal though secret declaration that he was accepting the treaty under duress. He then signed the authorization document and had the Duke of Alba and Ruy Gómez de Silva sign as witnesses. Because he had not been allowed to participate in the preparation of the treaty, Philip considered that he was bound only to the marriage contract and nothing more.[35]

One major difficulty remained unsettled. The English negotiators wanted Philip to appear in England to sign the marriage documents, or at the very least to have a proxy marriage performed *per verba de futuro*, with details to be decided later. By this means they hoped to force him to accept even more restrictive terms. Philip insisted that the proxy marriage be performed *per verba de presenti*, leaving nothing to be decided later. With this caveat, Philip signed the powers as requested by his father, then sent them to Charles himself, rather than to the imperial ambassador in London. "I have signed both powers but thought it best to send them to your Majesty," he said. "When you have seen them and know what is thought here, your Majesty may arrange and command that something be done."

Somehow Charles managed to inform Mary of Philip's objections, and she apparently agreed with him, at least in part. Charles immediately wrote to reassure his son, saying, "The Most Serene Queen confidently states that, as to the secret matter, it will be done as we wish." Thus, while Mary almost certainly knew about Philip's reservations, her Council and negotiators certainly did not. In any case, it is not exactly clear what was covered by Mary's agreement to the "secret" terms.

One of Philip's principal concerns was the clause specifying that England would not enter into the emperor's war against France. Philip had urged his father to have this provision omitted from the treaty, but the clause remained in the document, no doubt because the queen's Council wanted it there. Mary may very well have agreed to ignore it and perhaps all the other objectionable clauses as well.[36]

So, the marriage was arranged. Originally happy with the terms of the contract, Mary agreed to change them to suit her betrothed. Philip, for his part, was unhappy with the whole agreement, but accepted the terms because that was his duty as prince and heir of the emperor.

Chapter 6

The Reluctant Bridegroom

God save her Majesty and his Majesty the Prince
of Spain, whom the most Serene Queen has chosen
as her King!

Charles gave an official authorization to his treaty commissioners on 21 December 1553. Mary signed the authorization for her treaty commissioners on the first of January, and both groups approved the terms on the twelfth. The English negotiators still wanted Philip to come to England, so he could sign the additional terms in person before the marriage took place. This he refused to do, explaining to his father that "regrettable consequences" might follow. What he meant is that the English negotiators might insist on additional changes that he would be unable to accept.[1]

Philip signed his own authorization documents in early January, but kept them back for a few days, then sent them to his father by overland courier. As a result, they did not reach Brussels until the end of the month. Charles immediately forwarded the documents to London, where the royal negotiators were swiftly running out of patience. Just a few days earlier the Count d'Egmont wrote to tell Philip, "We are waiting from one hour to the next for the powers from Your Highness."[2] By the time they arrived, the situation in England had changed dramatically.

For months the French ambassador, Antoine de Noailles, had been stirring up the discontent that still rankled in the breasts of some few Englishmen who were bitterly opposed to the Spanish marriage and the Catholic religion. Their numbers were small, but Noailles seems to have convinced a few of them that they could depend on France to back their efforts. These conspirators were led by Sir Peter Carew and the Earl of Devon, Sir Thomas Wyatt in Kent, and the Duke of Suffolk, among others. As with most rebel groups, their aims were not clearly defined, but all seemed to agree on deposing Mary and putting Elizabeth and Courtenay on the throne. The plots had been an open secret for months, though no action was taken until the Council summoned Carew to London from the West Country. Once the summons arrived, Carew declared himself to be a rebel, and with that, a number of the London plotters were clapped into the Tower.[3]

Much to Carew's surprise, the people of Devon ignored his call to arms, and in great panic he departed immediately for France. Wyatt, closer to London, managed to organize a force of several thousand men and began to move his army toward the capital. When he did so, all but one of the imperial delegates fled to the continent, Renard alone remaining in the city. Several Council members advised Mary to flee as well, but she refused. Instead she marched to the Guildhall with her closest supporters and gave a stirring address to the people of London.

Speaking frankly, Mary told the people that Wyatt and his followers wanted to capture her, but more importantly, the Tower of London, with all its treasure and arms and the property that belonged to the citizens. He was using the marriage as a pretext, she said. Her main reason for choosing to marry the Prince of Spain was that he was the country's best defense against French aggression. "The Prince of Spain can defend the realm, as no other could," she said, "against the King of France, who has already seized Scotland."

Then promising to submit the matter once more to Parliament and the Council, Mary gave her final challenge. "This being my mind and firm intention, I beg you my beloved subjects, tell me whether I should expect loyalty and obedience from you," she said.

"Otherwise, tell me that you will side with that criminal traitor against me, your queen." With these rousing words Mary rallied the people of London once more to her cause. One witness said, "They all cried with one voice: 'Faith and obedience to our queen.'" Another recalled that people started shouting, "Long live the queen and long live the Prince of Spain." Still another reported the crowd crying, "God save her Majesty and his Majesty the Prince of Spain, whom the most Serene Queen has chosen as her King!"[4]

Within a few days the rebellion was over. Wyatt, Suffolk, and Crofts were prisoners, along with their supporters. Courtenay abandoned the plot before it ever started and spent most of his time thereafter declaring himself the helpless pawn of evil men. About 500 rebels were condemned to death. A hundred or so were executed, including Jane Grey and her husband Guilford Dudley, neither of whom had a role in the uprising. On 22 February the remaining 400 were marched to the tilt yard at Westminster with collars and halters about their necks. There they knelt, begged Mary for forgiveness, and she pardoned them.[5]

During the month of January Renard and Charles had urged Philip to go to England with all due speed and "consummate" the marriage. Now they wrote to tell him that it was unsafe to do so. No doubt this is what he wanted to hear. Even though their advice changed quickly,[6] Philip continued to show a monumental indifference to England and Mary. He did not bother to write to her or even to send her the traditional betrothal gift. Nevertheless, Mary gathered the ambassadors and Council members together on 6 March for the formal exchange of oaths to ratify the treaties. Afterwards, Mary and the Count d'Egmont stood before the Bishop of Winchester and completed the betrothal *per verba de presenti*, as called for in the treaty.[7] The ring she wore was a diamond Charles sent to welcome her into the family as "our own daughter."[8] Mary responded in kind, sending her betrothed a letter in which she said, "I am your Lady, your most loyal and most submissive Lady."[9]

Renard's report of the ceremony left Charles with the impression that Philip had been declared King of England, so he passed the information along to his son. "You have been proclaimed and sworn as king," he said in his letter of 30 April, "to the satisfaction of everyone." The misimpression was widespread. Francisco de Vargas, the Spanish ambassador in Venice, wrote to give Philip the news he had received from England, "All the kingdom awaits your Highness with great rejoicing, saying, 'Long live Philip, King of England and France, Prince of Spain.'" The Duke of Medina Sidonia wrote from San Lucar, congratulating Mary on her "most welcome" marriage to "the prince and king." The French ambassador sent home a report describing the new titles approved by Parliament: "Philip and Mary, by the Grace of God, king and queen of England, France and Ireland, Defenders of the Faith, princes of Spain, dukes of Brabant, counts of Flanders and other Low Countries, &c."

Before this time Philip had considered the marriage to his aunt a duty to be borne for the sake of the empire and the Catholic faith. The new title changed things. As regent of Spain Philip customarily signed official communications "*Yo el principe*," or "I the prince." With his changed status, Philip could be "*rey-principe*," or "king-prince," or maybe just "king." On 12 May, basking in his new title, he wrote to members of the Privy Council and signed himself "*Philippus Rex*," or "Philip the King." As it turned out, all the reports were wrong. Even though the treaty was approved and people in Mary's court referred to him as king, the royal title would not take effect until after the marriage, with a formal coronation scheduled a month or so later. Luckily for everyone, Philip's correspondence went through Renard, who noticed the blunder and kept the letters from being delivered to the Council members.[10]

The note from Mary and the report that he was king finally moved Philip to do what he should have done much earlier. Along with the letters to the Privy Council Philip sent a chest of jewels for his bride. The central gift was "a huge flat diamond, beautifully worked into a roseate setting, and valued at fifty thousand ducados." Besides this he sent "a necklace of eighteen diamonds, worked with such meticulous precision that one follows the next with captivating elegance; value: thirty thousand ducados." The third piece of jewelry evidently became Mary's favorite, for she wore it in several portraits: "a great diamond with a pearl pendant, to wear on the breast. These two pieces were the most beautiful and lovely that could be found in the universe, such was their delicacy and appearance; value: twenty-five thousand ducados." There were also other rings and jewels set with diamonds, emeralds, and rubies. The whole lavish display of gifts was intended to impress the bride and her subjects with the majesty and generosity of the Spanish prince, and they no doubt did.[11]

While everyone in England kept pressing for Philip to arrive, some of the delay was actually caused in London. Parliament did not approve the marriage treaty until 12 April, even though Philip had made it abundantly clear that he would not leave Spain until he had seen the ratified treaties. Then, once Mary's commissioners had the treaties in hand, they dawdled on their journey to deliver the documents. They left England in the middle of April and did not arrive in Spain until nearly four weeks later. At that point Philip decided it was useless for them to come to see him in Valladolid, so he arranged for them to be entertained in Corunna and Santiago de Compostela, while he finished his preparations for departure.[12]

By 12 May most of the scattered Spanish fleet was at last in or near Corunna, where Philip was to board for the journey to England. Still, one important task remained. Charles had named Philip's sister Juana as regent of Spain during Philip's absence in England. The nineteen-year-old princess was still in Portugal, where she had just given birth to a son. Though she was recovering from childbirth and heartbroken over the tragic death of her bridegroom, Juana put her affairs in order and left at once for Spain. On his way at last, Philip met Juana at Alcántara, where he found the princess on the verge of exhaustion and bathed in tears. Comforting her as best he could, Philip spent a few days advising her about the most pressing matters of government. Then he turned toward Santiago de Compostela to greet the English ambassadors. Along the way he stopped in Benavente for one last visit with his son Don Carlos. Finally, on 25 June Philip was in Santiago, where the English diplomats awaited his arrival. Although an emissary had taken Philip's ratification to London in May, the English diplomats may have had some knowledge of the secret disclaimer, for they insisted on witnessing his signature to the additional articles of the treaty. Whatever the case, Philip went through the process once more,

Fig. 14　Don Carlos, Philip's son

promising faithfully to observe all the conditions he had once found so humiliating.[13] The new ratification was so specific that Philip very likely decided to abandon his secret *"escriptura ad cautelam"* of 4 January 1554. In the document of 25 June Philip said,

> We approve, praise, and ratify these presents and everything contained therein, in the manner and form in which they have been agreed upon; in good and genuine faith we solemnly promise on our princely word to see them observed, every exception or contrary declaration notwithstanding; and we have confirmed the same, swearing on the Holy Gospels, which we have touched.

No doubt the greatest disappointment for Philip was the knowledge that he was not yet king, nor had anyone sworn allegiance to him. In some annoyance he signed the document as plain *"Philippus."* No title.[14]

Very likely the English diplomats gave Philip one more bit of bad news: because of recent events, Parliament had acquired extensive authority to determine who should rule England. Henry VIII owed his crown to a declaration of Parliament and not to his own claim to the throne by right of inheritance. When Henry VIII decided to name the successors to his throne, he asked Parliament for legislative authorization, then used that authority to write the succession into his will. More recently lawyers in England had raised the possibility that a woman could not rule permanently in her own right, so that upon marriage, Mary's throne would pass to her husband. To cover this possibility and to please the queen, Parliament had declared that a woman could possess the crown as fully and completely as any previous English ruler.[15] Thus, Parliament seemed to have assumed the power to determine succession to the throne. If Philip hoped to be anything more than titular King of England, he would very likely need parliamentary approval. Certainly Philip was discouraged about this development, but he seems to have felt that everything would be taken care of when he was crowned King of England.

A few days after his meeting with the English embassy Philip arrived at Corunna. The streets and inns were packed with people who wanted to take part in festivities honoring the prince and see the great fleet prepared for his journey. A good 3,000 soldiers heading for the emperor's army in Flanders were ready to board the ships anchored in the harbor at Corunna, and more were arriving every day. Some had been there for weeks, waiting for Philip. Merchants came daily with cartloads of provisions, battling for dock space with sailors trying to load the horses, guns, armor, and countless pieces of equipment needed by Philip's huge entourage. Wives and children, forbidden to accompany the men, came to say goodbye. Philip brought his own household, in their hundreds, plus his personal guard – a hundred halberdiers from the Guarda Española, another hundred from the Guarda Alemana, and a third hundred of his German archers. In addition to a retinue of nobles, he brought his own spiritual advisors: his chief chaplain, the Bishop of Salamanca, plus a dozen assistant chaplains and four theologians, including two Franciscans, one Dominican, and another bishop. All of them brought their own retainers – the nobles their servants, and the religious their choirs and chapel furnishings. Some wondered whether the 125 vessels in the Spanish fleet could hold it all. In fact, there was not room at the docks for everyone. When Philip left, some twenty ships remained behind to load 4,000 soldiers who would make up the rear guard and then go to the continent to reinforce the emperor's army. In the meantime they would also serve as guards for the treasure shipment Philip was bringing to help pay the costs of his father's war with France.[16]

Just before Philip embarked, a messenger arrived from his father in Flanders, bringing news that a French attack on Marienbourg had ended disastrously; Philip must come to his aid as soon as decently possible. Troops were needed, but money was just as important. Charles had mentioned this before, but Philip always managed to find a reason for delay. Though silver and gold arrived every year from the Spanish possessions in the New World, the treasure quickly left Spain, usually in the hands of the merchants and bankers who supplied and financed the emperor's wars with other European monarchs.[17]

Philip's fleet left port on Friday, 13 July, aboard the *Espíritu Santo*, a huge vessel flying banners and pennants of various sorts, all of which were hauled down once the fleet left port. The winds were good, but the sea was rough, and many became ill. "I left La Coruña on Friday," Philip wrote to Antonio de Rojas, his old tutor. "That first day I was so sick that it took me three days in bed to recover." Ruy Gómez de Silva said, "I nearly died of seasickness." Even so, both recovered nicely, and the ships kept sailing. After four and a half days with a good wind the Spanish fleet met thirty-eight English and Dutch ships that had been patrolling the sea lanes between England and France. The combined fleets made port at the Isle of Wight, on 19 July, where Philip had, earlier in the spring, been directed to land. As it turned out, plans had changed, so the Spanish fleet sailed on to Portsmouth. Arriving there at two in the afternoon, the fleets traded cannon salutes with the fortress, while messengers scurried back and forth between ship and shore. One of the dispatch boats carried a letter from Philip to his bride. Another brought his emissary, the Marquis de Las Navas and several young English noblemen who offered to serve as gentlemen of Philip's chamber.[18]

It was a stunning reception for the young prince, perhaps not as grand as he had seen in his journey through the courts of the Holy Roman Empire, but still one worthy of a new king. This was the problem. Philip might be able to control the Privy Council and rule the country, but he was depending on Mary to keep her agreement and see that he was crowned King of England.

Chapter 7

The Marriage of England and Spain

Philip will you have Mary as your wife, to cherish and love her at all times, in poverty or improved circumstances, in favorable health or stricken by some disease, and have no dealings with other women, surrendering to her your body and your entire kingdom?

As morning broke on 20 July 1554, a barge, richly decorated in black and white and trimmed in gilt, left Southampton. Several other vessels joined the barge, which began rowing toward the Spanish fleet riding at anchor about three leagues away. On board were the imperial ambassadors Renard, Courrières, Alba, Juan de Figueroa, Philip's own envoy the Marquis de Las Navas, and the Earls of Arundel, Derby, Shrewsbury, and Pembroke. All sat or stood on one or another of the thick carpets, but left vacant the brocaded chair that was reserved for Prince Philip. Arriving at the flagship about noon, they found Philip and his company eating lunch, so they waited for them to finish. Figueroa then gave Philip two special letters from his father, one of them informing Philip that as a wedding gift he had been named King of Naples, one of the richest states in the empire, and Duke of Milan as well. It was an important gift, no doubt intended to remove Philip's annoyance about the unfortunate restrictions that seemed to surround his title as King of England. As a result of the gift Philip and his bride would be equal in prestige.[1]

With the letters read and lunch finished, Philip and several of his closest companions boarded the barge and headed for the dock at Southampton. As the rowers bent to their oars, the ships of the combined fleets and the batteries on shore fired a thundering salvo, then fired again when the barge came to the pier. Just before the Spanish party disembarked at Southampton, the Earl of Arundel came aboard the royal barge. There he inducted Philip into the Order of the Garter, presenting him with a gift from Mary consisting of two versions of the Garter insignia, one of which was set with diamonds for ceremonial wear. After listening to Arundel as he recited the rules of the Order of the Garter, Philip went ashore wearing his new decoration. There the royal horse guard was assembled on foot, led by Anthony Browne – later Lord Montague – Philip's new Master of the Horse. In his hands Browne held the reins of a white filly draped in crimson velvet with embroidery of pearls and gold. Having previously sworn his oath of service before Las Navas, Browne bent his knees before Philip to say his vow once again in Latin. The Spanish prince responded graciously, also in Latin, then raised Browne to his feet. With that ceremony completed, Philip mounted the filly, and Browne led the procession to the Church of the Holy Rood, where Philip entered and knelt to pray. After this he was led to a building next door, where an apartment had been prepared for his use with the usual adornment of canopies, carpets, and tapestries, some of which had belonged to King Henry VIII.[2]

Letters from his father during the previous few months had repeated the same paternal directives: Philip must send money as soon as possible, and Philip must be attentive to his prospective bride. Charles understood that the money could not be sent until Philip had it in his possession, but he did not understand Philip's attitude toward Mary, which had bordered on gross neglect. Early in the proceedings a friend wrote to say, "For the love of God, try to look pleased." A little later Charles rebuked Philip, saying, "Son, since you are going on with this marriage, I beg you to follow the instructions I sent you by the Count of Agamonte; if you don't do

Fig. 15   Philip riding a white filly, led by Anthony Browne

as I say, I would rather not have begun this business." Half
expecting the worst of Philip, Charles asked his ambassador to keep
an eye on the reluctant prince. "Duke, for the love of God, be
careful to see that my son behaves properly; for if he does not, I
tell you I would rather never have started this business at all."[3]
They need not have worried. Once Philip had put his signature on
the marriage documents brought by the English ambassadors, he
determined to act as an attentive bridegroom should.

On the day the fleet arrived in England Philip sent Arundel
to Winchester with a diamond gift for Mary, while Renard went
along to find out what arrangements had been made for the
marriage and to determine when Philip should plan to arrive. The
very next day Renard returned to Philip, saying that he was to
remain in Southampton until Monday and that the wedding would
happen on Wednesday the twenty-fifth, the Feast of St. James,
patron of Spain.

By this time nearly all the diplomats and nobles who usually
lived in London had arrived in Winchester for the wedding. The
one major exception was the French ambassador Noailles, who was

deliberately omitted from the guest list because of his involvement with Wyatt and the other rebels. Even so, Noailles had a series of agents who kept him informed. One of them reported that Philip met on Friday evening with the leading members of the Privy Council, who all swore to be loyal to him as their king. After they had done so, Philip told them (doubtless in Latin or French) that he had been called by the grace of God "to wed the queen their mistress." "As a good servant of God," said Philip, "he could not refuse to obey His divine will." He came not as "a prince of Spain and a stranger, but as a native Englishman," an apparent reference to his ancestor, Edward III. Finally, he commended the councilors for "their good willingness to be faithful, obedient, and loyal," promising in return that "they would find him to be a very good and loving prince."[4]

The next morning Philip rode to Mass at the cathedral in a driving rain, accompanied once again by the mounted English guardsmen, and wearing a borrowed hat and cloak to keep the rain from ruining his beautiful clothes. After lunching alone, as he usually did, Philip asked Figueroa for a formal reading of the emperor's gift. When the ambassador finished, Philip announced with great solemnity that he kissed his father's hands for the great honor bestowed on him, but said he would like to keep the matter secret for a while. The next day he told Figueroa that he had had second thoughts: it would be best to publish the news now, rather than let the secret leak out somehow. The formal announcement would take place as soon as Philip had had the opportunity to discuss the details with Mary. Charles had specified that a ceremony of coronation precede the wedding, but Philip vetoed that idea, saying that it would be best to confer with Mary first. He wanted nothing to annoy his English subjects or to diminish the importance of his role as King of England. Once his decision was made, Philip sent Ruy Gómez to Mary with another jeweled gift as well as a note that told her what he had in mind.[5]

The rain continued on Monday and for the rest of the week, pelting the wedding party on the muddy road from Southampton to Winchester. If the rain dampened anyone's enthusiasm, it was not apparent to Philip and his company. Mary provided an honor guard – archers, bowmen, and pikemen, mounted and vested in Philip's livery – to guide the party along the road to Winchester. Counting the nobles and gentlemen, there were nearly 3,000 in the parade, all dressed in fine clothes and colorful uniforms. About a mile from the city they arrived at a monastery where Philip stopped to change out of his wet clothes and prepare for the formal entry to Winchester. When he emerged an hour or so later, Philip wore a black silk doublet chased with gold, white velvet shoes, and a white waistcoat. Over this he wore a coat of black velvet, trimmed in gold lace. Thus refreshed, the prince and his company rode on to Winchester. Just outside the city he was greeted by an honor guard of eight or ten young noblemen, clad in crimson doublets with sashes made from cloth of gold. Their horses were richly caparisoned, and at the rear rode a gentleman similarly dressed and leading a fine horse with beautiful trappings. This, he said, was a gift from Queen Mary for Philip's entry to the city. As he rode through the gates of the city, another guard of a dozen or so, clothed in scarlet, presented Philip with the keys to the city and the castle. After a ceremonial welcome, Philip rode on to the cathedral, where several bishops and dozens of priests had assembled to greet his party. Walking in procession to the main altar, everyone knelt while Philip said his prayers and the choir sang a *Te Deum* in thanksgiving for his safe arrival. With this accomplished, the prince retired to his quarters in the dean's palace next door to the cathedral. His bride had her own quarters across the garden in the palace of the bishop.[6]

Later that evening Philip and Mary met for the first time, and both appeared to be pleased with one another, not a common thing in royal marriages and certainly not something that was expected in this one. Hoping to impress his bride, Philip had changed his clothes once again, this time wearing a black velvet coat, cut in "the French style" and chased in silver and gold; beneath this he wore a jerkin of white leather also trimmed in gold and silver; his leather shoes were also white. "He really looked handsome," said one observer.[7]

Mary wore a black velvet gown, trimmed with an open ferret of black silk and a front of silver brocade embroidered with seed pearls and larger pearls. On her head the queen wore a sort of cap of black velvet with gold fastenings. In the fashion of the day, she had a high collar of the same materials about her neck. There was a diamond girdle about her waist, a necklace of diamonds over her shoulders, and her fingers sparkled with jeweled rings. It was obvious to nearly everyone that Mary deserved her reputation for wearing fine clothes and finer jewelry. However, one of the gentlemen in Philip's company was not impressed, either with Mary's looks or with her taste in clothes. "The queen is no beauty," he said, adding, "she dresses very badly."[8]

This was more than unkind. Both Mary and her younger half-sister Elizabeth looked alike in many ways. Both had the same fair skin, inherited from their father, with hair so light as to make it seem they had no eyebrows. Beyond this, Mary was small and slight and much paler than the women usually seen in Spain. But her small stature and light complexion were a good match for those of her bridegroom, who could only be called handsome by stretching the term to its very limit. With this in mind, one of Philip's men wrote: "The queen is very nice although older than they told us." The Venetian ambassador gave a more diplomatic assessment: "If not for a slight decline due to age, one might say she was somewhat pretty."[9]

Once the demands of royal courtesy had been observed, Philip and Mary retired to a private corner where they could discuss the matter of royal precedence. Now King of Naples, Philip appeared to think that his coronation as King of England would come with the wedding or shortly thereafter. Mary apparently did nothing to change this impression. Instead, she asked him to have a formal reading of the "Privilege of Naples" the next evening before the lords of the Council, who could scarcely fail to be impressed.

Since Philip did not speak or understand English, though he had some ability in French, and Mary had a little Spanish, they conversed in two languages. Mary used French while Philip spoke in Spanish. Before the evening was over, Philip asked Mary to teach him how to say good night in English. After practicing the words with her a few times, Philip rose from his chair and said, "Good night my lordes all." Then he turned to the ladies, bade them a similar good night, and with his party went back across the garden to his own lodging.[10]

The next afternoon Philip visited Mary once more, wearing a suit she had sent him early that morning. Not surprisingly, it fit him perfectly, nor was anyone surprised that the men of the honor guard were perfectly attired in Philip's livery. All this had been arranged months earlier through careful negotiations between the ambassadors. After speaking with his bride for some considerable time, Philip departed, stopping in the cathedral for the vespers of the Feast of St. James, the major patron of Spain. That evening Philip crossed the garden again to visit his bride. There, in front of a small group of his own gentlemen and a few of Mary's ladies, Philip ordered Figueroa to read the proclamation from Charles, granting him the kingdom of Naples. Once this was done, Philip said, as he had done earlier, that he kissed the emperor's hand for his great generosity. Figueroa called upon those present to bear witness to what had taken place, and Philip returned once more to his own lodging. After the Spanish party departed, Mary met with Bishop Gardiner, the Lord Chancellor, and others of her Council. All agreed that a ceremony of coronation should be held the next morning, just before the wedding. Philip was informed of the change and immediately agreed.[11]

The driving rains continued on 25 July, delaying wedding guests and dampening their magnificent clothes. Philip appeared at the church at about ten in the morning, well before most of the guests and long before the bride herself entered the building. He was wearing another suit that Mary had ordered for him – white again – and the Garter. Over everything he wore a mantle made of cloth of gold, decorated with pearls, studded with precious stones of various sorts, and trimmed in crimson velvet. The bride was robed once more in black, over which she draped a mantle of cloth of gold, matching the one she had sent to Philip. The bride and groom met in the nave of the cathedral, where Mary had been led in procession by the Earl of Derby, who carried the sword of state, symbolizing her royal dignity. Both then went to their respective thrones, Philip on the left and Mary on the right, where they confessed their sins and were shriven. Then they proceeded further into the church, where five bishops waited, including the chancellor of the realm, Bishop Gardiner, who would preside at the ceremony.[12]

At this point Ambassador Figueroa appeared, carrying the silver-cased vellum sheet he had brought from Brussels. Reading in Latin from the document, Figueroa proclaimed that Emperor Charles V had made his son Philip King of Naples:

> His Imperial and Kingly Majesty my lord, . . . in order to show how he continues in true and heartfelt paternal love for Your Majesty and also because he wishes to honor the marriage which you have contracted with the Most Serene Queen of England by some outstanding gift, and to show his munificence and love to Your Majesty and to the same Most Serene queen, gives, releases, renounces and transfers to Your Majesty, the aforesaid Most Serene Prince, the Kingdom of Naples, which by the Grace of God, among his other kingdoms, he possesses, as it stands at this moment.

The ambassador then presented the vellum document to Philip, who responded as he had twice before, promising "undying gratitude to the Emperor His Catholic Majesty and most gracious lord for his signal grace and munificence, which he will repay with filial devotion and singular submission." After this Philip handed the document to Mary, as they had arranged, and she gave it to Bishop Gardiner. The bishop opened the silver cover for a moment and paused to read the introductory text. Then he looked up and explained to the congregation in English what the ambassador and Philip had said in Latin. Finally, another sword of state was brought in and presented to the Earl of Pembroke to carry before King Philip, while the Earl of Derby carried Queen Mary's sword of state and led the royal couple to the altar.[13]

Walking to the choir hand in hand, Philip and Mary paused while Bishop Gardiner recited the terms of the treaties that were part of the marriage contract each had signed earlier in the year.

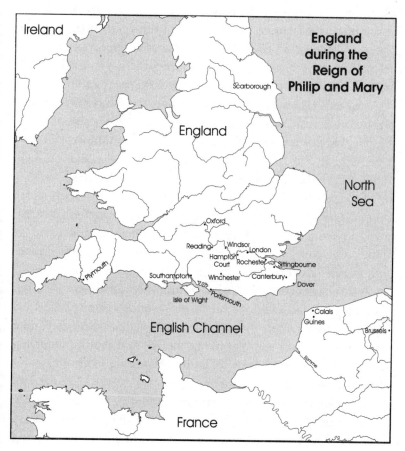

Map 2   England during the Reign of Philip and Mary

He then asked (in Latin) whether anyone knew of a reason why the two should not be joined in marriage. After a brief pause the congregation answered, "Nullus est." (There is none.) Then the bishop said, in Latin once more, "Philip will you have Mary as your wife, to cherish and love her at all times, in poverty or improved circumstances, in favorable health or stricken by some disease, and have no dealings with other women, surrendering to her your body and your entire kingdom?" Philip answered, "Yes." (Ita est.) He then placed several gold coins on the missal as a token of his wealth. The same question was asked of Mary. Her answer was the same, and she also placed gold coins on the missal. After the ring was placed there and blessed, Mary put it on, a plain gold band, which she said English maidens used to wear at their weddings. Then Philip kissed her, and they were married.[14]

During the Mass the bride and groom were seated under canopies placed on opposite sides of the high altar, so that when the time came for wishing peace to one another, Philip crossed to Mary's side, gave her the kiss of peace, and returned to his throne. Both received the Eucharist, though the rest of the congregation did not. Instead, they were given Holy Bread and cups of wine after the Mass was over, according to the former English custom. Once this was done, four heralds came to the foot of the altar, where one who was dressed in the brocade of the King of Arms announced the titles of Philip and Mary in Latin, French, and English:

> Philip and Marie, by the grace of god, king and Quene of England, France, Naples, Hierusal[em], & Ireland, def[en]ders of the faith, Princes of Spain and Secyll, Archidukes of Austria, Dukes of Mill[an], Burg[un]dy and Brab[an]t, Counties of Haspurge, Fla[an]ders, and Tirol.[15]

The religious ceremony over, the newly-weds departed hand in hand for the bishop's palace, where a feast lay spread upon the tables of the banquet hall. The king and queen sat at the royal table, raised on a platform several steps above the other tables. They were surrounded with dishes of gold set with precious stones, but whether they ate or drank is not recorded. The music was mellow, and soon the crowd of ambassadors, councilors, noble ladies, and gentlemen was mellow as well. After a time the heralds appeared and proclaimed the royal titles once more, crying, "Largesse, largesse, largesse." Once they were given their traditional reward of a few coins, the heralds then departed. Afterwards, Philip and Mary danced until nine in the evening, while "the dukes and noble men of Spain danse[d] with the faire ladyes and the moste beutifull nimphes of England."[16]

Finally, the celebration was over for the day, but the royal couple still had one duty to perform. Strolling once again in procession, the king and queen went hand in hand to the bridal chamber, where the bishop blessed the marriage bed, according to the custom of the country. Then all the guests retired to their respective apartments. "The remainder of this night," said a Spanish gentleman, "those may imagine who have gone through it."[17]

Philip was up early next morning, but Mary remained in her chamber all day with her ladies-in-waiting, again following the custom for royal brides. Philip went to Mass, lunched alone, though in public, and chatted with visitors. A day later he began work once more, signing papers for the formal transfer of Naples, conferring with the captains of his fleet, and giving orders for the ships to go to Flanders with the troops and money for Charles. Visitors called on the royal couple, including the Duchess of Alba, who played a sort of game of musical chairs with the queen. The duchess wanted to sit on a lower chair than Her Highness, but Mary insisted that they be seated on the same level. Finally they compromised, both sitting on low stools. Some of the guests went to see the sights of Windsor, the most famous of which was the Round Table of King Arthur, "who is said to be enchanted there."[18]

By the end of the month, with the wedding ceremonies concluded in Winchester, the newly-weds began their slow procession to London. Citizens in the towns along the way had enjoyed holidays during the royal marriage celebration, and the arrival of the cavalcade was the signal for further festivities. Stopping first in Basing, they spent a night and the next in the house of the Lord Treasurer. According to one account, the feasting

Fig. 16   Philip and Mary

was beyond compare. "I have not sene the like," said John Elder, "for the tyme in my dayes." Staying a single night in Reading, the king and queen moved on to Windsor, entering the town on Friday, 3 August, while the Earls of Pembroke and Derby carried the two swords of state before them. The following Sunday Philip stood in the great church, once more wearing the robe of the Order of the Garter. This time the queen herself placed the jeweled collar about his neck and completed the ceremony making her husband a Knight of the Garter. The entertainment at Windsor included a day of hunting in the forest, with game trapped at a barricade, "a great toyle of 4 or 5 myles longe." At the end of the week the two rode on to Richmond, staying there for several more days, while the pageants were prepared for their arrival in London.[19]

At last the great day arrived. On 17 August Philip and Mary went by boat from Richmond to London, landing at the stairs of St. Mary Overie, now Southwark Cathedral. There the Lord Chancellor met them and took them to his house for dinner. Afterwards they crossed through the park to the house of the Lord Chamberlain, where they spent the night. Next day, accompanied by the usual crowd of nobles, ambassadors, privy councilors, and others, they crossed London Bridge, with the Lord Mayor leading the way and brandishing his mace. The first stop was at the drawbridge, where two huge images, *Gogmagog Albionis* and *Corineus Britannus*, held a great silver tablet. The long Latin inscription hailed Philip as the "noble Prince, sole hope of Cesar's side, by God apointed all the world to gyde." While the royal party stopped to read the message, the cannon batteries of the Tower of London roared a thunderous salute.[20]

Somewhat further along, on Gracechurch Street, the Steelyard merchants had prepared a pageant. This consisted of a number of paintings with inscriptions in Latin, one of which is sufficient to give the tenor of the whole. "Worthy Philip the fortunate and most mighty Prince of Spain, most earnestly wyshed for." At Cheapside a great genealogical tree listed the descent of the royal couple from Edward III, who was depicted as an old man with a long white beard, lying at the root of the tree. Perhaps the most spectacular display was the one at St. Paul's, where an acrobat came hurtling head first down a cord from the steeple "as an arrow out of a bow," and landed in a featherbed at the bottom.[21]

Depending on the source, the display at Fleet Street was either an inspiring tribute to the new king and queen or a deliberate insult prepared by an angry Protestant. John Elder said the pageant depicted:

> a quene & a king representing their highnes, having
> of their right side *Iusticia* with a swerd in her hande,
> and *Equitas* wyth a payre of ballaunce. And of theyr
> left side Veritas wyth a boke in her hande, whereon
> was written, *Verbum Dei & Misericordia* with a hearte
> of golde.[22]

An anonymous manuscript, now published by the Camden Society, seems to transfer some of these details to a mildly subversive pageant. In that manuscript, where the paragraph was crossed out, and the location was "the counduit in Graciouse strete," the scene was said to show Henry VIII with a book in his hand labeled *Verbum Dei*. Pretty tame stuff, perhaps, but the depiction is said to have annoyed the bishop so much that he came back later and forced the painter to change it. Apparently that good prelate thought the book should have been shown in Queen Mary's hand, since she had restored the "Word of God" in the church.[23] Still, if this was subversion, most people did not notice it. Instead, they saw a king and queen who were obviously much taken with each other, and Philip's followers saw that the English were able to arrange pageants and parties nearly as grand as those that had greeted Philip during his tour of the empire.

Good relations between Mary's court and Philip's followers did not last long. Philip had brought his own enormous household, seemingly unaware that Mary had appointed an English establishment to serve him, at his expense, of course. Both groups vied for the king's attention. Finally, after several days of trying to elbow their way into the king's presence, most of his old courtiers began to give up in disgust and ask for permission to go to Flanders or back to Spain. English servants were equally frustrated. Those

Spaniards who stayed found things very different from what they were at home. Merchants took advantage of the difference in coinage to cheat the newcomers. An official exchange rate had been established earlier, but it was set on the advice of the local merchants, very favorable to them and disadvantageous to the visitors. "There are great thieves among them," said Philip's mayordomo, "and they steal openly. They have this advantage over Spaniards, that we do it by cunning and they by force."[24]

Chapter 8

Philip of Spain, King of England

*The first and most important subject which I wanted
to achieve was to win approval on religious matters.*

Philip

Once she had seen her husband, Mary determined that Philip
would be a real king. On 27 July, just two days after the wedding,
the Privy Council met in Winchester to adopt measures that would
make everyone understand that Philip was an integral part of the
government. Matters of state requiring the sovereign's approval
were henceforth to carry the signatures of both Philip and Mary.
A new state seal was ordered, bearing both names. At the end of
each meeting a summary in "Laten and Spanyshe" was to be
prepared for the king's use. Council and parliamentary sessions
would be listed under the new regnal name, *"Anno primo et secundo
Philippi et Marie Regis et Regine,"* or, "The first and second year of the
reign of Philip and Mary, king and queen." To start things off right,
Mary sent an order to the Lord Privy Seal, the Earl of Bedford,
telling him to brief Philip on all current matters of government.[1]

> fyrste . . . tell the Kyng the whole state of this
> Realme, wt all thyngs appartaynyng to the same as
> myche as ye Knowe to be trewe
> Seconde . . . obey hys cõmandment in all thyngs

> thyrdly in all thyngs he shall aske your aduyse, . . .
> decl[are] your opinion as becometh a faythfull
> conceyllour to do
>
> Marye the quene

Both councilors and diplomats soon became accustomed to Philip's presence. In early September Renard reported to the emperor that "the king has begun transacting business with the Council."[2] Philip attended all the regular Council meetings, usually two days per week. The discussions were sometimes long and often tedious, but Philip was used to this. He could sit for four or five hours at a time, listening to the opinions of the members, then making his own brief and succinct remarks. Over time he seems to have gained an understanding of English, so that he could follow the conversations with relative ease. Even so, he gave his own opinions in Spanish or Latin, the latter of which most educated people understood. Beyond his work with the Council, Philip held regular audiences, which anyone could attend.[3]

In one of his first acts as sovereign, Philip received the French ambassador's credentials. Then, after consulting the Council, he had the chancellor inform the French diplomat that England would observe the peace treaties with France so long as there was no provocation to do otherwise.[4] An Italian ambassador reported: "The King hears and dispatches almost all state affairs, as it befits his dignity and authority that he should."[5] The transition was accomplished with the complete approval of the queen, the chancellor, and the Council. And with their approval Philip announced to one petitioner that Mary and her entire kingdom were "bound to be guided by my will."[6]

One reason for Philip's success was his considerable skill in government, but another, perhaps equally important, was his liberal use of money. Almost as soon as he arrived in England, Philip put the leading lords and government officials on his personal payroll, with cash gifts and annual pensions. Going even further, he paid a considerable sum to retire Queen Mary's most pressing debts, pleasing the lenders and putting the kingdom on a stable financial footing.[7] Perhaps most importantly, Philip managed to shrug off the grave, even haughty, demeanor that people had found so unpleasant

Fig. 17   The Great Seal of Philip and Mary

during his trip through the capitals of the empire. Now he appeared to be patient, kind, friendly, and above all generous. He was a good listener and gave his time freely to anyone who wanted to speak with him.[8] Ambassador Renard managed to find signs of discontent here and there, but Philip was as pleased as he could be. Writing to his sister in early September, he reported that the people of London had greeted his arrival with "universal signs of love and joy."[9]

During their month-long honeymoon, Philip had treated his bride with all the attentive care she could possibly have expected, at the same time showing amazing deference to the members of the English court. One of the emperor's ambassadors wrote to say that "everyone loves him," and this was very likely true. Of course, the one who loved him most was the queen. Ruy Gómez saw the royal couple alone one day, Mary "speaking bashful words of love, and Philip answering in kind." Mary was thoroughly smitten, romantically in love with her husband, and she thought he returned her love in equal measure. In this she was probably wrong. While thoughtful and polite in the extreme, Philip was not really in love with Mary, though she was too innocent to realize this. Still, he appeared in public with the queen on many occasions, paid her unfailing courtesy, and showered her with little attentions. This seemed to be sufficient for Mary, who was totally inexperienced in matters of the heart.[10]

When Philip first began to attend meetings of the Privy Council, he saw quickly that there were problems. For a few days he watched, just to get a better understanding of the way governmental affairs were conducted in England. Mary's original appointees, named to reward them for supporting her during the brief period when Jane Grey was queen, were men who had little or no experience in government. Those named later had much more experience but were correspondingly less loyal. As a result the Council was an unwieldy group, divided in loyalty and too diverse for effective administration. Since all government operations depended on approval by members of the Privy Council, Philip saw that drastic measures were needed to improve efficiency in that body. Paget, who had become one of Philip's closest advisers shared this opinion.[11]

A second problem, perhaps more serious in Philip's mind, was formal coronation. While both law and custom seemed to make him sovereign, and while the marriage treaty recognized that he was in fact King of England, the treaty also placed serious restrictions on his ability to rule effectively. Philip and his entourage soon understood that he would never command the full respect of his English subjects until he was anointed and crowned, just as Mary had been a year earlier. Most of the diplomats stationed in London thought his coronation was imminent, and for a time Philip did as well. However, a third problem, the religious question, added several layers of complications.[12]

During the reign of her brother Edward, Mary's faith had made her extremely popular with the Catholic gentry. Almost as soon as she was proclaimed queen in July 1553, many of her supporters began to order local priests to resume saying the Latin Mass. Some priests complied immediately, but many others remembered the bad times under Henry and Edward and decided to wait for a change in the law. This came on 18 August, when Mary issued a proclamation on religion. Declaring her own preference for the Mass, Mary would allow the new religion to continue in places where the people preferred it. As a result, the Mass and other sacraments were quickly restored in heavily Catholic areas like Yorkshire. In London the changes were much more moderate. In Protestant strongholds in Kent there was outright refusal to accept any change, and this was allowed to continue.[13]

The arrangement worked for a time, allowing Philip to concentrate on the most pressing religious matter, the disposition of the former abbey lands. Most of the convents and abbeys confiscated from religious orders under Henry VIII had come into the hands of the gentry. Many of the new owners were members of the English church, but nearly as many were Catholic, and almost all of them were determined to retain possession of their new estates. Thus, both groups were opposed to any reconciliation with Rome, since that would require them to return everything that had once belonged to the church. This became clear in April 1554, when a bill on the subject was introduced in Parliament. Paget himself led the opposition, and the bill failed to pass.[14] If Philip was going to be successful, he would need to take a new approach. His surprisingly widespread popularity seemed to guarantee that something could be done.

Dazzled by the lavish wedding and the grand entourage of their new king, Englishmen in late summer became very optimistic about the Spanish marriage. Moreover, it seemed that there would soon be an heir to the throne. One of Mary's physicians told Renard in great confidence that Mary was with child. Seizing his opportunity, Renard quickly spread the good news, and most of the country rejoiced.[15] With his public approval at a new high, Philip and his advisers thought it was time to assemble Parliament and settle all the major questions in one grand session.[16]

Along the way some arms would need to be twisted. Working through the imperial legates in Rome, Charles and Philip told Pope Julius III that England could be brought back into the church, but only if he would send a representative to London to work out a compromise on the issue of church property. Julius quickly agreed, selecting Cardinal Pole as his legate, and giving him authority to make the necessary concessions.[17]

While the cardinal made his way across Europe, Charles and his advisers made an effort to find out what the legate intended to do. By the time Pole stopped in Brussels they understood that he had no intention of making things easy for the holders of church property. In Pole's mind, the question was entirely a legal one: since Henry VIII had no right to confiscate church lands, his government could hardly convey a valid title to the new owners. Pole intended to consider each case separately, sending problem cases to Rome for final disposition. This process would involve considerable expense for the new owners and months or years of uncertainty. After lengthy discussions during which the cardinal refused to budge, Charles decided to detain Pole in Brussels until he changed his mind. At the same time Mary and Philip made it clear to the cardinal that he was not yet welcome in England. He had been banished from the country during the time of Henry VIII, and approval of Parliament would be needed before he could return. To help matters along, Philip dispatched Renard to Brussels to tell the cardinal bluntly that church property would have to be surrendered, if reconciliation were to proceed. At the same time, Philip sent instructions to the imperial legate in Rome, securing a broader mandate for Cardinal Pole.[18]

Surprisingly enough, these negotiations were the easy ones for Philip. Getting his proposals through Parliament proved to be much more difficult. The proposal for coronation met unexpectedly firm resistance. For at least two centuries the coronation of English royal consorts had been almost automatic, and Mary could easily have made the coronation of Philip a part of the wedding ceremonies. She failed to do so, no doubt because she did not realize she would grow to love him so much. But she could have corrected the omission later, and why she did not has never been entirely clear. One possible reason is that both Edward VI and Mary drew their authority from acts of Parliament. Their father Henry VIII did not determine the order of succession until Parliament had given him authority to do so. And when a question was raised about a woman's ability to rule England, Parliament solved the problem by declaring that a queen could be sovereign in exactly the same way as a king.

With Philip there was a special problem. His authority as king was limited by treaty. However, if Philip were anointed as king, he might logically claim the throne, regardless of the terms of the marriage treaty. Once crowned, Philip could claim to be king in his own right, with his children inheriting the throne, whether they were Mary's progeny or not. English legislators were not anxious to have a Spanish Hapsburg succeed to the English throne.[19]

Searching for some basis for compromise, Philip's agents in Parliament suggested that Philip might be made king without right of succession, the coronation to take place in January. Paget in this case was one of Philip's strong supporters, for he considered the queen too docile to deal with the Council. And not just the Council; he thought the country itself needed a king's firm hand. By the end of December some of Philip's supporters managed to have the Lower House approve a bill that in the event of the queen's death would make Philip permanent guardian of their children; but a separate provision to allow Philip to rule for life in such an event

Portrait du Cardinal Polus

D'apres le Tableau de Raphaël, ou de Fra Sebastien del Piombo, qui est dans le Cabinet de M. Crozat:
haut de 3.pieds 5.pouces, large de 2.pieds 10 ½ pouces, point sur toile, gravé par Nicolas de Larmessin.

Fig. 18   Cardinal Pole

was firmly rejected. In the end the coronation bill failed to pass, and the whole idea had to be dropped.[20]

While disappointed, neither Charles nor Philip was greatly worried about the failure of the coronation bill. The conditions Philip faced in England paralleled almost exactly those that had prevailed when Charles himself first came to the Spanish throne. Charles had overcome all the obstacles, largely through the force of his own personality. Both father and son were firmly convinced that Philip could do the same. "When the king our son is crowned," Charles said with great assurance, "he will be able to manage the affairs of that place with greater authority."[21]

While he wanted very much to be crowned as King of England, Philip's main concern for his first Parliament was to settle the religious question and the related matter of church property. "The first and most important subject which I wanted to achieve was to win approval on religious matters," he said to Vargas once it was all over.[22] After much talk and negotiation and with little sign of concessions from Cardinal Pole, Philip decided on his own to meet with members of the Parliament, the queen, the Council, and his own theologians to have a full discussion of the property issue. It was not an easy matter to settle, but Philip had faced the same problem in Spain, where his father had negotiated papal permission for sale of church lands. The issues were not simple. Many in England who held church property had bought it from the crown more or less in good faith or had received property grants in payment of debts or in return for services. None of these new owners thought they should have to compromise. After much discussion, Philip gave them his personal guarantee that possessors would remain undisturbed in their titles. This concession satisfied everyone, and as a result Parliament withdrew the Act of Banishment that had been directed at Pole years earlier. Pole was then brought to London and allowed to present his diplomatic credentials.[23]

Pole arrived in the capital on 24 November amid much fanfare. Four days later he addressed Parliament, talking for the best part of an hour. On 29 November Parliament agreed to repeal the legal restrictions on the church along with the laws denying the authority of the pope. Once this was done, the members presented a petition asking for absolution. This was necessary because the English schism had been accomplished by act of Parliament. Pole then absolved the members in a great ceremony, where all knelt and some were moved to tears.[24]

These were major accomplishments for the new king. The issue of church property was settled. The English church was once more in communion with Rome. And even without a coronation ceremony, the Spanish king was recognized as de facto ruler of the country.

Chapter 9

Expecting an Heir

The pregnancy will end in wind, and nothing more.
Giovanni Michiel

During the parliamentary session Philip had consulted on numerous occasions with members of each house and with the Privy Council, helping to iron out differences on the question of church property and to persuade recalcitrant members on other issues as well. This was almost second nature for Philip, for in Spain he had grown accustomed to work with councils and *cortes*. No doubt he had intended to be in the thick of things all along, but it was Mary's intent as well.[1] As signs of her pregnancy grew more obvious, Mary withdrew from governmental affairs, leaving nearly everything to Philip, whose "wise guidance" she credited with the successful outcome of the religious negotiations. So it was something of a surprise to both of them, when, in late December as the parliamentary session was about to end, the emperor wrote saying that he expected Philip to come to Brussels. Charles wanted his son to assist with the war against France, and more importantly, he wanted to begin the transfer of the Netherlands and Spain to his son.[2]

It was unwelcome news to Philip and Mary. He was enjoying his role as King of England and refused to be rushed. Instead, he told Charles that he simply could not leave until he had seen that all the laws recently passed by Parliament were put into effect. Left unsaid, but certainly understood, was the fact that Mary had begged him to remain in England until the birth of their child. She believed that his presence kept her safe from the numerous intrigues that surrounded the court, and she told her husband, a little hysterically, that she and the child might die if he were not there. More than this, she felt his presence was vital for "the good governance of the country."[3]

During the next few months Philip remained in England with Mary, changing residence as she did, and attending to both governmental and social obligations as the need arose. The royal couple lived in the same palace, but in separate apartments, as was then the custom for European royalty. The king spent his days very much as he had done in Spain, rising at about eight and reading in bed for a while, usually administrative papers. At around nine thirty he rose and was shaved by one of his barbers, then dressed with the help of his personal staff. Following this, he met Queen Mary and her entourage and attended Mass. Later he received petitioners or conducted other business. Philip lunched alone, as did Mary; then he spent the rest of the afternoon conducting additional business. On occasion the working day could also be interrupted by formal receptions, plays, masques, or dances. But by nine in the evening, after a light supper, both Philip and Mary retired once more to their separate apartments.[4]

Not only did they have separate apartments, but both Philip and Mary also had separate household staffs. For a while a good number of Philip's Spanish staff stayed on, but the king soon managed to whittle it down to a reasonable size, while allowing most of the English staff to continue to serve him. Household protocol was very elaborate, involving numerous noble retainers and servants. All of the English staff had to be trained in the Burgundian ceremonies adopted by Philip in 1548. There were kings-of-arms and mace-bearers, stewards, and chamberlains. The Duke of Alba as *mayordomo mayor* was in charge of everything and had his own emblem of office. He alone was allowed to hand the napkin to the king.[5]

Of course Philip and Mary did not spend all of their days at work. There were frequent diplomatic receptions, hunting parties, fishing excursions, walks in the garden, and other forms of entertainment. And the entertainment could be quite elaborate. Philip's favorite was the *juego de cañas* or the game of canes, which involved dozens of mounted soldiers, along with their pages and lackeys. This bloodless combat did not impress Philip's hosts on his tour of Europe, but the English spectators thought it was a great show.

One of the first games took place on Sunday, 7 October, according to the account of an anonymous Spaniard. Others followed on 25 November and 2 December. An English diarist compiled a brief description of the November game, while the Spanish informant recorded additional details about the December contest. From these it is possible to get a fairly good understanding of the *juego de cañas*, the whole purpose of which was to demonstrate skill in horsemanship and the arts of war.[6]

On Sunday 2 December, the combatants gathered in the large plaza of Whitehall Palace. The games had become extremely popular, so seating and standing room had to be found for more than 12,000 spectators. Once the crowd settled down, the queen arrived, accompanied by the lords and ladies of her court. The women were dressed in garments embroidered in silver and gold with hats similarly decorated. All the fabrics were provided at the expense of Philip, who gave orders to his stewards that the ladies should have whatever they asked for. When everyone was seated, the games began.

First came the two captains, Juan de Benavides and Luis Venegas, entering from opposite sides of the plaza, trailed by their attendants, some playing drums and trumpets. All of them wore silk and damask trimmed in gold, the first group in white and the others in green. Meeting in the center of the enclosure, they repeated a challenge and reply that each side had made a few days earlier. Then they circled and left the plaza, to be replaced by great numbers of cavalry, riding on mules, richly harnessed, the riders clad in colorful garments and bearing banners embroidered with the arms of each leader. Both groups circled the plaza as though looking for a field of battle. Stopping to drape some of the banners in front of the seats occupied by their own partisans, the two groups finally gathered at opposite ends of the plaza and waved their colors as a signal that the field was secure.

At this sign the mounted knights charged into the plaza, two by two in a dozen squadrons of ten, each side wearing its own distinctive colors. Their coats had one long sleeve (for the arm that carried the shield) and a short one decorated in some sort of costly fringe. Both groups then began riding forward, two by two, suddenly baring their swords and charging their opponents, all the while wheeling through complicated maneuvers and executing threatening slashes at the supposed enemy. Then they returned to their original positions, sheathed their swords, and armed themselves with canes ten or twelve feet in length. Then the groups took turns charging at one another. Those armed with spears tried to strike a body blow on their opponents, who used their shields to turn the canes aside. The whole demonstration lasted about an hour. Spectators who could not appreciate the display of horsemanship and skill at arms could no doubt enjoy the colorful pageantry. Those who had come to see bloodletting were disappointed, for the contest ended without injury either to man or beast.[7]

When the games ended, the celebration went indoors, where the queen gave a grand dinner in the palace. She and Philip were seated at one side of the hall, with the titled lords and ladies, both English and Spanish, on the other. The lesser ladies and gentlemen dined in a separate hall. When the king and queen had finished eating, a Spanish officer entered the hall with a squad of armed knights and a great fanfare of trumpets. He handed a written challenge to the English King of Arms, who read the challenge in both English and Spanish: "Don Fadrique de Toledo, *comendador mayor*, and Don Fernando de Toledo, and Don Francisco de Mendoça, and Garcilasso de la Vega y Çuñiga challenge [all comers] to a tourney the following Tuesday; three blows of the pike and seven of the sword." The English knights accepted the challenge, for they could hardly do otherwise. The evening ended with dancing and a masque; in these Philip danced first with the admiral's wife, and then in the torch dance with Mary as his partner.[8]

The masque occasion involved eight mariners and their torchbearers, all clad in garments made at least partly from cloth of gold and silver. Their masks were "lyons faces of molded worke of paste & cyment trymmed with hear for the brestes and backes of the said maskers." On their heads were helmets, also made of paste and cement, with crests like griffons and "Cerberus in the form of a greyhound."[9] Not a typical day, perhaps, but something like this happened frequently enough to keep life at court from being boring.

Yuletide festivities in the palace ran from Christmas Day to the Epiphany and involved several elaborate plays. The first was the "maske of viij patrons of galleis like venetian Senatours with vj gally slaves for their torcheberers." Another masque involved "vj venusses or amorous ladies with vj Cupides & vj torcheberers to them." The Cupids carried bows with arrows clamped in place and wore quivers with additional arrows. The costumes included everything from head to toe, helmets and crowns and caps, silk shirts and girdles, buskins and wicker baskets. Gilding was done with real gold and silver.[10]

The plays did not end at the Epiphany. Later in January there was a masque involving six actors dressed like Turkish magistrates, each with his personal archer. Another, on Shrove Tuesday, featured eight "goddesses huntresses" with "viij turky wemen their torcheberers."[11] All entertainments were typically accompanied by the usual *juego de cañas*.

Determined to make himself more acceptable to the ruling elite, Philip continued the round of feasts and celebrations that kept both king and queen in the public consciousness. For the most part he was successful, but there were rumblings, as there were in most of the capitals of Europe. Members of Philip's Spanish household were occasionally in a turmoil over rumors of rebellion and assassination, but most of these came to nothing.[12] Still, there were controversies and plots, and some of the conspirators were thoroughly nasty people. In London an assassin entered St. Margaret's Church on Easter Sunday, 1555, and attacked the priest who was distributing the Blessed Sacrament. Crying, "What doyst thou geff them?" the man hacked at the priest, cutting him on the head and the arm and nearly severing his hand. The attacker, a former monk named William Flower, was immediately subdued and led to jail. After a summary trial, the hand he used in attacking the priest was cut off; then he was executed by burning.[13]

At least one plot was very serious: an attempted mass murder. In Suffolk several arsonists tried to burn a church while the congregation was praying inside.[14] But other incidents were comical and were treated as such by the authorities. Robert Mendham of the parish of Saint Giles in the Field shaved his dog's head in the form of a tonsure, mocking the monastic practice of shaving the top of the head. For his efforts Mr. Mendham was ordered to present himself at church on Sunday and "openly confesse his folly."[15]

Some clashes were not at all religious, but grew out of the natural antipathy that natives have for foreigners. Philip's large entourage had to be billeted in the city, since there was no room for them in the palace. This meant that Englishmen and Spaniards met frequently, and not under the best of conditions. For example, Philip's retainers thought they were being overcharged for rent, while their English hosts often thought they were being overrun by outsiders. Tempers boiled over from time to time, and the two sides found themselves at swords-point. Such tiffs were commonplace. Philip knew how to deal with them, since there had been similar incidents during his tour of the imperial capitals. In fact, Charles had sent a Spanish alcalde to England to sit with an English jurist, each one to punish offenses committed by his own countrymen. The system worked marvelously well, and after a few miscreants on each side were severely dealt with, the squabbling stopped.[16]

From the beginning of her reign Mary had displayed great leniency in matters of religion. She wanted respect for the church and religious peace.[17] However, as time passed, certain members of the Privy Council began to see heresy as a serious problem for the government. They saw religious dissent as treason, and in fact, many dissenters did promote violence and insurrection. Early in 1555 Gardiner, the Bishop of Winchester, who was Lord Chancellor, summoned some of the most notorious heretics to appear before him for trial. Two recanted and were released, but another four did not, and they were sentenced to death. The manner of execution was typically English – burning at the stake.[18] Thus began a series of executions – perhaps two hundred in all – that historians have used to justify the sobriquet "Bloody Mary."

Philip thought that the executions, while unfortunate, were justifiable under the circumstances.[19] He certainly approved of the punishment meted out to William Flower.[20] And this was very likely Mary's attitude as well. No doubt Catholics who had been persecuted under previous regimes thought it only just that their oppressors should be punished in the same ways, but their attitudes seem to have changed as the executions continued.

On one issue there was no disagreement: Mary's pregnancy. Everyone was ecstatic about the possibility of a royal heir, though for a time some doubted that Mary was really pregnant. Simon Renard, the emperor's ambassador in London was one of the doubters. For two months he began his references to her pregnancy with "If." Finally, in mid-November he felt it safe to confirm the fact. "The Queen is veritably with child," he said. "She has felt the babe, and there are other likely and customary symptoms, such as the state of the breasts."[21]

A week later, when Cardinal Pole arrived in London to reconcile the country with the Catholic Church, Philip and Mary were so moved that they wept with joy. The cardinal greeted the pious queen with the Angelic Salutation: "*Benedicta inter mulieres, et benedicta fructus ventris tui.*" Upon hearing the greeting, the infant moved in Mary's womb, or so she said.[22]

The custom at the English court demanded that expectant mothers withdraw from public view. Accordingly, Philip and Mary moved to Hampton Court Palace at the beginning of April, so Mary could spend the final month of her pregnancy, surrounded by all the important ladies of the kingdom. As the end of April drew near, a rumor spread across the country that she had been delivered of a son. The report seemed so certain that bonfires were lit in the streets of London. There were public toasts to the health of the new prince, and church bells rang out the joyful news. As it turned out, the report was false, so all the fires were extinguished, and the revelers went home.[23]

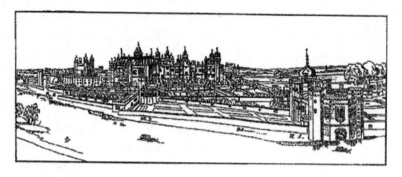

Fig. 19   Hampton Court Palace

During this brief flurry of excitement, word came to London that Queen Juana, Philip's grandmother, had died in Spain. Because her grip on reality was always fragile, the unfortunate queen had spent most of her life confined in the castle at Tordesillas. Whether she was really crazy is still a matter of dispute, but many family members greeted her death with a feeling of relief, and Philip was one. Juana was Mary's maternal aunt, so Philip tried to keep the news from her, not wishing to have her upset. Even so, Mary soon found out. She too was relieved, and the royal couple began to plan for an appropriate memorial Mass to be said in St. Paul's Cathedral, London. There was no question of allowing Mary to attend, and it seems likely that Philip was absent as well, for he sent Gómez Suárez de Figueroa, the Count of Feria, to be the chief mourner. As was the custom, the sovereigns furnished cloth for mourning cloaks to clergy, nobility, and members of the diplomatic corps, as well as to the people who made up their entourage. When the Venetian ambassador reported this, he called the gesture an act of "generosity" and "very handsome," adding that the cost must have been at least 6 or 7,000 ducats. After the obsequies ended, the lords of the realm and the other guests went to the bishop's palace for a lavish dinner.[24]

April passed, and the baby did not appear, so the royal physicians began to recalculate the expected date of birth. At first they predicted it would occur no later than 6 June; then they said the baby might not appear until 20 July. Both dates came and went, and though Mary experienced stomach pains on two or three occasions, labor did not commence.[25] Around the palace there were constant prayers and public processions, but it soon became clear that Mary was not pregnant at all. There was no public announcement, but none was necessary. On 2 August the king and queen left Hampton Court, going to Oatlands for a few days. The crowd of noble ladies who had gathered to witness the birth of the royal child went home. The palace, thoroughly disrupted by the crowd of visitors, was scrubbed and adorned once more. The Venetian ambassador, Giovanni Michiel wrote to his government, saying the pregnancy had been an illusion. "Her Majesty's belly has not grown in size, but rather decreased," he said, adding somewhat crudely, "the pregnancy will end in wind, and nothing more."[26]

Mary's was a false pregnancy, or pseudocyesis. According to modern studies, this occurs "at a rate of 1 to 6 for every 22,000 births."[27] Hers was a classic case, with all the signs of pregnancy: amenorrhœa (cessation of menstrual flow); morning sickness; enlargement of the breasts and flow of milk; even movement in her swollen abdomen. The cause could have been physical, perhaps an excess of hormones such as estrogen and prolactin. But there might also have been an emotional component. Psychiatrists now tend to think that the psychological element is predominant and that the condition can occur when a woman desperately wants to have a child.[28] In Mary's case, according to one author, the hormonal imbalance, could have resulted from the depression, loneliness, and severe deprivation that she suffered as a child.[29] Whatever the reason, Mary had not been pregnant.

During the months of her "pregnancy," Mary was not idle. Earlier in the year Noailles, the ambassador of the King of France, had prevailed upon her to summon Henry II and Charles to a peace conference. The emperor, reluctant to commit himself to such a course, agreed only after considerable pressure from Philip and Mary. The French king agreed because he understood that a Hapsburg heir sitting on the throne of England would be one enemy too many. Deciding to hold the conference at Marcq in the English Pale of Calais, Mary sent her invitations at the end of

March 1555, and the delegates met early in May. Mary was seen by both sides as a neutral party; but Philip could not attend the conference because his father was one of the combatants. Even so, he wanted very much to have the war end so staying at Hampton Court, he met daily with the Privy Council, receiving reports from the delegates, and deciding on steps necessary to bring the warring sides to agreement.[30]

The meeting hall at Marcq was an interesting structure, consisting of five large wooden buildings, constructed in England, transported in sections to the site, and assembled there. Each delegation was housed in a separate wing, all of which were connected by hallways, leading to a central salon where the meetings were held. Despite these elaborate preparations the delegates could not reach a compromise. When he had agreed to attend, Henry II felt considerable pressure to bring the war to an end. However, the failure of Mary's pregnancy, changed things. By 7 June it was clear that no settlement would be reached. On 9 June all the delegates left Marcq and returned home. As soon as the English delegates arrived at court, Philip insisted that they repeat for him every detail of the negotiating process. He wanted to understand exactly what the French were after, so he could deal more effectively with them in the future.[31]

When he first arrived in England, Philip had intended to stay for a very short time – perhaps a couple of weeks – just long enough to consummate the marriage. But he found that he liked the place and liked his queen and liked governing the country. When the emperor first wrote to insist that Philip was needed in the Netherlands, he refused to go. A year later things were different. Every plan of Philip and Mary had depended on her successful delivery of a royal heir. Now there was good reason to doubt that this would ever happen.

Beyond this, the emperor's health had continued to deteriorate, and he kept insisting that his end was near. He wanted to abdicate in favor of Philip, leaving him in charge both of Spain and the Low Countries. And he wanted his son to come to the Netherlands immediately in order to begin the transition. By the summer of 1555 Philip knew that he could delay his departure no longer. A small fleet – twelve ships and a galleon – was quickly readied to carry him to the continent.[32]

Before leaving, however, Philip took care to see that his place in government of England, shadowy though it might be, would not be compromised by his absence. First, "in order to improve and greatly expedite deliberations of the council," Philip named a select group consisting of Cardinal Pole, the chancellor, the Count of Pembroke, Controller Rochester, the Lord Treasurer, the Bishop of Ely, the Count of Arundel, Paget, and Secretary Petre. These nine men were to consider all matters of state, including finance, debts, and in general anything touching on the "honor, dignity, and state of the Crown."[33] In major decisions they were to be guided by Cardinal Pole, who otherwise was told not to participate in routine council business.[34]

Philip also prepared careful instructions for summoning a new Parliament. There were several issues to be decided. The English government was still hovering on the brink of bankruptcy, and of course, Philip hoped that a new Parliament would finally satisfy his wish to be crowned King of England. Even so, his main concern was still the Catholic religion. In discussions with the Council, Philip argued that all members of Parliament must be good Catholics, men who would see to the faithful practice of religion in their own districts, and men who would attend Mass every day.[35] Since Mary was so firmly opposed to his departure, Philip arranged that she would begin once more to participate in Council deliberations. This, he hoped, would keep her so busy that she would not be able to think about his absence.[36]

Having done his best to see the government put into safe hands, Philip prepared to depart. From all indications, he intended to return quickly. For one thing, he left most of his personal entourage in England, taking only a few trusted advisers along for the trip to Brussels. Beyond this, Philip expressly told the Council members that he would not be gone long, and therefore they prepared for his "shorte retourne." On 26 August Philip and Mary journeyed to London, where they stopped for lunch. As usual in their travels, Mary went by litter with Philip on horseback beside her. After lunch they continued to Greenwich, where Philip intended to board one of the ships that awaited him there. The plan had been that Mary would make the trip from London to Greenwich by barge, but at the last minute she insisted on going by road with Philip and the rest of the court. [37]

She understood why Philip must leave, and she said so in a letter to Charles. Still, on 29 August, she had to fight back tears as she walked with him through the halls of Greenwich Palace, waiting at the head of the stairs as he kissed all the ladies-in-waiting, just as she had taught him to do on the night they first met. Returning then to her apartment, Mary watched in tears as his barge moved away, refusing to leave her window overlooking the river until the vessel had disappeared from sight. Philip, for his part, took his post on the highest part of the vessel, waving his hat and saluting her until he could see her no more. It was a sad end to a year that had begun with great joy.[38]

The failure of the pregnancy and the failure of the peace conference brought a dismal end to Philip's first stay in England. Even so, he had achieved much. Mary's rule was stabilized, and largely through his personal efforts the country had been brought back into the Catholic Church. This he accomplished by pressing Rome to give up its claims and by guaranteeing the new owners that they could keep what they had. Other plans had gone awry. The members of Parliament, though grateful to Philip for his efforts on their behalf, had balked at the proposal to anoint and crown him as King of England. More serious was the lack of a Hapsburg child to inherit the throne of England. The emperor's great plan to unite England and the Low Countries under a single ruler looked doubtful in the extreme. Moreover, both Philip and Mary, both so popular in the fall of 1554, suddenly seemed less attractive to many people in England.

Chapter 10

Leaving a Kingdom,
Gaining an Empire

King of Spain, England, France, Ireland, etc.

After leaving Greenwich, Philip's party stopped at Sittingbourne, where the local dignitaries gave a grand reception and dinner in his honor. The parties continued the next day at Canterbury, where the entourage stayed until 4 September, waiting for a favorable wind. When this came, Philip and his companions went to Dover to board the ships. The crossing was quick and uneventful, and Philip's fleet arrived in Calais an astonishing two and a half hours after leaving the English coast. In the custom of the time, he was presented with the keys to the English castle and town of Calais, plus cash gifts of 2,500 ducats, all of which Philip donated to the soldiers stationed there. Similar gifts received at Sittingbourne and Canterbury were given to the poor, whose numbers had multiplied in England since the time of Henry VIII.[1]

On 8 September Philip arrived at the emperor's house in Brussels, where Charles came out to welcome him. As Philip knelt to kiss his father's hand, Charles seized his son's arms, drew him to his feet, and kissed him affectionately. It was an emotional reunion for both of them, and onlookers could see that Philip's eyes were brimming with tears. In the following days Philip talked with Charles for several hours each day, in brief episodes, for the emperor was shockingly frail. Their discussions covered all aspects of the transfer of power, but also the ceremonies planned for the funeral of the emperor's mother Juana.[2]

The memorial Mass for Queen Juana was held in Brussels on 17 September, with arrangements paralleling those made for a similar ceremony in London. As usual, diplomats jostled one another for position in the processions. In one dispute the English and Portuguese ambassadors each claimed precedence over the other and refused to compromise. Angered at the unseemly display of temper, Philip and Charles refused to settle the quarrel, and asked both diplomats to remain at home. English ambassador John Mason refused, saying he could not accept such an affront to his queen. Instead he announced his intention to attend the ceremony with all the other Englishmen resident in Brussels. When Philip heard this, he sent the Earl of Arundel to reason with Mason. Arundel told his fellow countryman that the King of Portugal seemed to have a closer relationship with the emperor, and that Philip simply didn't have time to sort it all out. Mason replied that he would remain at home, but only because "the consort of his mistress" asked him to do so. This was too much. Once the obsequies were over, Ruy Gómez informed Mason that Philip was furious at his rude behavior. Mason then tried to apologize, but it was too late. Henceforth he would be known as "agent" of the Queen of England, rather than ambassador.[3]

A few days after the funeral Charles sent letters to the rulers of the various states in the Netherlands, reminding them that they had previously accepted Philip as his heir and summoning them to meet in Brussels for the solemn transfer of authority.[4] Thus, the crowns of Spain and the Netherlands that Philip had worked for all his life would finally be his. With this in mind Philip wrote to tell Mary that he was reluctant to return to England, where he had not been crowned and therefore could rule only with her consent. "He cannot adapt himself to it," said the ambassador of Venice, "for he is forced to reside there in a form unbecoming his dignity." Unable to convince the Council (or Parliament, as it turned out) that Philip should receive the crown, Mary did what she could to soothe her husband. Mason would be called home quickly, she told Philip, for she needed no one to represent her to her husband.[5]

Though worried, Mary seems not to have told the Privy Council that Philip had threatened to stay in Brussels. On 23 September the members of the Council declared that Philip's return to England was imminent. "The Kinges Majestie [is] in sum towardnes to returne shortly homewardes," they said, and ordered Sir Richard Southwell to prepare to escort him back to England.[6] But Philip was determined to make his point. He sent orders for the rest of his household to leave England and join him in Brussels.[7] In some panic, either real or feigned, Mary wrote to Philip, saying that his absence from England had allowed the formation of a "violent opposition" group in Parliament. Therefore, she "hesitated to propose his coronation" just yet. Instead, she would arrange it herself once Parliament was dissolved. Thinking this might be imprudent, Philip immediately sent word that Mary should not do anything to bring about his coronation unless she was certain of its success. Within a few days the members who opposed his coronation learned of Mary's plan or something like it. They raised such a ruckus that Lord Chancellor Gardiner had to make a public declaration that it was completely false, only a vicious rumor.[8] Nevertheless, such rumors continued, and opposition continued as well.

Charles's plans ran more smoothly. With only moderate squabbling among rival princes, the States General of the Netherlands met on 21 October. In their presence Charles conferred upon Philip the title of Grand Master of the Knights of the Golden Fleece. Four days later Charles published his Act of Abdication, ceding the Netherlands to his son Philip.[9] The formal transfer took place in "the great hall" located across the park from the emperor's villa. After presenting the document to the assembled nobles, Charles spoke at length, describing his lifetime of service "through toil, inconvenience, and peril," both "by sea and land." When he finished, Philip once more knelt before his father intending to kiss his hand, but Charles would not allow him to do so. Instead they repeated the tearful embrace of the son's arrival in Brussels. Philip then apologized for his lack of skill in languages and introduced the Bishop of Arras who read the new ruler's acceptance speech in French, a language Philip understood but did not speak well. The next day, 26 October, the leaders of the states of Flanders and Brabant met with Philip in the same hall and swore their fealty to him. Philip, in turn, confirmed all of their appointments for another year. All the rest of the states swore their fealty to Philip a day later.[10]

Philip reveled in his new position in the Netherlands, and let Mary and the English Council know it. Mary wrote to say there were still difficulties within the government over his proposed coronation. Philip wrote back, feigning indifference and saying she seemed to want it more than he did. At the same time, he told Mary that she ought to reopen peace negotiations with France, warning the French king that, should the negotiations fail once more, England might enter the war on the side of the emperor.[11]

Mason, who had not yet left for England and who apparently still hoped to stay in Brussels, took it upon himself to urge Mary to do as Philip asked. Emphasizing his point, Mason reminded Mary that the Anglo-Spanish treaty of 1542 required England to enter the war against France. It all turned out just as Mason had hoped. Philip was so pleased with Mason's attitude that he made the former ambassador a member of his inner circle, with the title of "councilor" rather than agent or ambassador.[12] And Mary had no problem reopening the talks with France, where negotiations had never really stopped, since there were ongoing discussions about prisoners and other matters.[13]

In January 1556 Charles abdicated the Spanish throne in favor of Philip, thereby conferring on his son sovereignty over the richest and largest empire in the world. Still smarting from Parliament's refusal of coronation, Philip instructed his newly reorganized Privy Council that his royal title would henceforth be "King of Spain, England, France, Ireland, etc." and that Queen Mary should be addressed in similar fashion. The members of the Council replied politely, declaring with some trepidation that the new titles would be contrary to English law and custom. Then, fearing that Philip would react badly to their letter, they sent the Bishop of Ely and the Lord Privy Seal to explain the matter in person. Philip, of course, was annoyed, but his response was measured. He sent his councilor, Juan de Figueroa, regent of Naples, to emphasize that the new title was more than a suggestion. When the Council declined once more, Philip sent Figueroa back with verbal instructions and a written outline of what he expected. "We suggest that you give him the same credence as you would if we were speaking," Philip told the Council. "This will please us greatly." Thereupon Mary intervened, issued the new instructions, and the Council sent Philip a letter of apology.[14]

While much of the official correspondence from Philip to the Council or to Mary seems to be missing, some still remains. But personal letters between Philip and Mary are rare.[15] As a general rule their very intimate messages were entrusted not to the regular couriers but to certain diplomatic officials and personal friends. These missives did not make their way into the official archives, and diplomatic informants were either ignorant of their contents or chose not to discuss them. Even so, the letters from Mary to the emperor contain many remarks about her great love for Philip and her intense desire to have him return to England as soon as possible.

> I thank you for remembering me where the return of the King, my husband is concerned, as I have seen not only from your letters but also by the messages brought by Lord Fitzwalter. Now that the abdication is over and the truce concluded, and the arrival of the King of Bohemia should contribute to permit the King, my husband, to return, I implore your Majesty most humbly, for the love of God, to do all that is possible to permit it. I see every day that the end of one negotiation is the beginning of another. I beg your Majesty to forgive my boldness, and to remember the unspeakable sadness I experience because of the absence of the King.[16]

Charles wrote an affectionate note in reply – carried by Sir Henry Jerningham, Mary's vice-chamberlain – and Mary wrote to thank him for his thoughtfulness. Then she added, "[Philip] is the chief joy and comfort I have in this world."[17]

Fig. 20   Philip in 1555, when he became King of Spain

The repeated references in diplomatic correspondence to Philip's impending return to England make it obvious that he received similar messages from Mary and answered with promises to return quickly.[18] What else he might have said is unknown, but the Venetian ambassador in London told his government, "She is constantly comforted by letters and messages from His Majesty."[19] In one case Philip sent Ruy Gómez de Silva to England and Spain on official business with these special instructions: "First of all go to England, where the Most Serene Queen, my very dear and much loved wife, resides, and give her the letter that you are carrying, written in my hand." He told Ruy Gómez to talk to Mary about his return to England and other business, but we are left to guess about the contents of the personal letter.[20]

Biographers of Philip and Mary, confronted with this absence of reliable information about Mary and lacking any love letters by Philip, usually say that Mary was warm and loving, while Philip was cold and impersonal. This is probably unfair to both of them. If Philip could have returned to England for brief visits, as most critics say, it is also clear that Mary might easily have made a brief trip or two to Brussels. But each had an overwhelming sense of duty. Philip understood he should not leave the Low Countries until his sovereignty was well established and peace with France was assured. Mary had much the same feeling about her duties in England.

Even so, Philip did not live in Brussels as a recluse. He was young and popular and perhaps not as faithful as he should have been. After a period when Mary did not hear from him for several days, she learned that he had been ill. In a panic she sent her chamberlain to visit him and find out how he was. As it turned out, he had been only slightly indisposed and had recovered quickly. But a certain Madame d'Aler, who was said to be quite pretty, had caught his eye. Philip went to her house twice for weddings, followed by masked dancing. According to the Venetian ambassador, Philip was "much in love" with her. When Mary's chamberlain returned home, he decided not to tell Mary about the parties and the romance, knowing this would only distress his queen.[21]

Fig. 21 Queen Mary, about 1553

As heir to various kingdoms, duchies, and principalities in Europe, Philip also inherited the enmity of Henry II of France and Henry's ally, Pope Paul IV. But in an astonishing display of diplomatic skill and with considerable help from Mary, Philip concluded a five-year-truce with France at Vaucelles in February 1556. The signatories were Charles as emperor, Henry II of France, and Philip as King of England. The pope was not included, probably because he would have disagreed. The treaty was signed early in the month but not proclaimed for another week or two.

Philip's signature on the treaty as King of England was a recognition of his role in the negotiations, but it was also an admission that England had a stake in the war. Henry II had given fairly continuous support to the Protestant plots against Queen Mary and to the claims of Mary Stuart, giving the queen ample reason to support the emperor. Recognizing the change of status, diplomats in both Paris and Brussels began referring to the war as one between the King of France and the King of England.[22] The Venetian ambassador in Rome, for example, called the truce a "suspension of hostilities between the Most Christian King and the King of England."[23] In England the treaty was looked upon as a "truce between the King our master and the French King."[24]

After returning from the peace negotiations at Marcq, Bishop Gardiner, Mary's chancellor, became seriously ill. Despite – or perhaps because of – attention from the royal physicians he died on 12 November. His death was a serious blow to the government. Not only did Gardiner know everyone of importance in England, he also knew when to twist an arm and when to offer a bit of friendly encouragement. "He understood the time and the place for encouraging and caressing and for the opposite, threatening and punishing." Few men in Mary's government were as skilled, or so said the ambassador from Venice.[25]

Before naming a new chancellor, Mary sought the opinion of her husband. Under the terms of the marriage treaty, appointments to office were at her disposal alone, but there was nothing to keep her from asking Philip's advice or to stop him from giving it. Though Philip was absent in the Netherlands, neither Mary nor the Council cared to act without his approval.[26] Upon receipt of the request from Mary, Philip asked Cardinal Pole whether he had a suggestion. Diplomat that he was, Pole replied,

> What we need (as I wrote before and now repeat) is a man unswerving in religion; one who fears God more than man; a man who loves justice; in short, one who brings to his office a strength of character reflecting that of Your Majesties, so that the chief and the subordinate may be in close agreement.[27]

In other words, the new chancellor should be a good Catholic who would support the policies of Philip and Mary. And he was. On 1 January 1557 their majesties announced that Nicholas Heath, archbishop of York, would be chancellor. Pole was delighted, describing Heath as "a person Catholic, lettered, and endowed with other good qualities."[28]

The office of Lord Privy Seal had been vacant for several months, following the death of John Russell, Earl of Bedford, in March. Lord Paget, a Protestant like Russell, was named to fill this post. According to Pole this appointment was made by both "their Majesties," but others thought it was Philip's work. The Earl of Pembroke said, "The King's Majesty hath appointed the Bishop of York lord chancellor, and my Lord Paget lord privy seal."[29] Clearly there was a feeling that Philip was still very much in charge, when the queen and Council had important business to transact.

While Mary kept insisting that Philip's firm hand was needed in the government of England, it was obvious that she was handling matters well. Some historians now argue that Mary deliberately created much of her own reputation as an ineffective ruler in order to achieve the goals she wanted, as well as to deflect attention from herself and blame others for the more intractable problems that plagued her government.[30]

Thus, Mary is said to have manipulated the Privy Council, the Parliament, the emperor, and her husband Philip in order to achieve her goals. She wanted legal recognition that a queen could rule, and Parliament gave it to her. She wanted England to be

Catholic, but without much interference from Rome. This arrangement Charles, Philip, and her reluctant cousin Cardinal Pole managed for her. She wanted to marry Philip but without making England a part of the Hapsburg empire. The astonishingly favorable marriage treaty settled that. And so far as the papacy was concerned, Mary's new husband and his father, as well as intractable landowners in Parliament, were responsible for the decision to leave monastic lands in the hands of the new owners. Having inherited an empty treasury from Edward VI, Mary needed someone to shoulder the blame for her early financial problems. An unwieldy Privy Council and an unruly Parliament were useful scapegoats here. In the same way, heretics and agents of the French government were allowed to take much of the blame for the several mild uprisings that occurred during Mary's reign.

It was not difficult for Philip to see what Mary was doing and to conclude that he was not really needed in London. He kept promising to return to England, while continuing to advise Mary and the Privy Council from Brussels. Brief delays while letters went back and forth actually caused little problem, and Philip could thus devote his main attention to the Netherlands, the rivalry with France, and the government of his new empire.

There was a flurry of excitement in the spring of 1556, when Henry Dudley and others concocted a wild plan to rob the royal treasury, execute the queen, and put Princess Elizabeth on the throne. Various French officials were also involved, including Henry II himself. As luck would have it, the plot was disclosed to Cardinal Pole, who alerted the Privy Council. The main conspirators were arrested or fled, and after a while it became clear that the threat was minor. Philip concluded once more that his presence in London was unnecessary.[31]

A serious problem for the emperor, and thus for Philip, arose when the Neapolitan Cardinal Caraffa was elected pope. Always an enemy of the Hapsburgs, Paul IV firmly opposed the policies of Charles V, especially Spanish rule in Naples and other parts of Italy. Before the papal election Philip had said that the cardinal was "entirely unsuitable" for the office of pope. Beyond this he apparently had no strong personal feelings about the cardinal, but by inheriting the Spanish throne and the emperor's territories in Italy, Philip also inherited the bitter feud between the Hapsburgs and the Caraffas.

Throughout the fall of 1555 and the spring of 1556 Philip tried to maintain peace, wanting time to consolidate his rule and recoup his finances. Mary had a similar goal, though she also thought it was her Christian duty to promote peace between her husband and the pope.[32] But the old enemies could not be reconciled, and it soon became clear that the Truce of Vaucelles would not last.[33] Soon the pope began arranging new alliances with France, with various states in Italy, and even with the Turks, all the while massing his troops along the Neapolitan borders of the Papal States.[34] Reluctant to wait for an attack in Italy or the Netherlands, Philip consulted his theologians about the morality of a possible pre-emptive war. Meanwhile, he dispatched envoys to the pope and to the King of France in a last, fruitless effort to keep the peace.

Finally, in the late summer of 1556, armed with a favorable opinion from his theologians,[35] Philip ordered the Duke of Alba to begin moving his soldiers into the pope's domain.[36] Alba's troops managed to isolate Rome without actually attacking the city, though battles raged at various fortified cities nearby. Defeated at nearly every point, Paul refused to consider a truce, and Alba finally broke off the fight for the winter. Early in 1557 the King of France broke the truce, sending troops to threaten Douai on the Flemish border.[37] At the same time he sent the Duke of Guise into Italy with fresh troops, lured by the promise that he might become King of Naples.[38]

There was some hesitancy in the French move against Douai, and it was not quite as clear a breach of the truce as Philip wanted. After a delay Philip realized that he would have to respond to Henry's attack in the north, if only to draw off some of the troops that Guise planned to use against Naples.[39] While there were threats and counter-threats in France, the real fighting had been confined to Italy, and with good reason. The harvest had failed throughout northern Europe, and many people in Flanders were starving. Neither monarch had the funds for a war on two fronts, nor did either have sufficient troops, which in any case would have to be recruited, trained, and fed.

Still, the threat from Henry was real, as Philip came to realize. He began to prepare for war, while continuing to talk about peace. As commander of his forces Philip appointed Emanuel Philibert, Duke of Savoy, naming him captain general. Then he sent agents to Germany and Spain for additional troops and money and began combing the ports of the Baltic for supplies.[40] At the same time Philip urged Mary and the Council to honor their obligation under the treaty of 1542 by declaring war on France. Certainly the French had given serious provocation, not only by their usual intrigues with English rebels and refugees, but with new threats against the English fortress at Calais.[41] Anxious to end the threats at home and to aid her husband in Europe, Mary asked the Privy Council to state in writing whether England might be required to go to war in France.[42]

> Whether by the treatie of p[er]petuall peace, made between the Emperors Ma[tie] and the Queenes Highness ffather anno 1542 or by thesclarisshment thereof made an° 1546 considering w[th]all such other treaties as have beene made of later tyme between the said Emp[or] and the King and Queenes Ma[ties] hir highnes be now bound to declare hir self enemie and to giue the aide mencned in the said first treaties in case the french King shall now brake the trewes and invade Spaine or the Low Countries wth the nombers mencned in the said first treatie and esclarisshement.

The members of the Privy Council answered that they thought the treaties of 1542 and 1546 had been superseded by the marriage treaty; that the war between Philip and Henry II was the same war as mentioned in the marriage treaty; and that the queen was therefore not obliged to honor the commitments made in the earlier documents. They said further that even if the earlier treaties were held to "remayne p[resen]tly in their full force" the queen was under no obligation to assist Philip until an actual invasion of Spain or the Netherlands occurred, and then only after Philip had certified the invasion and requested her help. Then they added, "Considering that the Queenes Matie is not hable to doe that the treatie requireth it is to be hoped that his Matie will not require that wch cannot be done."[43]

Of course, Philip considered the war with France to be entirely new. The earlier conflict had been between Henry II and Charles V. That conflict had ended in a truce that was supposed to last for at least five years and that Philip had hoped would be permanent. The new war had been started at the instigation of Pope Paul IV and was aimed at the conquest of the kingdom of Naples.[44] Unable to make his case convincingly by letter, Philip decided to go to England and confront the Council in person. Early in February he sent Ruy Gómez, who was instructed to speak to Paget in confidence, carefully explaining the reasons for war and stressing the need for English money and troops. Paget would then lobby the members of the Privy Council on his own. Mary was not to be involved. However, Ruy Gómez was ordered to explain privately to Mary that he was traveling on to Spain. There he would ask the emperor to come out of retirement long enough to help gather fresh troops and more money to finance a war; he was to tell her that Philip thought Charles might even use his personal influence to make Henry II and Paul IV see that the war was a bad idea.[45]

Early in March the Venetian ambassador in Paris heard a rumor that Ruy Gómez had told Mary about her husband's financial plight and that she had promised to send him £100,000. Soranzo was unable to verify the rumor,[46] and for a couple of reasons it seems unlikely to be true. First, Mary did not have the funds; and, second, Philip had strictly charged Ruy Gómez not to mention money to Mary. "You will not try to negotiate this matter for me with the queen or anyone else but Paget."[47]

On 17 March 1557 a messenger arrived at Greenwich with the long-awaited news that Philip was on his way to England. At Calais he boarded an English ship, where some of the chief nobles of the realm had been waiting for several days to take him to England. The vessel was "thoroughly decked and apparailed with all convenient furniture," ready to leave as soon as he arrived. Once Philip reached Dover, he found two gentlemen waiting to greet him, one to keep him company and the other to carry the news of his arrival to Mary. This was repeated at every step of his journey, so that he and the queen had constant news of each other. On the twentieth at five in the evening he arrived at Greenwich, where Mary and a great crowd of people awaited him. As he approached the gate of the castle a ship carrying sixteen "vere grett" guns fired a thirty-two gun salute, each cannon firing twice. Then the crowd greeted the two of them with the cry, "God Save the Kyng and the Quen."[48]

The royal couple remained at Greenwich for two days, no doubt happy to see each other again, though Philip was still suffering from a cold he had caught before he left Brussels.[49] At court the king's return was a signal for the usual round of dances and masks. One such celebration took place on St. Mark's Day, 25 April. It was "A Great Maske of Allymaynes pylgryms and Irysshmen with theire incydentes . . . in his highnes court at whightehall."[50]

During Philip's absence there had been constant gossip about him in the English court, and all of Mary's young ladies-in-waiting were wary of the king. Young Magdalen Dacre, later Viscountess Montague, recalled Philip's unwelcome attention and told her biographer about it.

> Once, when she was young and lived at court, King Philip who had married Queen Mary opened a window where she happened to be washing and, young man that he was, playfully reached his arm inside. Some might have taken this as a special honor, and have been pleased. But she knew that maidens were like flowers, which lose their beauty at the slightest touch. Thinking her own purity more important than the King's majesty, she grabbed a staff that was leaning nearby and struck the King sharply on the arm. The King wisely took no offense, but actually held her in even greater esteem for doing so.[51]

Mary, of course, was faithful to her husband. Whether Philip returned the compliment is unclear, but Mary thought he probably did not. She said as much to the Venetian ambassador, who promptly reported the conversation to his government: "She does not think the King is chaste, but at least, she says, he is not in love with any other woman."[52]

In his first discussions about the war with France, Philip found the members of the Privy Council hard to convince. They seemed to feel that England had valid complaints against the French king, but they wondered about the breach of the truce and doubted there was sufficient reason for war. Philip kept insisting until at last they offered, though very reluctantly, to send the cavalry and infantry required under the treaties, but they refused to declare war. As far as they were concerned, Philip and his army could handle the fighting.[53] Things were at an impasse when startling news came from the north of England. On 27 April 1557 Thomas Stafford, with ships and men from France, seized Scarborough Castle, about 150 miles north of London.[54] Calling himself, "your protector, governor, and defendor," Stafford issued a proclamation calling on all "that love the common wealthe, honoure, and libertie" to join in his attempt to overthrow Philip and Mary.[55] As invasions go, it was not much of a threat. Stafford and his men were easily caught, imprisoned, and executed. Even so, it was an overt act that the Council could not ignore,[56] just what Philip and his advisors wanted. One of his advisors wrote to the Duke of Savoy:

> As for the breach of the truce, the French have spared us the trouble, for they have sent a ship carrying a refugee from this kingdom, who had rebelled against the Queen, and have seized a castle on the Northern coast of England, which castle it appears is of small importance. The necessary steps have been taken to deal with this matter, and it will result in war being declared, unless it is decided to wait somewhat longer.[57]

The Privy Council in fact decided to wait somewhat longer for a formal declaration of war, though they agreed on some immediate aid. Five thousand infantrymen and 1,000 cavalrymen would be sent to aid Philip, along with an additional 3,000 men to reinforce the English garrison at Calais. The actual declaration would come after the troops were raised and equipped. The English fleet needed particular attention, for the ships had been sadly neglected.[58] More seriously, Stafford the rebel had been traveling in a fleet dispatched by France to carry reinforcements for the garrisons in Scotland.[59] If Philip's army in the Netherlands was a threat to France, Henry's army in Scotland was a similar threat to England. The Privy Council would need to bolster defenses on the border and keep a fleet in the Channel to intercept further French reinforcements.[60]

In order to provide immediate help for Philip, Mary sold several large tracts of crown land and gave the money (perhaps £10,000) directly to her husband. She could scarcely have done less, as Philip had spent enormous sums of Spanish and imperial money in England since the marriage, paying all his own household expenses for the past few years, making generous gifts to members of the court, and granting enormous pensions to members of the government. In spite of this there was grumbling at court about good English money going to support the Spanish king.[61]

The Privy Council lost no time authorizing the troops to join the king in Europe and to reinforce the English garrison at Calais. The fleet was ordered to recruit an additional 6,000 men to serve at sea, guarding the Channel. As Philip had expected, the nobility responded to the call to arms with great enthusiasm, an important development, since they were responsible for raising and equipping troops in their own districts. It was a great personal achievement for Philip, since leadership of an English army would strengthen his claim to be King of England.[62] Everything took less than a month, and on 1 June 1557 Mary signed a declaration of war, setting out all the grievances that England had with France. Mary's proclamation was taken to Paris by the royal herald, where on 7 June the French king noted that it was not signed by Philip and had it read aloud.[63] The declaration was proclaimed on the same day in London "with trumpeters blohing and a x [*sic*] harroldes of armes."[64]

Philip remained in England for a few more weeks, seeing that preparations for war went ahead without delay, and attending court ceremonies. He and the queen went to Hampton Court twice for hunting excursions, and on the last occasion Philip "kylled a grett stage with gones." At last, on 3 July Mary rode with Philip toward Dover, where he embarked once more for the continent.[65]

During his eighteen-month absence from England, Philip had become ruler of a vast empire, the Spanish possessions in Europe and America. These new responsibilities completely overshadowed his role as King of England and made him less inclined to devote time to English affairs. This might have changed had Parliament approved his coronation, but that did not happen. And when the Privy Council refused for such a long time to provide aid in Philip's new war with France, one that clearly involved English interests, the king realized that he had lost the influence he enjoyed before he left England.

Chapter 11

War and Death

Miserere nobis, Miserere nobis, Dona nobis pacem.

Mary

Arriving in Calais on 6 July 1557, Philip went immediately through Gravelines to Brussels. The Earl of Pembroke was scheduled to follow with an army of English soldiers and to fight under Philip's command. Once they arrived, Philip intended to lead them in an attack on the French stronghold at St. Quentin. Speed was essential. The Duke of Guise was on his way back from Italy, and Philip wanted to capture the place before Guise and his army could arrive. But Pembroke had other ideas. He arrived at Calais, and there he stopped. Having brought a mountain of baggage and a few unnecessary guns, he refused to go further. Instead, he sent word that Philip must supply him with horse teams for the artillery, carts for his baggage, and more money than Philip's treasurer had for the entire army.[1]

Busy with organizing the rest of his forces, Philip sent Juan de Ayala to reason with the Earl. It was a difficult job. The number of carts Pembroke wanted varied from day to day, the total number fluctuating between twenty and 800; the number of horses ranged from seventy to 150. Beyond this, the Earl and his commanders were demanding to be paid – in cash – before marching further inland. Moreover, a host of "supernumeraries" had joined the English army, all needing to be fed, housed, clothed, and paid. To some of Philip's staff it seemed that half the unemployed laborers and most of the penniless peers in England had joined the army and come to France. After days of endless arguing, the Earl finally agreed to send the extra people back to England, though he did not do so. Instead, he invented other demands. When he was asked to sign vouchers for the money to pay his troops, the Earl refused. He wanted cash, and he wanted it in advance.[2]

Despite frequent messages and visits from Philip's officers, it took nearly two weeks of negotiation to get Pembroke to move forward from Calais. At last, on 30 July, the English army began to move. But not very far. Disgusted with all the delay, Philip's advisers said the king had better proceed without Pembroke's forces. German mercenaries were about to arrive, and trained Spanish soldiers were near at hand. They might be enough for the battle.[3]

This, of course, would ruin Philip's plan to lead an English army in battle. In desperation, Philip decided to send the Spanish and Germans to surround St. Quentin, while he waited at Cambrai for Pembroke to appear. "My army is before St. Quentin," Philip said in a note to Pembroke. "It is very important that I should join that camp as soon as possible," he continued, adding, "I wish to have you accompany me."[4] As it turned out, the battle was over before Pembroke arrived. On 10 August the Constable of France, Anne de Montmorency, arrived in front of St. Quentin with thirty companies of French troops and his own German mercenaries. The Duke of Savoy attacked immediately with German and Spanish troops. In a series of bold strokes his forces destroyed the French army, killing 3,000 and capturing 7,000, including the Constable and other leaders. An anonymous soldier described the French losses this way: "All the infantry was taken prisoner or killed in the open country."[5] It was an enormous victory, one that would have added luster to King Philip and his English army, if only they had been present.

Philip and the English forces arrived at St. Quentin on 12 August, but the castle and outer defenses were under Savoy's control. All that remained was to encircle the town, then begin the bombardment. Pembroke had picked up several pieces of the heavy artillery that Philip had brought to Cambrai. Added to his English

Map 3   England and France at war

guns, these were put into position and began shelling the town. The final assault came on 27 August, when Philip's troops breached the walls and entered the city. A sentence from the report of a Spanish soldier said, "Both sides fought most choicely, and the English best of all."[6] This line or something like it was the basis for a rumor that quickly went back to London: Pembroke's English army was the first into the breach. The report was not true, but Philip allowed it to stand. It became part of the legend of St. Quentin as a great English victory.

Among the prisoners taken at St. Quentin was the Grand Admiral of France; among the English dead, Lord Henry Dudley. Though Philip ordered his men to treat the captives with magnanimity, his mercenaries could not be restrained. The town was set afire, the enemy prisoners were slaughtered, and corpses were piled in the streets.[7] Nevertheless, when the news of the battle reached London, Philip was hailed as the leader of a victorious English army.[8]

With the enemy so soundly defeated, a more daring and experienced commander might have marched on Paris, but Philip did not. Nearly all the troops in his army, including Pembroke's, had been paid from his treasury, and he was out of funds. In any case Alva's negotiations with the pope were going well, and Philip thought it likely that the French would sue for peace. By the middle of September Paul IV agreed to terms of peace, declaring that "the war had been waged due to misinformation." In a sudden burst of comprehension His Holiness said he believed King Philip and the Duke of Alva had always been "his obedient sons [who were] excellently disposed toward him."[9] News of the peace agreement reached Philip on 3 October. Moving quickly, he decided to consolidate his gains with the capture of a few additional forts on the route to Paris. More importantly, he reduced the size of his army, sending most of them home for the winter. The bulk of Pembroke's troops, enlisted for only four months service, were among those who departed.[10]

As it turned out, Henry II was in no mood either to sue for peace or to rest for the winter. While his enemies took time off to shelter from the bitter cold, Henry began to plan a surprise move that might just change the course of the war. What he had in mind was the capture of the English enclave at Calais. Usually called the Pale, Calais was more than a town and a castle. It was an area of a hundred square miles on the Channel coast between France and the Netherlands that provided English merchants with access to those two markets. Calais had been in English hands for two hundred years, and Henry wanted it back. As soon as Guise arrived in Paris, Henry asked him to consider the project. Reluctant at first, Guise dispatched two engineers to look the town over. Entering the place in disguise, they saw that it was poorly defended and that the castle was falling into ruins. Guise decided Calais could be captured with a quick and vigorous attack.[11]

How much of a surprise this was to the English defenders is a matter of dispute. Philip's modern detractors insist that he could have saved the place by quick action. The problem for Philip was that Calais was under the control of the Privy Council. Critics in England had been saying for some time that Philip was just waiting for an opportunity to garrison English forts with Spanish troops, something forbidden under the marriage treaty. This and Philip's increasing difficulties with the Privy Council made it impossible for him to occupy Calais with his own soldiers. Instead, he warned the commander, the queen, and the Privy Council as soon as he received word of the French intentions. Meanwhile, he kept a small Spanish force ready to assist as soon as he was asked to do so. As it turned out, the English commander refused his offer of reinforcements,[12] while the Privy Council failed to send English troops in a timely manner.[13]

What happened was this. Early in December rumors in Paris said that a French attack on Calais was planned and troops were moving in that direction.[14] On 18 December Philip's commander at Hesdin (some forty miles from Calais) received word from a spy in the French army that Calais was definitely the objective. He immediately sent word to Lord Wentworth at Calais and to Lord Grey, who commanded the English forces at Guisnes. Grey received the message on 22 December; if Wentworth received his warning at the same time, he apparently chose not to take it seriously. The Privy Council received a copy of the warning on 24

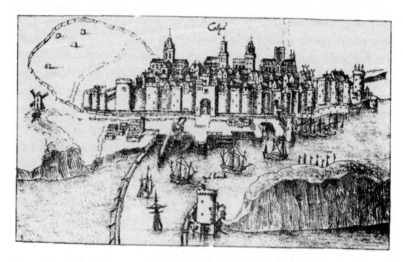

Fig. 22   Calais in 1557

December and immediately cancelled a prior order intended to reduce the garrisons around Calais.[15]

On 26 December Wentworth advised the queen that the French planned to establish a supply point at Ardres, and the next day he informed her that the supplies were intended to support a French attack on Hesdin. Since Ardres was only a few miles from Calais, he conferred with Lord Grey. They concluded that Guisnes and other small bases should be abandoned in the event of a French attack and asked for additional troops from England.[16] The queen replied that Guisnes was not to be abandoned unless absolutely necessary and said that reinforcements were being dispatched.[17] Finally, on 29 December, Wentworth wrote to say that the French army was at Hesdin and that the immediate threat was ended. With this information, Mary canceled the order for reinforcements to go to Calais.[18]

After that everything changed. On 31 December scouts sent out by Lord Grey saw the French forces advancing rapidly toward Calais. That night Wentworth sent word to Philip that the French army was poised to attack Calais. "I did not wish to fail to inform you," he said, "and to beg you to take the necessary measures."[19] In a letter to Queen Mary on the night of 2 January Wentworth said he could hold out "for a season," with proper rations. In these several messages there is little to show that any of the parties saw the French threat as more than a serious annoyance. It was winter, after all, and Wentworth and Grey were capable of putting up a good defense behind their fortifications.[20] When Wentworth's letter reached London, the reinforcements were ordered out once more. Philip, on the other hand, seems not to have received Wentworth's letter. On 2 January Philip sent a special messenger to warn him that the French were definitely headed toward Calais and asking him to send an immediate warning to the queen.[21]

> Today we have extremely reliable evidence that the French, our common enemies, are determined to attack the town and have directed their entire force to that purpose. Therefore we have dispatched our messenger with the greatest possible speed. We strongly advise (as you no doubt agree) that you see to the defense of the place with your usual care and vigilance, staying alert, and preparing in such a way that the town may be well defended and the plans of the enemy utterly defeated. Moreover, in order that the Most Serene Queen our dear wife may know, you should write by special messenger without delay and not worrying about the expense, so that the kingdom will understand what aid you require.

Obviously, Philip thought the threat was real, but he also thought the town ought to be able to defend itself, at least for the time. Even so, he added a promise to send any additional help Wentworth might request.

> If you require anything from us for the greater security and defense of the town, or any assistance in repelling the enemy, you will advise us of it, and we will give immediate orders, because we are willing and eager to help. Nothing can be done that is more important to England and our people. The

> Queen and Ourselves expect to see in you that
> loyalty and strength of spirit which is so agreeable
> to us.

That very day Wentworth wrote to tell Philip that he might soon require assistance, specifically, 300 or 400 harquebusiers from one of Philip's garrison towns. The best help Philip could give would be to tell the commanders to send help whenever he might ask for it. Later that same day he wrote once more, saying that Philip's warning letter had just arrived. He needed reinforcements, he said, though an attack by sea might be best. This last was added because the French had occupied the English fortifications commanding the entrance to the harbor.[22]

On 3 January 1557, Wentworth wrote to Philip saying that he had received the warning letter and asking for reinforcements. At the end of his message Wentworth wrote, "I am determined to die at my post."[23] The very same day a relief force of 200 harquebusiers from Gravelines tried to fight through the French lines to Calais but was unable to reach the town.[24] Philip apparently did not receive Wentworth's most recent letter, for he later told Lord Clinton he had "offered aid which was refused."[25]

Meanwhile in London there was a scurry of activity, organizing a relief force and dispatching it to the coast. On 3 January the Earl of Rutland with a shipload of English fighting men was supposed to sail from the port of Dover, just a few hours from Calais. However, the ship did not sail, because the sailors were afraid of the French artillery surrounding the harbor at Calais. The Spanish sailors were not so timid. On the fifth or sixth Philip's admiral, Luis de Carvajal, entered the harbor with supplies and reinforcements. French cannon fire made it impossible for Carvajal to land his troops, but he stayed in the port, waiting for a chance to land. Finally, on 7 January, fearing that Carvajal's fleet could be lost, Philip ordered him to withdraw and join the English fleet in the Channel.[26]

Even then, Philip left his admiral with the option of landing the reinforcements if an opportunity should present itself, but by that time it did not really matter. That same day, before Philip's

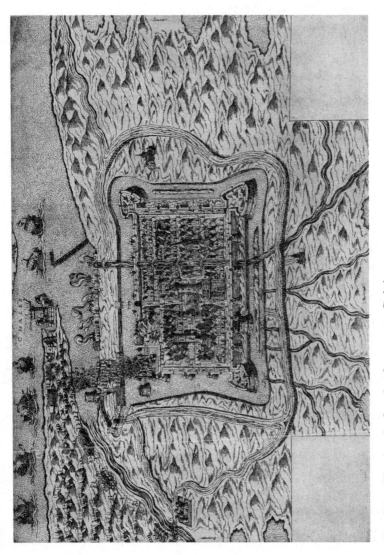

Fig. 23   The battle for the fortress at Calais

order could arrive, Wentworth surrendered Calais to the French army. He later claimed to have been out of food and munitions, but when French forces occupied the place, they reported finding large quantities of stores of every sort.[27]

Once Calais was taken, the French turned their attention to Guisnes, where Lord Grey was in command. This town, the last English outpost in the Pale, held out a while longer, eight days instead of seven. There was a plan to send reinforcements, but as luck would have it, a great storm blew up on the night of 9 January, pounded the English fleet, and put it out of action.[28] Two days later the government disbanded the relief force.[29]

Astonished at the lack of concern for Calais and Guisnes, both Philip and the Duke of Savoy wrote, urging that a new English relief force be assembled. Philip even offered to have the Spanish fleet carry the soldiers to Guisnes. Meanwhile, the Duke of Savoy informed Mary that he was sending Spanish and Burgundian soldiers to assist in the defense of the town. Shamed into action, the Queen and Council ordered the Earl of Rutland to have 5,000 soldiers ready to embark on 31 January, with more to follow.[30]

The delay was fatal, and the obvious lack of concern in London was reflected in the discouragement of the English troops at Guisnes. The Spanish and Burgundian soldiers fought with great bravery and suffered huge losses. The French asked the garrison to surrender, and the offer was refused. Once they heard what had happened, the English troops mutinied. As Thomas Churchyard reported, "When the Soldiours sawe, thei could not haue the Castell yeelded: thei threatened to flyng my Lord Grey ouer the walles."[31] Consequently, Lord Grey, who had promised on 4 January to fight "even to the death"[32] capitulated less than three weeks later.

Almost everyone thought the Pale of Calais had been lost through treachery on the part of some or all of the officers. On 21 January, before he knew of the loss of Guisnes, Philip wrote to the Privy Council,[33]

> We think you will have heard from Juan de Ayala,
> whom we sent to you a few days past, entrusting
> him to tell you of the assistance we were sending to

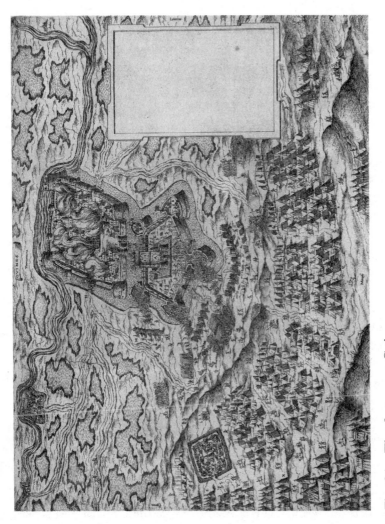

Fig. 24   The fortress at Guines

> relieve the siege of the town [Calais]. We felt certain
> it might have been successful, if the men charged
> with defense of the town had exerted themselves the
> least bit to defend it.

George Ferrers, the chronicler of Mary's reign, said, "It could not have come to passe without some secrete trechery."[34] The Duke of Savoy said Calais was lost due to "gross neglect" by all levels of the English command, while an officer on his staff wrote darkly of "the treason which it is said was practised inside the English Privy Council."[35]

The Count of Feria, dispatched to England by Philip in order to spur the Privy Council into action,[36] reported that Lord Grey was being feted as a hero. When Feria objected, Cardinal Pole pointed out that it was not unusual to surrender a fortress. After all, a Spanish commander had surrendered a fortress in North Africa. Admitting this was true, Feria said, "A gentleman inside that fortress had surrendered, not being able to defend it. When he arrived in Castile, they cut off his head."[37]

While all this was discouraging to Philip and his officers, the thing that surprised them most was the lack of enthusiasm in the Privy Council for retaking the Pale of Calais. When Feria insisted that the Privy Council give a formal reply to Philip's offer of aid in recapturing the Pale, the Council offered a long list of excuses, but declined to fight for the place. The Privy Council was reluctant to raise the troops; volunteers were hard to find; the French were threatening to be a permanent presence in Scotland; and there was simply not enough money to defend England and at the same time mount an attack on the Continent.[38] All the excuses led Granvelle to remark that "one would like to see more spirit, more resentment about Calais and more memory of the ancient virtues of their forebears."[39] Feria tried to move the Council into action, but finally reported to Philip in disgust, "They all raise difficulties about whatever is proposed and never solve anything."[40] The attitude in London seemed to be that Philip would have to reconquer Calais anyway in the course of his own fight against the French armies.[41]

By all accounts Mary was firmly on the side of Philip, urging the Council to raise the troops and provide the funds necessary to retake Calais. Clearly, she was still in love with Philip, though there is considerable difference of opinion about Philip's attitude toward Mary. This may have had something to do with a new development in their marriage. In December 1557, after Philip had been absent for six months, Mary managed to convince herself that she was pregnant once more. Cardinal Pole informed him of this and Philip replied,

> I received your two letters of the fourth of this month. The one by your own hand in which you write news of the pregnancy of the Most Serene Queen, my dear wife, has produced here the greatest increase in joy and contentment. It is the one thing in the world I have most desired, and it is so important for the welfare of our religion and our realms. Therefore I have given and do give appropriate thanks to Our Lord for his grace and mercy.[42]

A week later, when Philip sent Feria to London, the envoy, as usual, carried a personal letter from the king to his wife.[43] In addition Feria had private instructions to congratulate the queen for Philip and tell her of "the most extreme contentment and joy he had received from knowing this."[44] Again all the signs of pregnancy were present. A visitor who talked to Mary in January said he had seen that she was pregnant. Beyond this he had overheard a conversation between Feria and one of Mary's ladies-in-waiting, who reported that the delivery would occur in late February or early March.[45]

Once more Mary was disappointed. By March everyone knew the truth. Feria wrote to Philip, "It seems to me she only thinks she is pregnant, though she won't admit it." Mary wanted Philip to visit and comfort her. "Everything she does is intended to make you come here,"[46] Philip understood and said so to Feria, though he said nothing to Mary. "About the Queen giving birth," he wrote to Feria, "it would be safest for a man to believe what he sees and to withhold judgment until then."[47] In any case, there was no question of his leaving Flanders before the war with France was settled, and Mary doubtless knew it.[48] In May Feria reported that Mary was reconciled to the facts. "She has realized that the pregnancy has come to nothing."[49]

This was troubling news. Mary was clearly very ill. A false pregnancy was rare, but two false pregnancies were unknown. While some of Mary's symptoms were typical of pseudocyesis, others were not: headaches, depression, and progressive vision loss. These continued and toward the end of the summer worsened. According to a modern medical diagnosis all of Mary's symptoms occur only in prolactinoma, a pituitary tumor.[50]

Even though Mary's doctors were unable to devise an effective treatment for her illness, the main facts about the queen's health were clear to those closest to her. And some who had been Mary's most ardent supporters were beginning to think the unthinkable. Simon Renard wrote in some distress that, should Mary die, "which God forbid," Elizabeth would be called to the throne "in virtue of the will of Henry VIII, confirmed by Parliament."[51]

Philip probably could figure things out for himself, without Renard's reminder. Since Mary's health was so poor, it was most improbable that they would have an heir. Philip had been urging her to accept the idea that Elizabeth was the logical successor to the throne of England. In some ways Elizabeth was the only acceptable alternative. Should Elizabeth not succeed, the next in line would be Mary Queen of Scots, recently wed to the son of Henry II. It was unthinkable to Philip that the French king could be allowed any claim to the throne of England. Philip told Mary that he was ordering Feria to talk to Elizabeth about the succession. "I doubt not," he said to Feria, "that it will turn out well."[52]

The main concern, both for Mary and for Philip, was that England should remain thoroughly Catholic. Philip had met with Elizabeth when she was living at court and had apparently decided then that she was faithful enough to inherit the crown.[53] When Feria finally visited Elizabeth, she assured him that she had every intention of keeping England Catholic, or so said Mary's lady-in-waiting, Jane Dormer.[54] Feria's own report of the meeting is less revealing: "I went to see Lady Elizabeth, as you ordered me to do. She was happy to see me, and I to see her, as I will explain to Your Majesty when I am there."[55]

The succession was a matter of conscience for Mary; Elizabeth simply was not the legitimate heir to the throne. Mary held – and said she had done so for nearly a quarter of a century[56] – that Elizabeth was illegitimate, and that Henry VIII was not her father.[57] Many people believed this. Anne Boleyn, it was widely reported, told her brother that Henry was impotent. The brother himself was suspected of being the real father.[58] Whether this was true is immaterial. The fact is that Mary believed it.

Mary also thought that Elizabeth would return England to the religious practices of Edward VI. Formerly a Protestant, Elizabeth insisted that she had become a good Catholic. But Mary and most of her court were certain the conversion was a sham. Worse, perhaps, Elizabeth was accused of involvement in Wyatt's rebellion. And though she begged in tears afterwards for forgiveness, the name of Elizabeth figured prominently in nearly every plot hatched by those who opposed Mary's rule.[59] Moreover, Elizabeth had a large group of Protestant supporters in England and among the English refugees on the continent.[60] There were moves at court from time to time to send Elizabeth to Brussels or to Spain, where she could be watched carefully, but Mary could never bring herself to do this. There were also attempts to marry her to a Catholic prince – perhaps the Duke of Savoy or Philip's son Carlos – but none of the suggestions pleased Mary, and none came to fruition.

While in England, Feria had frequent conferences with members of the Council, urging them to raise men and money to continue the war with France and especially to recapture Calais.[61] However, the members were adamant. They refused to consider any attempt to retake Calais, saying that they had neither the men nor the money.[62] It was enough for them to thank Philip for the steps he was taking to recover Calais on his own.[63] A few members of the Council continued to meet privately with Feria for secret discussions, and as a result it was decided that Philip could recruit and pay 1,000 sappers in England and take them across the Channel for service with his army.[64]

By the end of April the English fleet was ready once more for sea, but standing idle. So Feria suggested that Philip summon Admiral Clinton to Brussels for talks.[65] The results were a little discouraging to Philip, although he did not say so to Clinton. The navy had been provisioned only for three months, and by the time Clinton arrived in Brussels, half their term had expired. Clinton said he could not be expected to provide any force for an invasion, though he had 5,000 fighting men who could be used for an occasional raid. Clinton would be able to reprovision Philip's troops if the army was near the coast, but he would need an additional three weeks to get the ships ready for sea. As a result of the discussions, Philip told Clinton that his first concern must be to patrol the Channel and prevent the French from landing in Scotland for a possible invasion of England. He also urged Clinton to tell the Privy Council that they must exert every effort to defend the realm.[66]

Clinton's report to the queen and Council was couched in less diplomatic language than Philip may have used. As the admiral remembered it, Philip said that if the Council were to approach the defense of the realm with the "slackness" they showed at Calais, "he would rather be at the defence thereof [with] his own person."[67] Surprisingly enough, the Council did accept some of the king's suggestions. The most important of these was an extension of time for the navy by another three months.

What Philip had in mind was a battle with Henry's army along the banks of the Somme. Clinton might then be able to supply Philip's army at Rue and perhaps ferry troops across the Somme to attack Henry on the south bank of that river. With the two kings thus engaged, Guise determined this might be a good time to march into Flanders. Gathering soldiers from garrisons stationed at Calais, Ardres, Boulogne, and Montreuil, Guise ordered Thermes, the commander of Calais, to occupy Dunkirk and use it as a springboard for an attack on Gravelines.[68] The plan almost worked. Dunkirk fell without much resistance, but the troops at Gravelines held out long enough for Clinton's fleet to arrive. Though he could not land his soldiers, Clinton's guns pounded the French positions. Already under fire from a relief force led by the Count d'Egmont, Thermes found his army isolated on a sandy beach between the town and the sea with a rising tide cutting off his retreat toward Dunkirk. Within a few hours, he surrendered.[69]

Further inland, a similar move by Guise at Metz and Thionville threatened the whole territory of Luxembourg. Thionville fell on 22 June.[70] Guise might have driven his army from there into Flanders, but the loss of his troops at Gravelines made him reluctant to advance much further. Instead, the war between Philip and Henry lumbered on for the remainder of the summer and into the fall. Meanwhile, the English fleet that had been of such great assistance at Gravelines, headed toward La Rochelle. Before reaching that place, a storm drove the ships into harbor near Brest. The English burned the town of Conquet and sacked the surrounding area. Then, with a few captured ships they headed for home.[71] Apparently no one gave any thought to the possibility of recovering Calais, which had been left nearly undefended when Thermes marched away to lay siege to Gravelines.

By early September Philip had most of his army near Doulens, preparing to attack Amiens. The defending French army was only twenty miles away. On 3 September, finding his troops short of supplies, Philip and some of his officers rode out to look for another place in French territory that had not yet been picked over by foragers. A French cavalry patrol soon appeared, was fired on, and a brisk fight ensued, with each side bringing up reinforcements until the French finally retired from the field. This is as close as Philip ever came to real combat. From all reports he enjoyed it greatly, but this was no longer an era for kings to lead their troops into battle. Moreover, both armies were exhausted, so delegations from each side began to confer about peace terms.[72]

The Constable of France, accompanied by Marshal de St. André came to Arras to negotiate with Philip's representatives: the Count of Feria, who had returned to Brussels; Granvelle, the Bishop of Arras; and Ruy Gómez. Perhaps because she was ill at the time with the flu-like sickness that was sweeping through England, Mary did not send her own representative to Arras. But late in September Nicholas Wotton, her ambassador to France, reported the bad news: the French refused to give up Calais, saying it properly belonged to the French crown.[73]

Hoping it was not too late to take action, Mary named Dr. Wotton, along with the Earl of Arundel and the Bishop of Ely to represent her interests at Arras.[74] Before they could do anything, the conference adjourned, to open again in October at Cercamp. At the end of October, after several sessions in which the French refused to surrender Calais, the English commissioners reported that nothing further could be achieved. The only alternatives were either to give up Calais or to continue the war. Since the matter was so important to the realm, they advised that it be taken up in Parliament. Meantime, they asked for permission to go home.[75]

When Philip heard what they had in mind, he told them emphatically that they should not leave. "It is the nature of the French, as you doubtless know," said Philip, "that the harder and more intransigent they are in the beginning, the softer and more agreeable they are at the end."[76] So the commissioners remained, though not at Cercamp, at least not all of them, lest the French think they were too eager to settle.[77]

At this point Philip received word from London that Mary was gravely ill. He had heard this before, so once again he dispatched Count Feria with letters and greetings for Mary and for the Council. This time it was not good enough. Most people – those who were firmly Catholic – thought Philip should have gone himself. People talked of his lack of affection for Mary and his apparent indifference in the face of her serious illness. They also thought he was responsible for the financial problems and unrest in England, saying that if he had been there these things would not have happened.[78] In effect, they wanted him to act like a king, but without a coronation.

When Feria arrived in London on 9 November, Mary was fading in and out of consciousness. She smiled faintly when Feria told her that he brought news from her husband, but she was not strong enough to read the letter Philip had written to her.[79] A day earlier she had sent two councilors to Elizabeth with a message: Mary would agree that Elizabeth should inherit the throne on two conditions. "First, she must swear to keep the old religion as Her

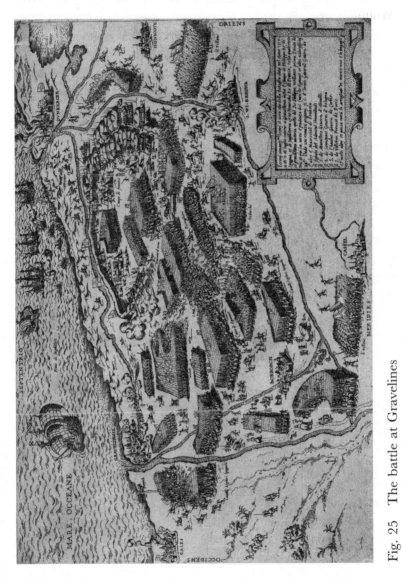

Fig. 25 The battle at Gravelines

Majesty has restored it; second she must pay the debts that [Mary] might leave."[80] For another week Mary remained at the brink of death, while physicians bled and purged her, the only treatments they knew. Finally, on 17 November while hearing Mass, Mary died. Her last recorded words were responses to the *Agnus Dei*: "*Miserere nobis, Miserere nobis, Dona nobis pacem.*"[81]

With her passing, Philip was no longer King of England. He had married in order to become king, and he was not interested in anything less. This was the whole point of his training, his main goal in life. Having inherited kingdoms and dukedoms from his father, news of whose death had just reached him,[82] Philip could not bring himself to accept a secondary role in England. And he did not know enough about love to love his wife. As a youth Philip had shown great love for his mother and enormous respect and admiration for his father, whose throne he would inherit. He understood the formalities of royal behavior, but he had not been taught that a king should love his wife. In fact, his training suggested the opposite. Considering his father's stern warnings and the experience of his first marriage, it seems probable that for Philip a marriage for love was simply out of the question.

Chapter 12

King of Spain

*I have resolved firmly to perform this service for
Our Lord God.*

Philip

After Mary's death the French king agreed to put off further peace
negotiations until it became clear what policy the new Queen of
England and her Privy Council would adopt.[1] Although he was no
longer King of England, Philip considered that he had an obligation
to England, because of the aid given by England in his war with
France, if for no other reason. While he hoped to arrive at a peace
settlement without renewing the war, he was determined to let
Elizabeth and the Privy Council tell him what they wanted to do.
In Philip's mind, it would not be possible to continue the war
during the winter, but if Elizabeth and her Council wanted to
renew hostilities in the spring and win back Calais, Philip would
join the fight. Not that Philip really wanted to do this; rather, he
felt bound by the same treaty he had cited to get the English
government into the war.[2]

Decisions about the war were not the only matters facing the
English government. There was still a strong feeling that a queen
could not rule alone. Elizabeth would have to choose a husband;
everyone wanted to know who it might be. There was still talk that
she should marry the Duke of Savoy. The emperor wanted her to

marry his own son, Philip's cousin. However, Elizabeth was not interested in either man.[3] Rather, she suggested to Feria that she might be interested in an offer of marriage from Philip himself, and Feria so informed his king.[4] Elizabeth's offer struck Philip like a blow. He did not see how he could refuse, though he told Feria that he felt "like a man condemned."[5]

Philip could think of numerous reasons not to marry Elizabeth. First, she was not really a Catholic, so the marriage would cause great scandal. And then, a marriage with Elizabeth would mean a "perpetual war with France," since that country had a claim on the English throne through Mary Stuart, the Queen of Scotland. Moreover, as he told Feria, there would be great expense involved in residing and entertaining in England, "as you know." And finally, there was a pressing demand from Spain for Philip to come home.[6]

On the other hand, Philip could see certain advantages in such a marriage, the main one being "the universal well-being of Christianity and the conservation of the Religion, which has been restored in that realm through the grace of Our Lord." For this reason, said Philip to Feria, "I have resolved firmly to perform this service for Our Lord God," though with certain conditions.

> First and foremost, you must assure yourself that the Queen will profess the same religion that I now hold and always shall, and that she will persevere in it and maintain and protect it in the realm. To this end she must do everything that seems to me appropriate to preserve and advance it. She must petition the Pope privately for absolution and for the necessary dispensation, doing all so that when I marry her she will be a Catholic, which she has not been to this time. . . . But you are not to put forward these conditions until you have understood her will and she has expressly said that she wishes to marry me. . . . What you say seems good to me: the discussion at first should be with the Queen alone, for she has opened the way.[7]

While Feria was digesting these instructions, it became clear that the queen and Parliament had no intention of keeping England Catholic. Consequently, Philip consulted with his closest advisers, the Duke of Alba, the Bishop of Arras, and Ruy Gómez. At their urging, he told Feria to warn Elizabeth that he would not be interested in marriage in a Protestant England.[8] No doubt she already understood his objections, perhaps from intercepting and reading his diplomatic correspondence. Before Feria could explain the matter, Elizabeth told him that she really had no interest in marriage.[9]

Ultimately, Elizabeth and the Privy Council decided not to fight for Calais, largely because there was no money to finance another season of war. Nonetheless, Elizabeth and Philip remained in close contact through Feria, she largely because of the peace negotiations, and he largely because of his worry about religious change in England.

The peace negotiations dragged on for several weeks, until the end of March, when a settlement was reached. The English delegates agreed to cede Calais to France for eight years, at the end of which time France would either give it back or pay England the sum of 500,000 crowns. When Feria reported this to Philip, he said that Elizabeth had pretended to be angry at her commissioners for agreeing to the terms. "But her anger was all feigned," said Feria, "and she is really quite pleased, and her people as well." No one really expected that France would give back Calais or pay the money either, and that is how it turned out.[10]

The treaty was a great victory for Philip, if not for England. He retained all his territories, isolating France, and placing Spain in a position of commanding importance in Europe. Beyond this, Philip acquired a new wife, the daughter of the French king. Explaining all this to Elizabeth, Feria told her that Philip was sorry their own marriage negotiations had not succeeded. She replied with some asperity that it was Philip's fault and not hers, for she had still been considering the matter. "Then she turned to tell me that Your Majesty could not have been very much in love with her," wrote Feria, "since you did not have the patience to wait four months [for an answer]."[11]

From that point Feria's influence with Elizabeth plummeted. By the end of the month he was writing to tell Philip that his spies had given him additional information about Elizabeth that made a marriage with one of the emperor's sons problematic: "She cannot bear children."[12] There was a persistent rumor about this. The exact problem is not clear, but it no doubt related to some physical deformity.

At least from the age of fourteen Elizabeth had been a shameless flirt, frolicing in bed with her guardian, Thomas Seymour, when his wife was pregnant. Perhaps it was innocent fun or perhaps not.[13] If not, the experience may have convinced Elizabeth – and her servants, who saw everything – that she was barren.

According to one suggestion, Elizabeth suffered from Androgen Insensitivity Syndrome. When this condition occurs, a male child has the external features of a female but with a shallow vagina and undeveloped ovaries. Such persons tend to be tall and thin, and physically very attractive.[14] In Elizabeth's case the evidence is contradictory. Those who liked her said she was perfectly normal; those who did not said otherwise.

Philip, on the other hand, was certainly not sterile, but he was said to be licentious. Not all the stories came from his detractors, though most of them did. A widespread bit of gossip says that he fathered one or two children during his stay in Brussels. A Venetian diplomat said there was one woman and one child. Others said there were two women and two children. Perhaps one of the women was Madame d'Aler. Whatever the case may be, both his friends and his enemies say Philip had affairs, just as his father did. Unlike his father, Philip did not give public recognition to any children who might have come from illicit liaisons.[15]

Philip remained in Brussels until late in the summer, hoping to be able to convince Elizabeth to keep England Catholic, and making arrangements about the government of the Low Countries. Finally in August 1559, with his funds nearly exhausted, he left for Spain. When his fleet arrived in port at Laredo, the ship carrying most of his papers was lost in a storm,[16] leaving historians with the task of filling in the story of his reign as King of England as best they might.

In June 1559 Philip's marriage to Elizabeth Valois was performed by proxy in Paris at the cathedral of Notre Dame. The girl was thirteen years old, pretty and vivacious, the eldest daughter of Henry II of France and his wife Catherine de Medici. The nuptial festivities were marred by Henry's death in a joust held to celebrate the wedding. The tragedy delayed her departure for several months. She finally arrived in December, and everyone fell in love with her, including Philip. They were married formally at the end of January in Guadalajara in the palace of the Duke of Infantado. The bride was so young – not yet of child-bearing age – that the two probably did not live together immediately as husband and wife.[17]

Instead, Philip resumed his romance with Eufrasia de Guzmán, a lady-in-waiting to his sister Juana. No doubt Elizabeth knew about the arrangement, and no doubt she was greatly annoyed. In the summer of 1564, when Elizabeth became pregnant, Eufrasia did as well, and she made no attempt to hide the fact. Instead, she continued to present herself at court, arrayed in all her finery. This was too much for the young queen, who became violently ill and took to her bed.[18]

Shocked to his senses, Philip hurried to his wife's bedside. He had already arranged a marriage between Eufrasia and the Prince of Ascoli, but Elizabeth obviously thought the affair was not over. In the event, she miscarried, but Philip became much more attentive, perhaps even faithful.[19]

Philip also took his young wife into his confidence, discussing matters of state with her. Very likely this was a result of his experience with Mary Tudor, who had shown him that a woman could be an effective administrator. Of course there were others with similar abilities. His sister Juana had been a remarkably good regent in Spain during Philip's absence. His half-sister, Margaret of Parma, served him well as regent in the Netherlands and might have done much better, if Philip had not placed so many restrictions on her authority.

During all this time Philip tried to maintain an amicable relationship with England and to be a protector for the new queen. One reason, of course, was that England sat on the flank of the sea route to the Netherlands. Another reason, equally important, was that the wife of Francis II, the new king of France, was Mary Queen of Scots, who also claimed the throne of England.

Despite his friendly demeanor, Elizabeth and her Protestant advisers remained suspicious of Philip's motives, treating Philip with mistrust and at times outright hostility. The relationship came close to breaking point when Elizabeth supported Protestant forces, first in France, where Philip had family ties, and later in the Netherlands, where Spanish merchants gained access to European markets. But there were also puzzling moves on Elizabeth's part that annoyed Philip greatly without advancing English interests. Most of them involved money.

Almost from the beginning of Elizabeth's reign the family of John Hawkins had been capturing or buying blacks in Africa and selling them to Spanish colonists in America. It was illegal, of course, since foreigners were not permitted to trade in the colonies, so Hawkins used various subterfuges, sometimes extorting licenses from local officials, other times pretending to be a Spanish subject. It mattered very little, as the colonists were eager to trade with Hawkins, who made enormous profits from this odious business.[20]

So great were the profits that in 1567 Elizabeth gave Hawkins two of her own ships to use in another voyage to the Spanish colonies. With fifty slaves left over from an earlier voyage and apparently kept in Plymouth, Hawkins sailed to the Guinea coast, where he captured another 4 or 500 poor souls. With these slaves and several shiploads of merchandise he sailed across the Atlantic, stopping to trade at the island of Margarita and the Spanish settlements of Rio de la Hacha, Santa Marta, and Cartagena. Sometimes the local officials greeted him warmly; at other times they insisted on a sort of sham battle, so they could later claim to have been forced to trade. Either way, they bought the slaves and goods, and Hawkins sailed for home.

The route out of the Caribbean led around the western tip of Cuba and into the Gulf of Mexico, where the English ships were caught in a terrible storm. Taking refuge in the Spanish port of San Juan de Ulloa, where he siezed the fort and set about repairing his ships. A few days later a Spanish fleet arrived. In the ensuing battle and flight one royal ship was captured, along with more than a hundred English sailors.

Before the survivors limped home to Plymouth, several ships arrived in England, carrying funds that Philip was in the process of borrowing from Genoese bankers and sending to the Netherlands. Chased by French Huguenot raiders, the ships took refuge in Plymouth and Southampton, where the authorities offloaded the treasure and sent it to London, allegedly for safekeeping. In retaliation Spanish authorities confiscated English ships and goods in the Netherlands. The Hawkins brothers then assessed their own damages and asked the English government to use the treasure as reimbursement for what they had lost in San Juan de Ulloa.

It was a nasty business all around, with English government officials and the queen herself seemingly involved in the slave trade. The embargo was extended in both countries, and Elizabeth authorized her subjects to attack any Spanish ship sailing through the Channel. Disgusted with the queen, Philip began to think seriously of deposing Elizabeth and putting Mary Queen of Scots on the throne.

At about the same time, October 1568, Philip's young French wife died in childbirth, which was the common fate of royal consorts. Still needing a son and heir, Philip looked for a new bride and in 1570 chose his cousin Anna of Austria. When a fleet was assembled in the Netherlands to bring the girl to Spain, English officials thought it looked like an invasion fleet and mobilized the nation for defense. The Spanish ships sailed quietly through the Channel, but Elizabeth was still worried and kept her own fleet close to home. As a precaution she sent an envoy to Madrid, asking for a new exchange of ambassadors.

At this point the disputes might have been settled amicably had not John Hawkins determined to deal privately with Spanish officials in an attempt to win the freedom of his imprisoned sailors. A good many of the men had died in captivity, and others had been taken to Mexico City. About forty of the survivors were transported to Spain, where they were imprisoned in the Casa de Contratación. In conversations with the Spanish ambassador in London, Hawkins discussed the prisoners and let it be known that he was unhappy with religious and political conditions in England.

At about this time two other men appeared in London. One was Roberto Ridolfi, a Florentine banker, and the other Thomas Stucley, an Irish adventurer. Like Hawkins, both men had their own plans, mostly involving Mary Queen of Scots. All of their plots, whether made together or separately, involved the removal of Elizabeth and the coronation of Mary as the rightful Queen of England. The various plans changed over time. In the final proposal Hawkins was to take his own ships and most of the royal vessels, transport Mary to the continent, and then join a Spanish fleet to bring an invasion force to England. English Catholics were expected to rise in support of a rebel army to be led by the Duke of Norfolk. The Duke of Feria was also involved, as was his wife, the former Jane Dormer, who had been lady-in-waiting to Queen Mary, Philip's wife. Jane assisted the English prisoners in Seville and urged Philip to release them. Feria himself represented Philip in dealings with the man Hawkins sent to negotiate for the prisoner release.

The plots, hazy to begin with, soon fell apart. Both Ridolfi and Hawkins were doubtless double agents, later, if not at the very beginning. After they betrayed Norfolk, he was arrested and later executed. Mary, already imprisoned, was kept in even closer confinement. Ridolfi, out of England at the time, never returned. Hawkins became treasurer of the navy.

From that time forward relations between England and Spain slid unhampered into war. In a three-year voyage, 1577–1580, Francis Drake sailed to Spanish ports along the Pacific coast, plundering as he went. Arriving home with a shipload of Spanish treasure, he shared it all with Queen Elizabeth, who knighted him, thereby turning a pirate into a gentleman and a national hero.

Drake's voyage was followed by other raids, in Portugal, the West Indies, the Cape Verde Islands, and elsewhere. It was all too much for Philip, who decided to send an army to invade England and put Mary on the throne. He gave orders for the preparation of an invasion fleet. The ships were almost ready to sail in 1587, when Francis Drake arrived in Cadiz. In a lightning stroke he captured four ships, burned twenty or thirty others, and loaded his own vessels with the supplies intended for the Spanish invasion force. Undeterred, Philip prepared a new fleet.

This armada was part of a grand scheme. The ships were to sail to the Netherlands, rendezvous with the armies held there by the Duke of Alba, and transport these soldiers to England. Nothing went right. Reaching the English coast in August 1588, the Spanish ships saw the English fleet in the harbor at Plymouth, but failed to attack. Nor did they attempt to destroy the English fleet later in their voyage through the Channel. Instead they sailed on toward Flanders, where they hoped to meet their invasion army and escort it across the Channel.

As it turned out, the Spanish ships failed to meet Alba's army. Instead they were driven away by the English fleet and sailed into the North Sea, where it was impossible to turn back. There the real destruction of the Armada began. Battered by storms, many of the ships were driven ashore on the coasts of Scotland and Ireland, and only about half of the fleet actually made port again in Spain.

From the time of Philip's return to Spain in 1559 until his death thirty-nine years later Philip remained in Spain, never once leaving to visit any of his vast dominions. He ruled the greatest and richest empire the world had ever known, some fifty million people scattered across two great oceans, four continents, and countless islands.

As with most monarchs of his day, Philip saw himself as a man appointed by God, and his divine duty was to bring England back to the faith. This he accomplished, and he considered it his greatest gift to the country. What made it all possible was Philip's skill as a negotiator and administrator. While the marriage treaty might have placed Philip in a secondary role in the country, he refused to allow this to happen. Instead, he negotiated with members of Parliament and sat in the meetings of the Privy Council, insisting that the members treat him as though he were King of England.

At first both Philip and his father thought they could see parallels between Philip's new role in England and that of Charles in his first year or two in Spain. Charles had overcome resistance in the cortes by the force of his own personality, and he thought

Philip would be able to do the same. Both father and son realized that Parliament had the authority to determine succession to the throne, but they thought this matter could also be adjusted. Already King of Naples at the time of the marriage, Philip was King of England only by treaty. Still, in this limited sense, he was king. The government recognized Philip as king and agreed that Philip's name should precede that of Mary in official documents and in the regnal name. However, Parliament refused to go any further and never approved Philip's coronation.

Thus, Philip's brief tenure as King of England was marked by success in administration, a religious restoration, and not much else. Philip and Mary did not produce an heir, so the emperor's grand plan to unite England and the Netherlands into a kingdom that would defend Spanish interests in northern Europe came to nothing. When Mary died and was succeeded by her Protestant sister Elizabeth, the country too became Protestant. Philip's great gift to the English people was firmly rejected. Instead there arose a global conflict between England and Spain that lasted for the next four centuries and may not yet be ended.

Notes

Introduction

1 "*Relacion de lo subcedido a la Armada de su Magestad desde los 22 de Julio hasta 21 de Agosto de 1588*," Vatican Library, Urbinates Latini 1115, fol. 229–30v. Ubaldino, "*Comentario della Impresa Fatta Contra il Regno D'Inghilterra del Re Catholica L'Anno 1588*," BL Royal 14. A. XI, translated in Waters, *The Elizabethan Navy and the Armada of Spain*, 96. Pierson, *Commander of the Armada*, 164. Martin and Parker, *Spanish Armada*, 187–88.

2 Pedro Coco Calderón, "*Relacion*," AGS Guerra Marina 221, fol. 190, 3N and 3Nv.

Chapter 1

1 Charles to the officials of the city of Ubeda, 21 May 1527, Archivo Municipal de Ubeda, legajo 258, from a photographic copy in Manuel Fernández Alvarez, *La España del Emperador Carlos V (1500–1559; 1517–1556)*, vol. XIX of Ramón Menéndez Pidal (ed.), *Historia de España* (Madrid: Espasa-Calpe, 1966), 1:12.

2 Manuel Colmeiro, "Ordenamiento de las Córtes de Valladolid de 1518," doc. no. VII in vol. IV, *Cortes de los antiguos reinos de León y Castilla* (5 vols.; Madrid: Real Academia de la Historia, 1861–1903), 260–84.

3 Roger B. Merriman, *The Rise of the Spanish Empire in the Old World and in the New* (4 vols.; New York: Macmillan & Co., 1925), 3: 66–124. John Lynch, *Spain under the Hapsburgs*, vol. I, *Empire and Absolutism*, 1516–1598 (New York: New York University Press, 1981), 38–51. Manuel Fernández Alvarez, *Charles V, Elected Emperor and Hereditary Ruler* (London: Thames & Hudson, 1975), 19–29, and 57–68.

4 AGS Libros generales de Cámara, núm. 46; transcribed by Claudio Pérez Gredilla in *Revista de Archivos, Bibliotecas, y Museos*, (1874), 4:104.

5 AGS Libros generales de Cámara, núm. 46; transcribed by Claudio Pérez Gredilla in *Revista de Archivos, Bibliotecas, y Museos* (1874), 4:104. A more ample description appears in a manuscript by Fray Juan de Osnaga, "*Relación de la guerra del Almirante de Francia contra el Emperador Carlos V*," 1544, published in P. Manuel Hoyos, *Historia del Colegio de San Gregorio de Valladolid* (Valladolid, 1928), 491. According to Fray Juan: "The Prince howled very loudly when they poured the water on him."

6 BL Cotton Vitellius C. XVI, fols. 132–34v; 235–35v; and 246–47.

7 Erickson, *Bloody Mary*, 37–38, and 80–81.

8 Peter Gwyn, *The King's Cardinal: The Rise and Fall of Thomas Wolsey* (London: Barrie and Jenkins, 1990), 502, 520, and 524.

9 Leviticus, 18:16. This is from the King James Version. Henry would doubtless have read the Vulgate: "*Turpitudinem uxoris fratris tui non revelabis quia turpitudo fratris tui est.*"

10 Even so, many modern scholars accept the arguments of Henry's experts at face value. See for example J. J. Scarisbrick, *Henry VIII* (Berkeley: University of California Press, 1968), 163–97. Others assert that the biblical prohibition was the key argument. See Edward Sturtz and Virginia Murphy (eds.), *The Divorce Tracts of Henry VIII* (Angers: Moreana, 1988), xvii.

11 Genesis, 38:6–10; Deuteronomy, 25:5–10.

12 According to Erickson (*Bloody Mary*, 102) Mary was immediately removed from the succession, and the new baby was proclaimed "rightful heiress" to the throne of England.

13 Erickson, *Bloody Mary*, 95.

14 This is based on the instructions given by Juan Luis Vives in his treatise, *De institutione fœminæ Christianæ, ad Sereniss. D. Catherinã Hispanã, Angliæ Reginam, libri tres, mira eruditione, elegantia, breuitate, facilitate, plane aurei, pietateque & sanctimonia, vere Christiani, Christianæ in primis Virgini, deinde Maritæ, postremo Viduæ, nouo instituendi argumento longe vtilissimi* (Antwerp: Michael Hoochstratanus, 1523), pages unnumbered. The book was translated later into English and published under the title, *A Very Frvteful and Pleasant boke callyd the instruction of a Christen woman, made fyrste in latyne, by the right famous clerk mayster Lewes Uiues, and tourned oute into Englysshe by Richard Hyrde* (London: Thomas Berth, 1541). Hereafter *Instruction of a Christen Woman*.

15 Erickson, *Bloody Mary*, 211–12.

16 Carlos G. Noreña, *The Life of Juan Luis Vives* (The Hague: Martinus Nijhoff, 1970), 70–71, and 79–80.

17 Vives, *De institutione fœminæ Christianæ*, preface.

18 Vives, *Instruction of a Christen Woman*, fols. 3, and 5v.

19 Ibid., fols. 8–9.

20 Noreña, *Life of Vives*, 80–81. Vives to Francis Cranevelt, 25 January 1524, in Henry de Vocht (ed.), *Literae Virorum Eruditorum ad Franciscum Craneveldium, 1522–1528* (Louvain: Librairie Universitaire, 1928), 90. Vives, *De ratione studii puerilis*, Epistola I, in *Introductio ad Sapientiam. Satellitium siue Symbola. Epistolæ duæ de ratione studii puerilis* (Bruges: Hubert de Crooc, 1526). The work of Vives in educational philosophy was largely forgotten in England until Foster Watson and William H. Woodward brought it back to the attention of scholars in the early 1900s. Watson referred to Epistola I of *De ratione studii puerilis* as *The Plan of Study for Girls*, perhaps to distinguish it from Epistola II, a treatise of similar title (but dated a few months later) dedicated to Charles, the son of Lord William Mountjoy. See *Vives and the Renascence Education of Women* (London: Edward Arnold, 1912).

21 *Introductio ad Sapientium. Satellitium*, no page numbers. The introduction is dated 1 July 1524 (*calendas quintiles .M.D.XXIII.*).

22 Henry Clifford, *Life of Jane Dormer Duchess of Feria*, Transcribed from the ancient manuscript in the possession of Lord Dormer by the late Canon E[dgar] E. Estcourt and edited by the Rev.

Joseph Stevenson (London: Burns & Oates Ltd., 1887), 80–82. Noreña, *Life of Vives*, 92. Henry de Vocht, *Monumenta Humanistica Lovaniensia: Texts and Studies about Louvain Humanists in the First Half of the XVIth Century: Erasmus, Vives, Dorpius, Clenardus, Goes, Moringus* (Louvain: Libraire Universitaire, 1934), 12, and 58.

23 Noreña, *Life of Vives*, 100–104. Following the lead of Foster Watson, several modern biographers have given Vives a leading role in Mary's education. See for example David Loades, *Mary Tudor: A Life* (Oxford: Basil Blackwell, 1989), 31–33, who sees Vives in the role of a leading educational advisor to the queen, her mother. See also Charles Fantazzi, "Vives, Juan Luis," *ODNB*, 56:571. Another writer blamed Vives for what she saw as Mary's unhealthily repressed sexual urges. See Erickson, *Bloody Mary*, 42–46.

24 John Pits, *Relationvm historicvm de rebus Anglicis* (Paris: Rolin Thierry & Sebastian Cramoisy, 1619), 729–30. Ethan H. Shagan, "Fetherston, Richard," *ODNB*, 19:453.

25 Du Wes, *An introductorie for to Lerne to rede, to pronounce, and to speake Frenche trewly, compyled for the ryghte hygh, excellent, & moste vertuous lady, the lady Mary of England, doughter to our moste souerayne lorde kyng Henry the eyghte* (London: Nicolas Bourman, [1540]), page A iii verso and following page. The author's attitude toward the divorce is seen in his dedication of part II of the text: "And to you most illustre, ryght excellent, and ryghte magnanime, lady and princesse my lady Anne by the grace of God Quene of Englande and of France with ryghte noble and moste vertuouse, your ryghte dere and well beloued doughter Elizabeth Princesse of Englande and of wales."

26 Claude Dodieu, Report of 8 May 1527, in *Letters and Papers, Foreign and Domestic, of the Reign of Henry VIII*, edited by J. S. Brewer (London: Her Majesty's Stationery Office, 1872), vol. IV, part II, 1412.

27 Katherine to Mary, 20 September (1544), BL Cotton Vespasian F III, fol. 37. E. J. Devereaux reproduced the Latin text of the letter in, "The Publication of the English *Paraphrases*

of Erasmus," *Bulletin of the John Rylands Library*, (Spring, 1969), 51:351. See also Agnes Strickland, *Lives of the Queens of England* (London: Henry Colburn, 1851), 3:229.

28 While the earliest printing is said to have been issued on 31 January 1548 (1549) Bishop Stephen Gardiner said in October 1547 that he had a complete copy of the book; this is possible, since each gospel was printed separately. In any case, the publication dates given in the early printings and editions are said to be untrustworthy. See E. J. Devereaux, *Renaissance English Translations of Erasmus* (Toronto: University of Toronto Press, 1983), 147–175. See the reconstruction of Gardiner's letter to the Duke of Somerset, 14 October [1547], in James A. Muller (ed.), *The Letters of Stephen Gardiner* (Cambridge: Cambridge University Press, 1933), 398.

Chapter 2

1 Doña Maria was born on 21 June 1528; the empress gave birth to another child, Fernando, in October 1529, but he lived only a short time. Menéndez Pidal, *Historia de España*, XIX, 1:50.

2 Antonio Guevara, *Epistolas Familiares*, ed. by Augusto Cortina (Mexico: Buenos Aires, 1946), Núm. XIII. *"Aprehendent septem mulieres virum unum."* The bishop's quotation is from Isaias. 4:1 (Vulgate edition).

3 The groom was fourteen and the bride eleven, though by her letters she seems to have been a fairly mature young girl. See the *Colección de documentos inéditos para la historia de España* (Madrid: Viuda de Calero, 1850), XVI: 222–23. (Hereafter *CDIE*.) The heart-breaking letters of the bride can be read in *CDIE*, 226–35.

4 Javier Vales Failde, *La emperatriz Isabel* (Madrid: Revista de Arch., Bibl., y Museos, 1917), 269–70. Failde reproduced the text of the document (from the archives of the Colegio de Doncellas Nobles, founded by Silíceo after he became archbishop of Toledo), modernizing the orthography.

5   Menéndez Pidal, *Historia de España*, XIX, 1:98, 104, 144. For a brief outline of Philip's studies, including the role of Estrella, see the letter of Juan de Zúñiga, 21 October 1541, AGS Estado-Castilla 53, fol. 366.

6   Menéndez Pidal, *Historia de España*, XIX, 1:89–93.

7   Bernabé de Busto was teaching the pages and other children of the court as early as 1532 and had for the past two years been urging the queen to begin Philip's education. See the '*Epistola del auctor*' in his *Introductiones grammaticas: breues e compendiosas: compuestas por el doctor Busto, maestro de los pajes de su majestad* (Segovia: n.n., 1532), n.p., which he hoped would move the queen to start the boy's schooling.

8   Pedro González de Mendoza to Charles V, 12 January 1531, AGS Estado 22, fols. 168–69.

9   See the letters of Juan de Zúñiga to Charles, 27 January 1540, AGS Estado 50, fols. 22, 24; 13 February 1540, AGS Estado 50, fol. 26; 25 February 1540, AGS Estado 50, fol. 27; 19 March 1540, AGS Estado 50, fol. 29.

10 Juan de Zúñiga to Charles, 25 March 1540, fol. 27.

11 Estefanía de Requeséns to the Condesa de Palamós, 23 April 1535; this and other letters from Juan de Zúñiga and his wife Estefanía de Requeséns are quoted in March, *Niñez y juventud*, 1:240, based on the originals in the Archivo de Palau in Barcelona.

12 Estefanía de Requeséns to the Condesa de Palamós, 5 December 1535, quoted in March, *Niñez y juventud*, 2:283–85. See also AGS Estado Castilla, Legajo 430, fols. 169–70, cited in Menéndez Pidal, *Historia de España*, XIX, 1:106–107.

13 Silíceo to Charles V, 2 May [1536], AGS Estado 38, fol. 259. See also the letter from Dr. Villalobos et al., 3 May 1536, AGS Estado 38, fol. 260. In a note dated 3 May Juan de Zúñiga said that the octave had passed and the sores were drying up, indicating that the illness was not terribly serious. Zúñiga to Charles, 1 May 1536, Estado 38, fol. 261. Lest Charles think that Zúñiga was not taking the matter seriously, the good servant added that he was writing the letter in the middle of the night.

14 The scabies attacks are mentioned in Silíceo to Charles, 4 February 1544, AGS Estado 68, fols. 367–68. See also March, *Niñez y juventud*, 1:78, 96, 97; II, 153, 264–65, 268–69, and 272.

15 Menéndez Pidal, *Historia de España*, XIX, 1:124. Parker in *Philip II*, 9, says flatly, "The prince's health was not good." In his biography, *Philip II of Spain*, 38, Pierson says the contrary: "Philip's health in his early years was relatively good." Both drew their conclusions from the same source, the various reports sent to Charles by Juan de Zúñiga and his wife Estefanía de Requeséns to her mother the Condesa de Palamós; both are quoted at length in March, *Niñez y juventud*.

16 Juan de Zúñiga to Charles, 13 September 1535, AGS Estado 31, fol. 83; and 1 May 1536, AGS Estado 38, fol. 261. See also Estefanía de Requeséns to the Condesa de Palamós, 13 September 1535, quoted in March, *Niñez y juventud*, II, 265.

17 AGS Casas y Sitios Reales 76, *Libro de la d[e]sp[ens]a del pri[nçip]e nro Señor del mes de agosto de myll e qui[nient]os e q[ua]r[ent]a a[ñ]os en* Vall[adol]id, [August 1544]; AGS Casas y Sitios Reales 78, *Libro de la d[es]pensa del prinçipe nro señor del mes de henero de myll e quyn[ient]os e quarenta y siete años.*

18 Pedro González de Mendoza to Charles, 12 January 1531, AGS Estado 22, March, fols. 168–69.

19 Guevara, *Epistolas Familiares*, Núm. XIII.

20 Pedro de Ribadeneyra, *Vida del P. Francisco de Borja, que fue Duque de Gãdia, y despues Religioso y .III. General de la Compañia de Jesus* (Madrid: Casa de P. Madrigal, 1592), fols. 15–19v. Frederick Baron Corvo, *Chronicles of the House of Borgia* (New York: E. P. Dutton & Co., 1901), 306–16. Menéndez Pidal, *Historia de España*, XIX, 1:137–39.

21 Menéndez Pidal, *Historia de España*, XIX, 1:141–44.

22 Parker, *Philip II*, 6–7. Pierson, *Philip II of Spain*, 16.

23 Kamen, *Philip of Spain*, 8.

24 Charles to Philip, 4 May 1543, quoted in March, *Niñez y juventud*, 2:13. The originals disappeared from the archives in the past century. March believed this copy was probably the

most dependable of the various versions available. See note 7, and 9–10.

25 Charles to Philip, 4 May 1543, March, *Niñez y juventud*, 14–16, and 22.

26 Charles to Philip, 6 May 1543, March, *Niñez y juventud*, 2:26–32.

27 Charles to Philip, 4 May 1543, March, *Niñez y juventud*, 2:19–20.

28 Charles to Zúñiga, 1 May 1543, Archivo de Palau, cartas secretas, quoted in March, *Niñez y juventud*, 1:304.

29 March, *Niñez y juventud*, II, 7. Menéndez Pidal, *Historia de España*, XIX, 1:156–62.

30 Menéndez Pidal, *Historia de España*, XIX, 1:155, 177–79. Maria's mother was the emperor's sister; her father was brother to the empress.

31 Sarmiento to Cobos, 25 July 1542, AGS Estado 373, [sic] quoted in March, *Niñez y juventud*, 2:61.

32 Silíceo to Philip, 1 November 1543, AGS Estado 62, fol. 15.

33 Philip to Charles, 4 February 1544, AGS Estado 64, fol. 141.

34 See the 1543 letter of Zúñiga describing the wedding festivities, quoted in March, *Niñez y juventud*, II, 81. There are other stories as well, as to who saw whom and when. Several are quoted in Menéndez Pidal, *Historia de España*, XIX, 1:189–91, and 194–97. It is no doubt safe to take Philip's word for the date and place. See his letter to his father, 4 February 1544, AGS Estado 64, fol. 141.

35 See John Elder's letter to Robert Stuarde, 1 January 1555, *The Copie of a letter sent in to Scotlande, of the arivall and landynge, and moste noble marryage of the moste Illustre Prynce Philippe, Prynce of Spaine, to the most excellente Princes Marye Quene of England, solemnisated in the Citie of Winchester: and howe he was recyued and installed at Windsore, and of his triumphyng entries in the noble Citie of London* (London: John Waylande, [1555]), n.p. [fol. F.v.].

36 William Coxe, *History of the House of Austria from the Foundation of the Monarchy by Rudolph of Hapsburg to the Death of Leopold the Second, 1218 to 1792* (4 vols.; London: Henry G. Bohn, 1847), 1:211.

37   Ludovic Lalanne (ed. and comp.), *Oeuvres Complètes de Pierre de Bourdeille, Seigneur de Brantôme* (11 vols.; Paris: Jules Renouard, 1876), 9:612–13.

38   Charles to Zúñiga, 17 February 1545, Archivo de Palau, cartas secretas, quoted in March, *Niñez y juventud,* 1:322. See also Lope Hurtado to Charles, AGS Estado 72, fol. 76–78.

39   Pierre Loyseleur and Hubert Languet, *The Apologie or Defence, of the Most Noble Prince William, by the grace of God, Prince of Orange* (Delft: n.n., 1581), 43–45. See also "Anatomia de España," Cambridge University Library, MS Gg.6.19 (1598) cited in Parker, *Philip II*, 203. The various charges are analyzed and refuted in Menéndez Pidal, *Historia de España*, XIX, 1:548–55.

40   See the two letters from the comendador mayor de Castilla to Charles, 13 August 1545, AGS Estado 69, fols. 54–56, and 58.

41   Cobos to Charles, 27 September 1546, Charles to Cobos, 11 August 1546, AGS Estado 73, fols. 203–206, and 239. There were recurring rumors on this point, one or two involving a lady-in-waiting. Isabel de Osorio, before she died in 1589, claimed that she had been Philip's wife. The court historian who reported her story explained it all by saying that the lady was mentally unbalanced. Much older than Philip, she was assigned to help care for him when he was a little boy. In time she came to love him so much that she began to imagine herself as his wife. Luis Cabrera de Córdoba, *Felipe Segundo, Rey de España* (Madrid: Imprenta, Esterotipia y Galvanoplastia de Aribau y Cia., 1877), 3:367. Extended treatment of the lady's story appears in Agustín G. de Amezúa y Mayo, *Isabel de Valois, Reina de España (1546–1568)* (Madrid: Gráficas Ultra, 1949), 1:393–401.

42   The Venetian ambassador Federico Badoero gives a good description of Philip's linguistic ability. See his 1557 report *"Relazione delle Persone, Governo e Stati di Carlo V e di Filippo II,"* *Le Relazioni degli Ambasciatori Veneti al Senato durante il Secolo Decimosesto* (ed.), Eugenio Albèri (Firenze: Società Editrice Fiorentina, 1853), ser. 1, 3:236. Hereafter Badoero, *Filippo II.*

43 Parker, *Philip II*, 12–14. See also Kamen, *Philip of Spain*, 6.

44 Kamen, *Philip of Spain*, 28–30. The document of investiture from AGS Patronato Real, 43–41, is pictured in color in Fernando Chueca Goitia, *"Felipe II, El Hombre," Philippus II Rex*, ed. by Pedro Navascués (Barcelona: Lunwerg Editores, S.A., c. 1998), 178.

45 Philip to Charles, 20 December 1546, AGS Estado 73, fols. 158–59.

46 Philip to Charles, 25 January 1547, AGS Estado 75, fol. 300. See also Philip to Charles, 1 June 1547, AGS Estado 75, fol. 75. Even so Philip soon changed his mind. See Helen Nader, *Liberty in Absolutist Spain: the Habsburg Sale of Towns 1516–1700* (London: Johns Hopkins University Press, 1990), 113.

Chapter 3

1 Chapuys to Charles, 29 January 1536, 17 February 1536, Pascual de Gayangos, *State Papers Spanish*, 5(2):26–29, and 39–45.

2 Death and Burial of Katherine of Aragon, n.d., *Letters and Papers, Foreign and Domestic, of the Reign of Henry VIII*, edited by James Gairdner (London: Her Majesty's Stationery Office, 1887) 10:104–106. Chapuys to Charles, 2 May 1536, Gayangos, *State Papers Spanish*, 105–108. Thomas Cranmer, *Sentencia definitiva in causa nullitatis matrimonii inter regem Henricum VIII. Et Annam Clivensem*, in David Wilkins, *Concilia Magnae Britanniae et Hiberniae, ab anno MCCCL. Ad annum MDXLV* (London: R. Gosling et al., 1737), 3:803–804. Chapuys to Charles, 19 May 1536, Gayangos, *State Papers Spanish*, 5(2):122–31.

3 Cromwell to Gardiner, 5 July 1536, BL Add. 25114, fol. 177.

4 Chapuys to Charles, 21 April 1536, Gayangos, *State Papers Spanish*, 5(2):85–102.

5 Chapuys to Charles, 19 May 1536; 1 July 1536, Gayangos, *State Papers Spanish*, 5(2):122–31, and 170–87.

6 Mary to Henry, n.d. (Thursday), Thomas Hearne, *Sylloge Epistolarum, a variis Angliae principibus scriptarum. Quibus & alia*

paucula sunt interspersa, e collectaneis Smithianis (una & altera dempta Epistola) descripsit, bound as part of *Titi Livii foro-juliensis vita Henrici Quinti, regis angliae* (Oxford: Theatro Sheldoniano, 1716), 140–43. Loades computes this date as Thursday, 22 June 1536. See his *Mary Tudor,* 101. The letters printed by Hearne were collected by Thomas Smith of Magdalen College, Oxford.

7   Chapuys to Charles, 1 July 1536, Gayangos, *State Papers Spanish,* 5(2):170–87.

8   For the various official attempts under Henry to change English Catholic religious practice, see Eamon Duffy, *The Stripping of the Altars: Traditional Religion in England, c. 1400–c. 1580* (London: Yale University Press, 1992), chaps. 11, and 12.

9   Mary to Cromwell, 23 June 1536, in Hearne, *Sylloge Epistolarum,* 144–46. Bishop of Faenza to Ambrogio (?), 26 June 1536, *L & P, Henry VIII,* 10:507.

10 Chapuys to Charles, 6 June 1536, Gayangos, *State Papers Spanish,* 5(2):137–62. Henry to Stephen Gardiner and John Wallop, 15 August 1536 and 12 September 1536, BL Add. MS 25114, fol. 198v, and 202. Chapuys to Charles, 12 August 1536, *State Papers Spanish,* 5(2):224–30. Henry to Richard Pate, 3 October [1540], PRO SP 1/163, fols. 52–54v (draft).

11 Henry to Gardiner and Wallop, 12 September 1536, Add. MS 25114, fol. 201ff. Great Britain, Statutes, 35 Henry VIII, chap. 1; *Henry the Eyght . . . beganne this thyrde Session of his moste high courte of parlyament . . . wherein were established these actes folowynge* (London: Thomas Bertheleti, 1544).

12 See for example Mary's letter of 24 August and 8 December 1538 to Thomas Cromwell, who had become her advisor; reprinted in Hearne, *Sylloge Epistolarum,* 135–36. In a letter to Charles V, dated 31 August 1538, Chapuys and Mendoza described the correspondence between Mary and Cromwell. Gayangos, *State Papers Spanish,* 6 (1):25–27.

13 Charles de Marillac to Anne de Montmorency, 27 December 1539, in Jean Kaulek (ed.), *Correspondance Politique de MM. De Castillon et De Marillac, Ambassadeurs de France en Angleterre (1537–1542)* (Paris: Ancienne Librairie Germer Baillière et Cie., 1885), 148–49.

14 Frederick Madden, *Privy Purse Expenses of the Princess Mary, Daughter of King Henry the Eighth, afterwards Queen Mary* (London: William Pickering, 1831), 176.

15 Philip of Bavaria to Henry, 27 February 1540, PRO SP 1/155, fols. 97–97v. There are two dates written on the reverse of the document, January 1540 and 27 February 1540, the latter of which seems to be the day Philip was granted an audience and presented the letter to Henry.

16 Mary to Cromwell, 17 December 1539, Hearne, *Sylloge Epistolarum*, 136–37. Thomas Wriothesley to Cromwell, 17 December 1539, Hearne, *Sylloge Epistolarum*, 149–51.

17 There are several draft agreements in BL Cotton Vitellius C. XVI, fols. 288–302v.

18 Madden, *Privy Purse Expenses*, 176. The inventory of jewels is dated 12 December 1542. Mary's notation on the document says simply: "The same deliu'ed to my Lorde Chauncello^r by the King' co'mandm^t."

19 Marillac to Francis I, 3 June 1542, in Kaulek (ed.), *Correspondance Politique*, 422–23. Surprisingly, the negotiations with Philip were renewed in 1546, after Philip came to England and visited Mary once more. Again the negotiations failed, at least partly because of religious problems. Mason to Henry, 11 May 1546, PRO SP 1/218, fols. 64–64v.

20 Mendoza and Chapuys to Charles V, 31 August 1538, Gayangos, *State Papers Spanish*, 6(1):25–27. Lope de Soria to Charles V, 25 February 1539, BL Add. 28591, fol. 49v (transcribed from AGS Estado 1314, fols. 144–47). Report of an address by Ridolfo Pio, Cardinal da Carpi, n.d., *L & P, Henry VIII*, 15:42. For references to the rumor of a possible marriage with Charles V, see the letter from the chancellor of France to Marillac, 26 October 1540; and the letter from Francis I to Marillac, 28 Feb 1541, in Kaulek (ed.), *Correspondance Politique*, 236, and 271–72. At one time it was thought that Henry might very well want his daughter to marry Reginald Pole or Pole's brother Henry; Chapuys to Granvelle, 8 July 1536, Gayangos, *State Papers Spanish*, 5(2):199. See the summary of a letter from the Count of

Cifuentes to Charles V, 4 February 1537, AGS Estado 866, fol. 5.

21 Copy of commission to Stephen Gardiner and Thomas Thirlby, 23 October 1545, PRO SP 1/209, fols. 96–96v. William Paget et al. to Gardiner and Thirlby, 10 November 1545, BL Add. MS 25114. fol. 342. Gardiner, Thirlby, and Edward Carne to Henry VIII, 20 November 1545, PRO SP 1/210, fols. 180–180v.

22 *Anno Secundo et Tertio Edovardi Sexti, Actes made in the Session of this present parliament, holden upon prorogacion at Westminster the fourth daie of Nouember, in the second yere of oure moste drad souereigne Lorde Edward .VI. by the grace of God kyng of England, Fraunce, and also of Irelande, defendor of the faith, and of the churche of England and also of Ireland, in yearth the supreme hed: and there continued & kept to the .xiii. Daie of Marchem in the .iii. Yere of oure saied souereigne lorde* (London: Richard Grafton, 1549), fols. ii–iiii verso.

23 Largely the work of Cranmer and Somerset, the Communion service spoke of "one oblacion, once offered" and of the service itself as "a perpetual memory, of that his precious death." *The booke of the common prayer and administracion of the sacramentes, and other rites and ceremonies of the Churche: after the vse of the Churche of England* (London: Edouard Whitechurche, 1549), fols. cxxviii and verso. For Cranmer's doctrinal ideas, see G. J. Cuming, *A History of Anglican Liturgy* (New York: Macmillan & Co., 1969), 79–81.

24 Duffy, *The Stripping of the Altars*, 457–77.

25 Van der Delft to Charles, 16 June 1547, Hume and Tyler, *State Papers Spanish*, 9:101.

26 David Loades, "The Personal Religion of Mary I," in Eamon Duffy and David Loades, *The Church of Mary Tudor* (Aldershot: Ashgate Publishing Ltd., 2006), 15. This is a curious work. Despite all the evidence to the contrary, Loades seems here to doubt that Mary was much of a Catholic. Ibid., 18. In another book he called Mary "a famous upholder of the traditional rites of the church, particularly the mass." Loades, *Intrigue and Treason: The Tudor Court, 1547–1558* (London: Pearson, Longman, 2004), 129.

Chapter 4

1   Badoero, "*Filippo II*," ser. 1, 3:236.

2   Luis Pfandl, *Felipe II*, trans. by José Corts Grau (2nd ed.; Madrid: Cultura Española, 1942), 192.

3   Menéndez Pidal, *Historia de España*, XIX, 1:11, 13, and 258–59.

4   Philip to Juan Vázquez de Molina, 30 November 1548, AGS Estado 76, fol. 111.

5   Juan Cristóbal Calvete de Estrella, *El Felicísimo viaje del muy alto y muy poderoso príncipe Don Felipe* (original, Anvers: Martin Nucio, 1552; reprint, Madrid: Sociedad de Bibliófilos Españoles, 1930), 35–40, and 51. Hereafter, Calvete, *Felicísimo viaje*.

6   Calvete, *Felicísimo viaje*, 57–59, 85–88, 203–204, and 306–11.

7   Ibid., 71–79.

8   Calvete, *Felicísimo viaje*, 90. Menéndez Pidal, *Historia de España*, 19(1):276.

9   Calvete, *Felicísimo viaje*, 99–100.

10 "A Booke of the Trauaile and Lief of Me Thomas Hoby, wᵗ diuerse things woorth the notinge," BL Egerton 2148, fol. 16v.

11 Calvete, *Felicísimo viaje*, 114–18, and 121–43.

12 Ibid., 146–49.

13 Ibid., 148–54.

14 Ibid., 167–74.

15 Ibid., 217.

16 Richard Morysine to the council, 28 February 1552 (1553), in William E. Turnbull (ed.), *Calendar of State Papers, Foreign Series, of the Reign of Edward VI, 1547–1553* (London: Longman, Green, Longman, and Roberts, 1861), 250. Hereafter *State Papers, Foreign*.

17 Michele Soriano, "*Relazioni di Filippo II Re di Spagna*," in Eugenio Albèri (ed.), *Le Relazioni degli ambasciatori veneti al Senato* (Florence: Società Editrice Fiorentina, 1853), ser. 1, 3:378. Reprinted in *Relazioni di Ambasciatori Veneti al Senato*, ed. by Luigi Firpo, vol. 8, *Spagna (1497–1598)* (Torino: Bottega d'Erasmo, 1981), vol. 8.

18   Antoine Perrenot de Granvelle, Bishop of Arras, to Maria, Queen Dowager of Hungary and regent of the Low Countries, 13 October 1550, Turnbull, *State Papers, Foreign*, 10:156n.

19   "A Booke of the Travaile and Lief of Me Thomas Hoby," BL Egerton 2148, fol. 93–94v. Paolo Sarpi, *Historia del Concilio Tridentino* ([London: John Bill], 1619), 371–72. *Pactos entre el Rey de los Romanos y el Príncipe dⁿ Felipe sobre la sucesion del Imperio con relacion al Rey Maximiliano a quien promete qᵉ le nombrara Gobernador de Alemania si despues de su tio llegase a ser Emperador*, 9 March 1551, AGS Estado 646, fols. 253–55.

20   For details of the arrangements made by Juan Martínez Silíceo, see his letter to Philip, 6 June 1551, AGS Estado 1467, fol. 99, transcribed in Constancio Gutiérrez, *Trento: Un Concilio para la Unión (1550–1552)*, vol. 1, *Fuentes (1549–1551) (Cartas, Despachos, Nóminas, etc.)* (Madrid: Consejo Superior de Investigaciones Científicas, 1981), 329–32. Menéndez Pidal, *Historia de España*, 19(1):305–306.

21   Menéndez Pidal, *Historia de España*, 19(1):307–310.

22   Luís Sarmiento de Mendoza to Charles, 24 November 1552, AGS Estado 376, fol. 1.

23   Charles to Maria of Hungary, 24 February 1552, Brussels, AR Etat et Audience 65, translated in Tyler, *State Papers Spanish*, 10:456.

24   Charles to Philip, 18 January 1548, Besançon, Collection de Granvelle 4; Jean de St. Mauris to Charles, 12 November 1548, Hume and Tyler, *State Papers Spanish*, 9:311–12, and 545. Charles to Philip, 3 April 1553, AGS Estado 98, fols. 137–38.

25   Charles to Philip, 3 April 1553, AGS Estado 98, fol. 137–38.

26   Charles to Philip, 12 August 1553, AGS Estado 506, fols. 25–28. Charles and Philip seemed to use *cruzados* and *ducados* interchangeably. See Philip to Charles, 22 August 1553, AGS Estado 807, fol. 24. Charles to Luís Sarmiento de Mendoza, 21 November 1553, AGS Estado 90, fols. 134–36.

27   These developments are reflected in the letters sent to Charles by the imperial ambassadors in London. See especially those dated 10 July 1553, 12 July 1553, [16 July 1553], 19, 20, and 22 July 1553, in Charles Weiss (ed.), *Papiers d'État du Cardinal*

de Granvelle d'après les Manuscrits de la Bibliothèque de Besançon (Paris: Imprimerie Royale, 1853), 4:22–24, 33–42, 46–53, and 57–58.

28 Ambassadors to Charles, 19 July 1553, 22 July 1553, in Weiss, *Papiers d'État du Cardinal de Granvelle d'après les Manuscrits de la Bibliothèque de Besançon*, 4:37–42, and 57–58.

29 Charles to Philip, 30 July 1553, AGS Estado 807.

Chapter 5

1 Charles to the Ambassadors, 22, and 29 July 1553, in Weiss, *Papiers d'État du Cardinal de Granvelle d'après les Manuscrits de la Bibliothèque de Besançon*, 4:54–61. Ambassadors to Charles, 2 August 1553, in Gachard and Piot, *Collection des Voyages des Souverains des Pays-Bas*, 4:88–89.

2 Charles to Philip, 30 July 1553, AGS Estado 807, fol. 29.

3 A very readable summary of these events may be found in Antonia Fraser, *Mary Queen of Scots* (London: Weidenfeld & Nicolson, 1969), 27–35.

4 Charles to Philip, 30 July 1553, AGS Estado 807, fol. 22.

5 Philip to Charles, 22 August 1553, AGS Estado 807, fol. 24.

6 Ambassadors to Charles, 4 September 1553, Tyler, *State Papers Spanish*, 11:206–207.

7 Ambassadors to Charles, 9 September 1553, in Gachard and Piot, *Collection des Voyages des Souverains des Pays-Bas*, 4:116.

8 Ambassadors to Charles, 2 August 1553, in Gachard and Piot, *Collection des Voyages des Souverains des Pays-Bas*, 4:89.

9 Ambassadors to Charles, 27 August 1553, Tyler, *State Papers Spanish*, 11:188.

10 Charles Wriothesley, *A Chronicle of England during the Reign of the Tudors, from A. D. 1485 to 1559*, ed. by William D. Hamilton, Camden Society New Series, vol. 20 (Westminster: Camden Society, 1877), 2:97.

11 'Robert Parkyn's Narrative of the Reformation,' ed. by Arthur G. Dickens, *Reformation Studies* (London: Hambledon Press, 1982), 308–309. Duffy, *Stripping of the Altars*, 524–28.

12 Ambassadors to Charles, 9 September 1553; Renard to Charles, 6 November 1553; in Gachard and Piot, *Collection des Voyages des Souverains des Pays-Bas*, 4:110–11, 191. For a complete list of Mary's Privy Council see Loades, *The Reign of Mary Tudor*, 404–11.

13 Ambassadors to Charles, 9 September 1553; 19 September 1553, in Gachard and Piot, *Collection des Voyages des Souverains des Pays-Bas*, 4:111, 126.

14 Renard to Philip, 3 October 1553, AGS Estado 807, fols. 2–3.

15 Renard to Charles, 12 October 1553, in Gachard and Piot, *Collection des Voyages des Souverains des Pays-Bas*, 4:138.

16 Giovanni Soranzo, "*Relazione di Giovanni Soranzo, 1565*," in *Le Relazioni degli Ambasciatori Veneti al Senato durante il Secolo Decimosesto*, ed. by Eugenio Albèri (Firenze: Spese dell' Editore, 1861), ser. 1, 5:114–15. Reprinted in *Relazioni di Ambasciatori Veneti al Senato*, ed. by Luigi Firpo, vol. 8, *Spagna (1497–1598)* (Torino: Bottega d'Erasmo, 1981).

17 Badoero, "*Filippo II*", ser. 1, 3:204, 251. Albèri, the editor of the series, said Badoero mistakenly referred to Don Juan of Austria, Philip's natural brother, rather than his son.

18 "Relazione di Giovanni Micheli," in *Relazioni dello Impero Britannico nel Secolo XVI Scritte da Veneti Ambasciatori* (Firenze: Società Editrice Fiorentina, 1852), 88.

19 Memorial from Renard to Mary, 11 October 1553, in Weiss, *Papiers d'État du Cardinal de Granvelle*, 4:126–31.

20 Renard to Charles, 21 October 1553, in Gachard and Piot, *Collection des Voyages des Souverains des Pays-Bas*, 4:160.

21 Renard to Charles, 15 October 1553; Ferdinand to Mary, 28 October 1553; in Gachard and Piot, *Collection des Voyages des Souverains des Pays-Bas*, 4:151, and 173–74.

22 Renard to Charles, 21 October 1553, in Gachard and Piot, *Collection des Voyages des Souverains des Pays-Bas*, 4:160.

23 Renard to Charles, 31 October 1553, in Gachard and Piot, *Collection des Voyages des Souverains des Pays-Bas*, 4:175.

24 Renard to Philip, 29 October 1553, AGS Estado 807, fol. 6.

25 Granvelle to Renard, 13 November 1553; Maria of Hungary to Renard, 19 November 1553; Weiss, *Papiers d'État du Cardinal de Granvelle*, 4:145, and 150–51; Eraso to Philip, 21 November 1553, AGS Estado 807, fol. 40. According to Pierson, *Philip II*, 30–31, this portrait is in the Galleria Nazionale, Palazzo Barberini, in Rome.

26 Renard to Maria of Hungary, 28 November 1553, *State Papers Spanish*, 11:397.

27 Renard to Charles, 17 November 1553; Renard to Charles, 21 October 1553; Ferdinand to Mary, 28 October 1553, in Gachard and Piot, *Collection des Voyages des Souverains des Pays-Bas*, 4:159–60, 171–73, 206–207. Charles to Renard, 21 November 1553, Weiss, *Papiers d'État du Cardinal de Granvelle*, 4:153–56.

28 Peter S. Donaldson shows how the terms of the treaty fit Gardiner's "Machiavellian" approach to the creation of a permanent Catholic dynasty in England. See his *Machiavelli and the Mystery of State* (New York: Cambridge University Press, 1988), 36–50.

29 Renard to Charles, 4 November 1553; 21 November 1553; and "Proposition a faire par l'empereur aux principaulx seigneurs et ceulx du conseil d'estat de pardeça, en la ville de Bruxelles, le 25ᵉ de Novembre 1553.", in Gachard and Piot, *Collection des Voyages des Souverains des Pays-Bas*, 4:183–84, and 215–19. Charles to Renard, 28 November 1553, Weiss, *Papiers d'État du Cardinal de Granvelle*, 4:157–67. Charles to Philip, 30 November and 16 December 1553, AGS Estado 807, Tyler, *State Papers Spanish*, 11:403–407.

30 Charles to Philip, 16 December 1553 and 26 December 1553, AGS Estado 807, fols. 25–26, and AGS Estado 98, fols. 374–75. Basically the same letters, the latter lacks the note about copying the Latin with care.

31 Eraso to Philip, 21 November 1553, AGS Estado 807, Tyler, *State Papers Spanish*, 11:382.

32 The original treaty was written in Latin, as were the associated documents. Philip's copy is in AGS Estado 807, fol. 36 (2ᵃ). A vellum copy with Mary's signature is in AGS

Patronato Real 55, fol. 28. For a printed Latin version of the treaty, see Thomas Rymer, *Fœdera, Conventiones, Literæ et cujyscunque Generis Acta Publica inter Reges Angliæ, et alios quosvis Imperatores, Reges, Pontifices, Principes, vel Communitates, ab Ineunte Sæculo Duodecimo, viz. Ab Anno 1101 ad nostra usque Tempora, Habita aut Tractata, ex Autographis, infra Secretiores Archivorum Regiorum Thesaurias, per multa Sæcula reconditis, fideliter Exscripta* (London: J. Tonson, 1728), 15:393–403. For a dependable English translation of the draft treaty, see Paul L. Hughes and James F. Larkin, *Tudor Royal Proclamations*, vol. 11, *The Later Tudors* (1553–1587) (New Haven and London: Yale University Press, 1969), 11:21–26.

33 One author makes the point that Charles was too ill to have much of a role in the negotiations and that major decisions were made by Granvelle and Renard, with the help of the emperor's sister, Mary. See M. J. Rodríguez-Salgado *The Changing Face of Empire, Charles V, Philip II, and Habsburg Authority, 1551–1559* (Cambridge: Cambridge University Press, 1988), 81.

34 "*Copia de la capitulacion de la casamiento,*" AGS Estado 807, fol. 36, 2ᵃ.

35 This is the famous "*escriptura ad cautelam*" that Philip signed on 4 January 1554. AGS Estado 807, 36 (1°). The document makes it pretty clear that Philip found most of the treaty objectionable, except, perhaps, the promise of marriage. Even so, historians have speculated about the clauses he particularly disliked. Hughes and Larkin thought he considered the financial terms excessively burdensome. (*Tudor Royal Proclamations*, 11:21.) In Pierson's opinion Philip "resented the sacrifice of Don Carlos's rights." (*Philip II of Spain*, 28–29.) Two historians have said that Philip thought the treaty terms were just fine. Kamen said, "There was . . . no problem about accepting them." (*Philip of Spain*, 55.) Erickson held a similar opinion: "Philip could hardly have asked for more advantageous terms himself – if he had been consulted." (*Bloody Mary*, 348.) Rodríguez-Salgado, on the other hand, considered that Philip found the whole treaty objectionable, (*The Changing*

> *Face of Empire*, 83), and Loades shared that opinion (*Mary Tudor*, 216.)

36 Philip to Charles, 6 January 1554, AGS Estado 103, fol. 72. Charles to Philip, 21 January 1554, AGS Estado 808, fol. 119. Rodríguez-Salgado interprets the reference to a "secret" as meaning only that Philip had insisted on her firm acceptance of the marriage contract by proxy (*per verba de presenti*) prior to leaving Spain, while the English wanted the proxy marriage to be less definite (*per verba de futuro*). See her book, *The Changing Face of Empire*, 83–84. Philip's real concern for the war against France is manifest in his father's letter of 16 February 1554, AGS Estado 808, which assures his son of Mary's "unshakable determination to carry out the alliance." Tyler, *State Papers Spanish*, 12:100.

Chapter 6

1 Charles to Philip, 16 February 1554, AGS Estado 808, Tyler, *State Papers Spanish*, 12:100.

2 Charles to Lamoral et al., [21] December 1553, AGS Estado 807, fols. 76–78, the date appears in a copy in BL 28597, fols. 134–37v. Various other documents are in AGS Estado 807, fol. 36, 2ª. Philip to Charles, 6 January 1554, AGS Estado 103, fol. 72. A letter from Eraso to Philip, 3 February 1554, AGS Estado 808, printed in Navarrete, *Colección de documentos inéditos*, 3:469–70 gives much the same information. Egmont to Charles, 21 January 1554, AGS Estado 808, fols. 2 (Spanish) and 3 (French).

3 Noailles to Henry II, 7 September 1553 and 24 November 1553, in Rene A. Vertot, *Ambassades de Messieurs de Noailles en Angleterre* (Leyden: Dessaint & Saillant, 1763), 2:143–45, 269–70. For a summary of Noailles's involvement in the rebellion, see E. Harris Harbison, *Rival Ambassadors at the Court of Queen Mary* (Princeton: Princeton University Press, 1940), 79–80, and 112–25. See also Renard to Charles, 23 October 1553, 14 November 1553, 29 December 1553, 18 January 1554, in

Gachard and Piot, *Collection des Voyages des Souverains des Pays-Bas*, 4:161–64, 203–204, 280, and 301–303. Ambassadors to Charles, 27 January 1554, AGS Estado 808, in Navarrete, *Colección de documentos inéditos*, 3:454–58. Ambassadors to Charles, 31 January 1554, in Weiss, *Papiers d'État du Cardinal de Granvelle*, 4:195–201.

4 Wriothesley, "Chronicle of England," 107–113. *"Relacion del successo de Inglaterra al Embax^{or} Vargas de Brusellas,"* 13 February 1554, AGS Estado 1322, fol. 32. Egmont, Lalaing, Courriers, and Nigri to Charles, 3 February 1554, Tyler, *State Papers Spanish*, 12:69–72. See the report of Giovanni Francesco Commendone, papal legate in London, *"Successi delle attioni del regno d'inghilterra,"* Biblioteca del Escorial, ms X–III–8, fols. 133–240; see also *"Diarium eorum quae post adventum legatorum caes^{ae} ma^{tis} in rebellione thomae wyort et aliorum act a gestaque sunt,"* Biblioteca del Escorial, ms &–111–23, fols. 68–73; both are reprinted in Cesare V. Malfatti, *The Accession, Coronation, and Marriage of Mary Tudor, as Related in Four manuscripts of the Escorial* (Barcelona: Alianza de Artes Gráficas, 1946), 120, and 134. The final quote is from a letter of Francisco de Aresti to Juan Vásquez de Molina, 29 January 1554, AGS Estado 507, fol. 167.

5 Renard to Charles, [8 February 1554], Weiss, *Papiers d'État du Cardinal de Granvelle*, 207–11.

6 Renard to Philip, 19 February 1554, AGS Estado 808, fol. 19(2°). Charles to Philip, 21 February 1554, AGS Estado 808, in Navarrete, *Colección de documentos inéditos*, 3:498–511. The letter from Charles is dated both 16 and 21 February. Ibid., 508.

7 Egmont and Renard to Charles, 8 March 1554, ARB, RA, Prov, 13, transcription in PRO 31/8/145, fols. 76–77.

8 Charles to Renard, 18 February 1554; Charles to Mary, 18 February 1554; ARB, RA, Prov, 13, transcription in PRO 31/8/145, fols. 291–95. Egmont and Renard to Charles, 8 March 1554, ARB, RA, Prov, 13, transcription in PRO 31/8/145, fols. 76–77.

9 Mary to Philip, 20 April 1554, BL Cotton Vespasian F III, fol. 26.

10 Charles to Philip, 30 April 1554, AGS Estado 508, fol. 106. Philip to a member of the Privy Council, 12 May 1554, AGS Estado 807, fol. 34 (draft in Latin); Philip to Charles, 15 May 1554, AGS Estado 103, fol. 134. See also Renard to Charles, 9 July 1554, Tyler, *State Papers Spanish*, 309. Vargas to Philip, 13 April 1554, AGS Estado 1322, fol. 16. Medina Sidonia to Mary, 20 April 1554, BL Cotton Titus B II, fol. 129. Vertot's informant said the title was announced as: *"Philippes & Marie, par la grace de Dieu, roy & royne d'Angleterre, France & Hirlande, deffenseurs de la foy, princes d'Espagne, ducs de Brabant, comtes de Flandres et aultres Pays-Bas, &c."* See *Suite de la relation de ce qui passe dans le Parlement & à la cour d'Angleterre*, 17 April 1754 (1554), in Vertot, *Ambassades de Messieurs de Noailles en Angleterre*, 3:169–70.

11 Andrés Muñoz, *Viaje de Felipe Segundo a Inglaterra, por Andrés Muñoz (impreso en Zaragoza en 1554) y relaciones varias relativas al mismo suceso*, ed. by Pascual de Gayángos (Madrid: Sociedad de Bibliófilos Españoles, 1877), 12–13. See also Martin A. S. Hume, "The Visit of Philip II," *English Historical Review* (April 1892), 7:261. Las Navas arrived in England on 9 June and presented the jewels to Mary on 21 June. See the letters from Renard Charles, 11 June 1554, Brussels, Relations avec l'Angleterre, Classement Provisoire 20, transcription in PRO 31/8/145, fols. 283–83v; Capelle to Eecke, 17 June 1554; Renard to Charles, 20 June 1554; and Renard to the Bishop of Arras, 21 June 1554, Tyler, *State Papers Spanish*, 12:275, 277, 283, and 286. Strangely, Renard reported that Las Navas brought only the large diamond. See his letter to Charles, 9 July 1554, Tyler, *State Papers Spanish*, 12:309.

12 Philip to Charles, 11 May 1554, AGS Estado 103, fols. 128, and 131. Introduced at the same time in both houses, the bills received their third readings on 10 April, with final approval on 12 April; the queen signed the bills on 5 May. *Journals of the House of Lords, beginning anno Primo Henrici Octavi* (London: House of Lords, n.d.), 1:451–52. *Journals of the House of Commons, from November the 8ᵗʰ 1547, in the First Year of the Reign of King Edward the Sixth to March the 2d 1628, in the Fourth Year of the*

Reign of King Charles the First (London: House of Commons, 1803), 1:33–34.

13 Philip to Francisco de Vargas, 11 July 1554, AGS Estado 1498, fol. 10. Muñoz, *Viaje de Felipe II*, 32, 39–49. Rymer, *Fœdera*, 15:393–403. Philip to Charles, 3 July 1554, AGS Estado 107, Tyler, *State Papers Spanish*, 12:286–88.

14 Rymer, *Fœdera*, 15:399, and 403.

15 Hannis Taylor, *The Origin and Growth of the English Constitution* (Boston: Houghton, Mifflin & Co., 1898), II:21–23. Dudley J. Medley, *A Student's Manual of English Constitutional History* (6th ed.; Oxford: Basil Blackwell, 1925), 80. Great Britain, Statutes, I Mary, Sess. 3, cap. I, *Statutes of the Realm*, iv, 222.

16 Muñoz, *Viaje de Felipe II*, 5–9, 29, 55–59, and 62–64. In Spanish naval tactics the main brunt of the sea battle was borne by infantrymen, who tried to board enemy ships and seize them in hand-to-hand fighting.

17 Charles to Philip, 29 June 1554, AGS Estado 507, fol. 14. Three letters from Charles to Philip, 16 February 1554, AGS Estado 808, fol. 111, 112, and 113. Charles to the Queen Dowager Mary, 17 July 1554; Renard to Charles, 19 July 1554, Tyler, *State Papers Spanish*, 12:314. Charles to Philip, 4 April 1554, AGS Estado 508, fol. 94. The circulation of the New World treasure is described at length by Francisco de Aresti in a letter to Juan Vásquez de Molina, 29 January 1554, AGS Estado 507, fols. 166–67.

18 Quoted in Menéndez Pidal, *Historia de España*, XIX, vol. 1, 344. Muñoz, *Viaje de Felipe II*, 64, 87–88. "Relation of What Passed at the Celebration of the Marriage of Our Prince with the Most Serene Queen of England," translated in Patrick F. Tytler, *England under the Reigns of Edward VI and Mary* (London: Richard Bentley, 1839), 2:430. Elder, *Copie of a letter sent in to Scotlande*, n.p. (fols. A.ii to A.iii). Renard to Charles, 14 March 1554; Juan Vásquez de Molina to Princess Juana, 18 July 1554, AGS Estado 103; Tyler, *State Papers Spanish*, 12:153, and 314. Ruy Gómez de Silva to Francisco de Eraso, 20 July 1554, AGS Estado 808, fol. 149.

Chapter 7

1   Commendone, *"Successi delle attioni del regno d'inghilterra,"* Biblioteca del Escorial, ms X–III–8, fols. 133–240; reprinted and translated in Malfatti, *The Accession, Coronation, and Marriage of Mary Tudor,* 125. Figueroa to Charles, 26 July 1554, AGS Estado 808, fol. 30. The other letter very likely informed Philip that the emergency was past, and he need not hasten to Flanders, after all.

2   The several first-hand sources agree in most respects, but differ in details. For example, the Order of the Garter was conferred on Philip either on his own ship, on the English admiral's barge, on the pier at Southampton, or in the Church of the Holy Rood, depending on which source you decide to use. Renard, who seemed to have an eye for detail, said the order was conferred just before Philip left the barge, and this is the version I have chosen. See the letter from Courrières and Renard to Charles, 26 or 27 July 1554, Weiss, *Papiers d'État du Cardinal Granvelle,* 4:277. Juan de Varaona, "Viaje de Felipe II a Inglaterra en 1554 cuando fue a casar con la Reina Doña María," Biblioteca del Escorial, est. ii, no. 4, printed in Navarrete, *Colección de documentos inéditos,* 1:564–66. Muñoz, *Viaje de Felipe II,* 64–67. Anne of Cleves, 20 July 1554, "Relation of What Passed at the Celebration of the Marriage," in Tytler, *England under Edward VI and Mary,* 2:430. There is an undated copy of this document, entitled, *"Relation de ce qui passé en la celebration du mariage de nostre prince avec la Serenissime Royne de Engletere,"* transcribed from a manuscript in the Archives de la Ville de Louvain, PRO 31/8/145, fols. 90–92. See also Elder, *Copie of a letter sent in to Scotlande,* fols. A.ii to A.iii. Commendone, *"Successi delle attioni del regno d'inghilterra,"* Biblioteca del Escorial, ms X–III–8, fols. 133–240; and *"Diarium eorum quae post adventum legatorum caes^{ae} ma^{tis} in rebellione thomae wyort et aliorum act a gestaque sunt,"* Biblioteca del Escorial, ms &–111–23, fols. 68–73; both reprinted and translated in Malfatti, *The Accession, Coronation, and Marriage of Mary Tudor,* 125, and 140–41. See also the report of Antoine de Noailles, in his letter to Henry II, 27 July

1554, in Vertot, *Ambassades de Messieurs de Noailles en Angleterre*, 3:283–89.

3   Manrique de Lara to Philip, 6 January 1554, AGS Estado 880, fols. 149–50. Charles to Alba, 1 April 1554, AGS Estado 508. Charles to Philip, 9 April 1554, AGS Estado 508, fol. 106.

4   Noailles to Henry II, 27 July 1554, Vertot, *Ambassades de Messieurs de Noailles en Angleterre*, 3:286. Several weeks earlier Noailles informed his king that he had seen the genealogy Mary had prepared to show Philip's descent in the English royal line. See his letter to Henry II, 4 May 1554, ibid., 3:192. Many of the French ambassador's informants are identified in E. Harris Harbison, "French Intrigue at the Court of Queen Mary," *American Historical Review* (April 1940), 45:531–51. The informant in this case may have been Sir John Leigh or even Henry Brooke (Lord Cobham), whose son George Brooke later became the ambassador's principal informant (ibid., 544–45). Elder, *Copie of a letter sent in to Scotlande*, fol. C.iii.

5   Figueroa to Charles, 26 July 1554, AGS Estado 808, fol. 30. Courrières and Renard to Charles, 26 or 27 July 1554, Weiss, *Papiers d'État du Cardinal Granvelle*, 4:277. Muñoz, *Viaje de Felipe II*, 67.

6   Muñoz, *Viaje de Felipe II*, 67–68. Malfatti, *The Accession, Coronation, and Marriage of Mary Tudor*, 125, and 141.

7   Muñoz, *Viaje de Felipe II*, 69. See also the "*Carta Segunda*" in ibid., 106.

8   Muñoz, *Viaje de Felipe II*, 70. Malfatti, *The Accession, Coronation, and Marriage of Mary Tudor*, 125, and 141. Juan de Varaona, "Viaje de Felipe II a Inglaterra" in Navarrete, *Colección de documentos inéditos*, 1:568.

9   Ruy Gómez de Silva to Francisco de Eraso, 27 July 1554, AGS Estado 808, fol. 147. See Giacomo Soranzo, "Relazione d'Inghilterra di Giacomo Soranzo, Tornato Ambasciatore da quella Corte il 19 Agosto 1554," in *Relazioni dello Impero Britannico nel Secolo XVI*, edited by Eugenio Albèri (Firenze: Società Editrice Fiorentina, 1852), part 2, 32.

10 Figueroa to Charles, 26 July 1554, AGS Estado 808, fol. 30. Juan de Varaona, "Viaje de Felipe II a Inglaterra" in

Navarrete, *Colección de documentos inéditos*, 1:568. The quotation is from Elder, *Copie of a letter sent in to Scotlande*, fol. A.iv verso. Muñoz has Philip saying "God ni hit," apparently a sixteenth century attempt to put the English phrase into phonetic Spanish. See his *Viaje de Felipe II*, 71. Numerous English writers have used the Muñoz quote to make Philip appear ridiculous.

11 Figueroa to Charles, 26 July 1554, AGS Estado 808, fol. 30. Elder, *Copie of a letter sent in to Scotlande*, fols. A.vi and verso. Muñoz, *Viaje de Felipe II*, 71.

12 The various descriptions of the ceremony differ considerably. I have relied largely on Figueroa, who wrote his report the very next day, while events were fresh in his mind. Figueroa to Charles, 26 July 1554, AGS Estado 808, fol. 30. Descriptions of the clothes worn by Philip and Mary appear in the "Relation of What Passed at the Celebration of the Marriage," in Tytler, *England under Edward VI and Mary*, 2:430; and in Elder, *Copie of a letter sent in to Scotlande*, fols. A.v verso to A.vi. Other details are from Commendone, *"Successi delle attioni del regno d'inghilterra,"* Biblioteca del Escorial, ms X–III–8, fols. 133–240; and *"Diarium eorum quae post adventum legatorum caes^{ae} ma^{tis} in rebellione thomae wyort et aliorum act a gestaque sunt,"* Biblioteca del Escorial, ms &–111–23, fols. 68–73; both reprinted and translated in Malfatti, *The Accession, Coronation, and Marriage of Mary Tudor*, 125, and 140–41.

13 A record of the proceedings was written out by the imperial notary Gonzalo Pérez, *Minuta del acto de la pñtacion que hizo el Regente Figueroa al Rey prin^e nrõ S^{or} del priv^o de la Refutacion del Rey^o de Napoles en su favor*, 25 July 1554, AGS Patronato Real 42, fol. 13. Descriptions of the clothes worn by Philip and Mary appear in the "Relation of What Passed at the Celebration of the Marriage," in Tytler, *England under Edward VI and Mary*, 2:432.

14 Commendone, *"Successi delle attioni del regno d'inghilterra,"* Biblioteca del Escorial, ms X–III–8, fols. 133–240; and *"Diarium eorum quae post adventum legatorum caes^{ae} ma^{tis} in rebellione thomae wyort et aliorum act a gestaque sunt,"* Biblioteca del Escorial,

ms &–111–23, fols. 68–73; both reprinted and translated in Malfatti, *The Accession, Coronation, and Marriage of Mary Tudor*, 130, and 143.

15 Ibid. Elder gives the title in English and Latin. See his *Copie of a letter sent in to Scotlande*, fols. A.vii verso and A.viii. Additional information may be found in John G. Nichols (ed.), *Chronicle of Queen Jane and Two Years of Queen Mary and Especially of the Rebellion of Sir Thomas Wyat* (London: Camden Society, 1850), Appendix IX, 167–70. Philip told the herald not to mention that he was Duke of Milan, saying, "That was old stuff." Charles had given him Milan in 1540. Figueroa to Charles, 26 July 1554, AGS Estado 808, fol. 30. Despite all this, most of the accounts include the duchy of Milan in the list of titles, probably because the list was copied from a standard form.

16 Elder, *Copie of a letter sent in to Scotlande*, fols. A.viii verso and B.i.

17 Figueroa to Charles, 26 July 1554, AGS Estado 808, fol. 30. The quote is from Juan de Varaona, "Viaje de Felipe II a Inglaterra," in Navarrete, *Colección de documentos inéditos*, 1:573.

18 Figueroa to Charles, 26 July 1554, AGS Estado 808, fol. 30. The quote is from "Carta Primera de lo Sucedido en el Viaje de S. A. a Inglaterra, Año de 1554," reprinted in Muñoz, *Viaje de Felipe II*, 96–97.

19 Wriothesley, "Chronicle of England," 121–22. Elder, *Copie of a letter sent in to Scotlande*, fol. B.iii.

20 Elder, *Copie of a letter sent in to Scotlande*, fols. B.iii verso and iv. This translation and the one that follows are Elder's.

21 Elder, *Copie of a letter sent in to Scotlande*, fol. B.vi.

22 Elder, *Copie of a letter sent in to Scotlande*, fol. C.iii.

23 Nichols (ed.), *Chronicle of Queen Jane and Two Years of Queen Mary*, 78–79. Sydney Anglo describes the pageants at greater length, emphasizing the use Protestant commentators later made of the *"Verbum Dei"* story. See his *Spectacle, Pageantry, and Tudor Policy* (Oxford: Clarendon Press, 1969), 326–39.

24 Ruy Gómez de Silva to Francisco Eraso, 29 July 1554, AGS Estado 808, fol. 148.

Chapter 8

1 Dasent, *Acts of the Privy Council,* New Series, 27 July 1554, 5:53. BL Cotton Vespasian, F. III, fol. 23.

2 Renard to Charles, 3 September 1554, Tyler, *State Papers Spanish,* 13:45.

3 "Relazione di Giovanni Micheli," in *Relazioni dello Impero Britannico nel Secolo XVI Scritte da Veneti Ambasciatori* (Firenze: Società Editrice Fiorentina, 1852), 93–94. Although Micheli wrote this report in 1557, he met frequently with the king during Philip's first residence in London.

4 Charles to Renard, 1 September 1554, Weiss, *Papiers d'État du Cardinal Granvelle,* 4:295–96. (Dated 2 September in Tyler, *State Papers Spanish,* 13:42.)

5 Stroppiana to Granvelle, 19 September 1554, Tyler, *State Papers Spanish,* 13:50.

6 Philip to Charles, 16 November 1554, AGS Estado 808, Tyler, *State Papers Spanish,* 13:98.

7 Anonymous letter of 2 October 1554, in Muñoz, *Viaje de Felipe II,* 120.

8 "Relazione di Giovanni Micheli," 93–94.

9 Courrières to Charles, 11 August 1554, Tyler, *State Papers Spanish,* 13:24. Ruy Gómez de Silva to Eraso, 12 August 1554, AGS Estado 808, fol. 143. Philip to Juana, 2 September 1554, AGS Estado 808, fol. 38, 1°.

10 See the report of various official meetings and festivities during the month of November in Muñoz, *Viaje de Felipe II.*

11 Paget later explained many of his ideas to Charles, recorded in a memorandum of 14 November 1554, Tyler, *State Papers Spanish,* 13:88.

12 Judith M. Richards shows that the Protestant minority was "most vocal in questioning the standing of Philip in England," though many Catholics shared the same opinions. See her article "Mary Tudor as 'Sole Quene'? Gendering Tudor Monarchy," *Historical Journal* (December 1997), 40:895–924. The quote is from the final page.

13 Duffy, *Stripping of the Altars,* 527–28.

14 Michael A. R. Graves, *The House of Lords in the Parliaments of Edward VI and Mary I* (Cambridge: Cambridge University Press, 1981), 194. The opposition was clearly organized by Paget, though he denied it. Renard to Charles, 6 May 1554, 13 May 1554, Tyler, *State Papers Spanish*, 12:238–40, and 251.

15 Renard to Charles, 18 September 1554, Tyler, *State Papers Spanish*, 13:51.

16 Charles to Eraso, [1 October 1554], Tyler, *State Papers Spanish*, 13:57. Charles to Renard, 15 November 1554, Weiss, *Papiers d'État du Cardinal Granvelle*, 4:333.

17 For a summary of the sparring between the various parties, see Thomas F. Mayer, *Reginald Pole, Prince and Prophet* (Cambridge: Cambridge University Press, 2000), 203–23.

18 Charles to ambassadors, 2 August 1554; Ambassadors to Charles, 8 August 1554; Philip to Eraso, 12 October 1554, Tyler, *State Papers Spanish*, 13:14–15, 22–23, and 63–64. Philip to Juan Manrique, 6 December 1554, AGS Estado 809, fol. 7. Ambassadors to Charles, 6 August 1554; Ambassadors to Philip, c. 15 October 1554 (?); Weiss, *Papiers d'État du Cardinal Granvelle*, 4:286–88, and 325–28. Queen Dowager Mary to Granvelle, 14 August 1554, in Gachard and Piot, *Collection des Voyages des Souverains des Pays-Bas*, 4:431–32.

19 Judith M. Richards, "Gendering Tudor Monarchy," *Historical Journal* (December 1997), 40:904, and 921. Mortimer Levine, "A Parliamentary title to the Crown in Tudor England," *Huntington Library Quarterly* (1962), 25:121–27. Mortimer Levine, *Tudor Dynastic Problems, 1460–1571*, vol. 21 of *Historical Problems: Studies and Documents*, edited by G. R. Elton (London: George Allen and Unwin, Ltd., 1973), 88–96.

20 Philip to Charles, 16 November 1554, AGS Estado 808, fol. 54. Simon Renard to Charles, 13 October 1554; Simon Renard to Charles, 21 December 1544, Weiss, *Papiers d'État du Cardinal Granvelle*, 4:319, and 347–48. Paget's ideas are contained in Granvelle's memorandum of 14 November 1554, Tyler, *State Papers Spanish*, 13:88.

21 Charles to Renard, 15 November 1554, Weiss, *Papiers d'État du Cardinal Granvelle*, 4:333.

22   Philip to Vargas, 6 December 1554, AGS Estado 1458, fol. 15.
23   Philip's draft instructions to Eraso, [14 November 1554], Tyler, *State Papers Spanish*, 13:93. Granvelle's memorandum of 14 November 1554, Tyler, *State Papers Spanish*, 13:88. For the sale of Spanish church property, see Helen Nader, *Liberty in Absolutist Spain: the Habsburg Sale of Towns, 1516–1700* (London: Johns Hopkins University Press, 1990), 113.
24   "Traslado de una carta que fue embiada del reyno de Inglaterra a la muy illustre condesa de Oliuares," no date, in Muñoz, *Viaje de Felipe II*, 127–139. Philip to Vargas, 6 December 1554, AGS Estado 1498, fol. 15.

Chapter 9

1   BL Cotton Vespasian, F. III, fol. 23. Dasent, *Acts of the Privy Council*, New Series, 27 July 1554, 5:53.
2   Mary to Charles, 7 December 1554, and late summer 1555, Tyler, *State Papers Spanish*, 13:117, 239. Charles to Philip, 7 December 1554, AGS Estado 508, fol. 237.
3   Granvelle to Renard, 5 January 1554, Weiss, *Papiers d'État du Cardinal Granvelle*, 4; Renard to Philip, [late December 1554], Tyler, *State Papers Spanish*, 13:130.
4   Parker, *Philip II*, 36–37. Woodward, *Philip II*, 7.
5   Glyn Redworth and Fernando Checa, "The Kingdoms of Spain: The Courts of the Spanish Habsburgs, 1500–1700," *The Princely Courts of Europe: Ritual, Politics and Culture under the Ancien Régime, 1500–1700*, edited by John Adamson (London: Weidenfeld & Nicolson, n.d.), 46–48.
6   The description in this and the following three paragraphs is based largely on Muñoz, *Viaje de Felipe II*, 118, 137–39. A general description of the game may be found in the *Diccionario Enciclopédico Hispano-Americano* (Barcelona: Montaner y Simón, 1913), 4:493–94. A very brief mention of the *juego de cañas* of 25 November may be found in Machyn, *Diary of Henry Machyn*, 76.

7   An Italian diplomat reported that the game "left the spectators cold, except for the fine clothes of the players, and the English made fun of it." G.T. Langosto da Stroppiana to Granvelle, 25 November 1554, Tyler, *State Papers Spanish*, 13:104–105.

8   Muñoz, *Viaje de Felipe II*, 139. Gómez de Silva to Eraso, 2 October 1554, AGS Estado 808; Tyler, *State Papers Spanish*, 13:60.

9   Albert Feuillerat (ed.), *Documents Relating to the Revels at Court in the Time King Edward VI and Queen Mary (The Loseley Manuscripts)*, vol. 44 of *Materialien zur Kunde des älteren Englischen Dramas*, edited by W. Bang (London: David Nutt, 1914), 161–65.

10 Feuillerat (ed.), *Documents Relating to the Revels at Court*, 166–70.

11 Ibid., 166–76.

12 Anonymous letter of 2 October 1554, in Muñoz, *Viaje de Felipe II*, 120–21.

13 Wriothesley, "Chronicle of England," 127–28. Machyn, *Diary of Henry Machyn*, 84–85. Flower was later eulogized by John Foxe as one of the martyrs who suffered under Philip and Mary. See *The Acts and Monuments of John Foxe: A New and Complete Edition*, edited by Stephen R. Cattley (London: R. B. Seeley, 1838), 7:68–77.

14 Renard to Charles, 3 September 1554, Tyler, *State Papers Spanish*, 13:45.

15 Dasent, *Acts of the Privy Council*, New Series, 15 September 1553, 4:349.

16 Muñoz, *Viaje de Felipe II*, 118, 121. Renard to Charles, 18 September 1554, Tyler, *State Papers Spanish*, 13:49–50.

17 To date there has not been an adequate treatment of religious practice during the reign of Philip and Mary, most studies following what Duffy has called the "Protestant historiography, authoritatively shaped by John Foxe." See his book, *The Stripping of the Altars*, 524ff.

18 Loades, *Reign of Mary Tudor*, 271–77, gives a traditional treatment to the persecution of heretics during Mary's reign. See also J. J. Scarisbrick, *The Reformation and the English People* (Oxford: Basil Blackwell, 1984), 47.

19 Philip to Ruy Gómez de Silva (?), 2 August 1555, Tyler, *State Papers Spanish*, 13:239. In this draft Philip seems to align himself.

20 See Philip's testimony in the Carranza trial. José Ignacio Tellechea Idígoras, *Fray Bartolomé Carranza: Documentos Históricos*, vol. 22 of *Archivo Documental Español* (Madrid: Real Academia de la Historia, 1966), 3:23, and 184.

21 Renard to Charles, 18 November 1554, Tyler, *State Papers Spanish*, 13:102.

22 "Blessed art thou among women, and blessed is the fruit of thy womb." Renard to Charles, 30 November 1554, Tyler, *State Papers Spanish*, 13:108. G.T. Langosto da Stroppiana to Granvelle, 25 November 1554, Tyler, *State Papers Spanish*, 13:104–105.

23 Giovanni Michiel to François Venier (the Doge), 6 May 1555, *Les Dépêches De Giovanni Michiel, Ambassadeur de Venise en Anglterre pendant les Années de 1554 à 1557*, edited by Paul Friedmann (Venise: Imprimerie du Commerce, 1869), 36–37.

24 Philip told his sister that the news had made him "reasonably sad." See his letter to Juana, 29 May 1555, Estado 809, Tyler, *State Papers Spanish*, 13:197. Michiel to the Doge, 21 May, 17 June 1555, Friedmann, *Les Dépêches De Giovanni Michiel*, 43–44, and 61; he used the words *"liberalita"* and *"stato bellisimo"* to describe the gifts. There are additional details in Machyn, *Diary of Henry Machyn*, 90. See also "Expenses of the Obsequies of the Queen of Spain" held in St Paul's Cathedral, 17 June 1555, National Archives (formerly PRO), SP 11/5, no. 40.

25 Silva to Eraso, 1 and 20 June 1555, AGS Estado 809, fols. 116, and 121–22.

26 Michiel to the Doge, 5 August 1555, in Friedmann, *Les Dépêches De Giovanni Michiel*, 93. The other stages in her false pregnancy are mentioned in his dispatches of 27 May, 1 and 17 June 1555, ibid., 47, 51, and 63.

27 Elizabeth Svoboda, "All the Signs of Pregnancy Except One: A Baby," *New York Times*, 5 December 2006, D1.

28 Adolfo M. Sierra, "La Neurosis de Deseo de Maria Tudor, Reina de Inglaterra," *Revista de la Asociación Medica Argentina* (30 June 1938), 590–92.

29 M. L. Osborn, "Mary Tudor and the Empty Cradle," *Midwife and Health Visitor* (1974), 10:313–16.

30 The negotiations are detailed at length in Harbison, *Rival Ambassadors*, 231–50. The invitation to the emperor is in Mary to Charles, 28 March 1555, Tyler, *State Papers Spanish*, 13:149. Michiel to the Doge, 6 and 11 June 1555, in Friedmann, *Les Dépêches De Giovanni Michiel*, 99–111. See also Loades, *Intrigue and Treason*, 195, which misinterpreted Michiel's remarks, concluding that Philip "was playing no part in the government."

31 Soranzo to the Doge, 23 May 1555, Michiel to the Doge (newsletter), 23 May 1555, Soranzo to the Doge, 9 June 1555, in Rawdon Brown, *Calendar of State Papers and Manuscripts Relating to English Affairs Existing in the Archives and Collections of Venice and in Other Libraries of Northern Italy*, vol. VI, part I, 1555–1556 (London: Longman & Co., 1877), 78–79, 80, 103. Hereafter Brown, *State Papers Venice*. Michiel to the Doge, 11 and 17 June 1555, in Friedmann, *Dépêches De Giovanni Michiel*, 56–58, and 61–63.

32 Michiel to the Doge, 26 June 1555, in Friedmann, *Dépêches De Giovanni Michiel*, 69–71.

33 Unsigned commission dated 29 August 1555, BL Cotton Titus B II, fols. 160–61.

34 Michiel to the Doge, 3 September 1555, in Friedmann, *Dépêches De Giovanni Michiel*, 114–15.

35 Undated, unsigned draft in Philip's hand, generally agreed to have been addressed to Ruy Gómez de Silva, 2 August 1555, Tyler, *State Papers Spanish*, 13:239.

36 Pole to Philip, 2 September 1555, Brown, *State Papers Venice*, vol. VI, part I, 176.

37 Dasent, *Acts of the Privy Council*, New Series, 28 August and 23 September 1555, 5:176, 184. Michiel to the Doge, 27 August, in Friedmann, *Dépêches De Giovanni Michiel*, 110–11.

38 Mary to Charles, n.d., Tyler, *State Papers Spanish*, 13:238–39. Michiel to the Doge, 3 September 1555, in Friedmann, *Dépêches De Giovanni Michiel*, 114–15.

Chapter 10

1   Michiel to the Doge, 3 and 9 September 1555, in Friedmann, *Dépêches De Giovanni Michiel*, 114–15, and 118–19. Duffy, *Stripping of the Altars*, 552.

2   Badoer to the Doge, 14 September 1555, Brown, *State Papers Venice*, vol. VI, part I, 186–87.

3   Badoer to the Doge, 14 September 1555, Brown, *State Papers Venice*, vol. VI, part I, 186–87.

4   Charles to the heads of states (form letter), 26 September 1555, Brown, *State Papers Venice*, vol. VI, part I, 194–95.

5   Badoer to the Doge, 13 October 1555, Brown, *State Papers Venice*, vol. VI, part I, 212.

6   Dasent, *Acts of the Privy Council, New Series*, 23 September 1555, 5:184.

7   Badoer to the Doge, 16 October 1555, Brown, *State Papers Venice*, vol. VI, part I, 215. Michiel to the Doge, 21 October 1555, in Friedmann, *Dépêches De Giovanni Michiel*, 136.

8   Badoer to the Doge, 27 October 1555, Brown, *State Papers Venice*, vol. VI, part I, 227. Michiel to the Doge, 27 October 1555, in Friedmann, *Dépêches De Giovanni Michiel*, 142.

9   Badoer to the Doge, 23 and 26 October 1555; Act of Abdication of the Netherlands in favor of Philip II by Emperor Charles V, 25 October 1555, Brown, *State Papers Venice*, vol. VI, part I, 218–22.

10   Badoer to the Doge, 26, 27 and, 31 October, 1 December 1555, Brown, *State Papers Venice*, vol. VI, part I, 222–23, 227, 235–36, 267. John Mason to Petre, 27 and 28 October 1555, *Relations Politiques des Pays-Bas et de l'Angleterre sous le Règne de Philippe II*, edited by Kervyn de Lettenhove (Brussels: F. Hayez, 1882), 1:1–8.

11   Badoer to the Doge, 27 October 1555, Brown, *State Papers Venice*, vol. VI, part I, 227.

12   Badoer to the Doge, 1 December 1555, Brown, *State Papers Venice*, vol. VI, part I, 267.

13   Soranzo to the Doge, 17 September, 3 November 1555, Brown, *State Papers Venice*, vol. VI, part I, 191, 238. Fernand

Braudel, *The Mediterranean and the Mediterranean World in the Age of Philip II*, trans. by Siân Reynolds (New York: Harper & Row, 1966), 2:937.

14   Philip to the Council, 11 February; Council to Philip, 23 February; Philip to the Council, 16 March and 23 April; Council to Philip, 28 April, 1556; printed in Lettenhove, *Relations Politiques*, 1:18, 22, 30, and 35. *"Vos hortamur ut ipsi eam fidem adhibeatis, quam nobis loquentibus essetis habituri; erit enim apprime gratum."* See also Badoer to the Doge, 29 March 1556, Brown, *State Papers Venice*, vol. VI, part I, 391. For information about Figueroa, see the *"Memorial de los méritos de Juan de Figueroa,"* Sancho Rayón, *Colección de Documentos Inéditos para la Historia de España*, 97:362–68. According to Kamen, "the 'regent' was a senior official who represented his country's interests in the King's council." See his *Philip of Spain*, 329.

15   Perhaps some were lost with Philip's other papers in a shipwreck in the bay of Laredo in September 1559. M. J. Rodríguez-Salgado and Simon Adams (eds. and trans.), "The Count of Feria's Dispatch to Philip II of 14 November 1558," *Camden Miscellany XXVIII* in *Camden Fourth Series*, 29:303.

16   Mary to Charles, 6 April 1556, Tyler, *State Papers Spanish*, 13:260.

17   Mary to Charles, c. 3 May 1556, Tyler, *State Papers Spanish*, 13:267.

18   See, for example, Mason to Mary, 23 January 1556; Thomas Gresham to Mary, 24 February 1556; printed in Lettenhove, *Relations Politiques*, 1:13, and 23.

19   Michiel to the Doge, 21 October 1555, in Friedmann, *Dépêches De Giovanni Michiel*, 136.

20   Philip to Ruy Gómez de Silva, 2 February 1557, AGS Estado 515, fol. 92.

21   *"Alla quale mostra portar amor grande."* Badoer to the Doge, 11, 15, and 18 December 1556, Brown, *State Papers Venice*, vol. VI, part I, 278, 281, and 285.

22   "Truce and abstinence from war and suspension of arms, etc., between the Emperor and the King of England, his son, and the King of France," 6 February 1556, AGS Estado 112;

"Copy of the letters patent of King Henry of France concerning a truce between the Emperor, his son the King of England, and the King of France, for a period of five years," 15 February 1556, AGS Estado 809; Tyler, *State Papers Spanish*, 13:258.

23 Navagero to the Doge, 28 February 1556, Brown, *State Papers Venice*, vol. VI, part I, 360.

24 William Ryce to Edward Courtenay, 22 February 1556, Brown, *State Papers Venice*, vol. VI, part I, 355.

25 Michiel to the Doge, 18 November 1556, in Friedmann, *Dépêches De Giovanni Michiel*, 154–57.

26 John Strype, *Historical Memorials, Ecclesiastical and Civil, of Events under the Reign of Queen Mary I*, vol. III, part I of *Ecclesiastical Memorials Relating Chiefly to Religion and the Reformation of it and the Emergencies of the Church of England under King Henry VIII, King Edward VI, and Queen Mary I* (Oxford: Clarendon Press, 1822), 469–70. Hereafter, *Historical Memorials*.

27 Pole to Philip, 26 November 1556(?), *Epistolarum Reginaldi Poli S. R. E. Cardinalis et aliorum ad ispum* (Brixiæ: Joannes-Maria Rizzardi, 1757), 5:49. While the letter is undated, a date of 26 November is assigned by Brown, *State Papers Venice*, vol. VI, part I, 263. See also Michiel to the Doge, 18 November 1556, in Friedmann, *Dépêches De Giovanni Michiel*, 154–57.

28 Pole to Morone, 7 January 1556, Brown, *State Papers Venice*, vol. VI, part I, 309.

29 Strype, *Historical Memorials*, vol. III, part I, 469–70.

30 Elizabeth Russell shows that Mary's reputation for lack of skill in government rests largely on the reports of Simon Renard, whom Mary "fed" with information that she wanted to have spread abroad. See her "Mary Tudor and Mr. Jorkins," *Historical Research*, (October 1990), 63:263–76. In his study of Mary's rule Penry Williams concluded that "she was reasonably, even remarkably, successful." *The Later Tudors: England, 1547–1603* (Oxford: Clarendon Press, 1995), 123.

31 Michiel to the Doge, 24 March, 7 April, 12 May 1556, Brown, *State Papers Venice*, vol. VI, part I, 383–85, 398–99, and 447.

32　See, for example, Pole to the Constable of France, 20 January 1556, Brown, *State Papers Venice,* vol. VI, part I, 323.

33　For example, Badoer to the Doge, 9 March 1556, Brown, *State Papers Venice,* vol. VI, part I, 366.

34　For example, Navagero to the Doge, 7 March, 1 May 1556; Soranzo to the Doge, 8 July 1556; Brown, *State Papers Venice,* vol. VI, part I, 365, 425, and 511–12.

35　Philip to Juana, 17 September 1556, AGS Estado 114, fols. 27, 31, quoted in Menéndez Pidal, *Historia de España,* XIX, 1:409. Cardinal Pole argued against any such move. See his letter to Philip, 24 June 1556, Brown, *State Papers Venice,* vol. VI, part I, 496–98.

36　Badoer to the Doge, 4 September 1556; Navagero to the Doge, 5 September 1556; Brown, *State Papers Venice,* vol. VI, part I, 595 and 596.

37　Badoer to the Doge, 9 January 1557, Brown, *State Papers Venice,* vol. VI, part II, 902. Harbison, *Rival Ambassadors,* 314.

38　William S. Maltby, *Alba: A Biography of Fernando Alvarez de Toledo, Third Duke of Alba, 1507–1582* (Berkeley: University of California Press, 1983), 98–109. Henry D. Sedgwick, *The House of Guise* (New York: Bobbs-Merrill Co., 1938), 75–76.

39　Philip to Ruy Gómez de Silva, 2 February 1557, AGS Estado 515, fol. 92.

40　Menéndez Pidal, *Historia de España,* XIX, 1:433–34.

41　Michiel to the Doge, 7, 14, and 28 December 1556; Badoer to the Doge, 9 January 1557, Brown, *State Papers Venice,* vol. VI, part II, 847, 867, 888–89, and 902.

42　BL Cotton Titus C VII, fol. 198–99v. The document contains four questions from the queen, asking the Council for an opinion about declaring war on France. There is no title or date, but the contents indicate a date of December 1556 or January 1557, probably the latter.

43　BL Cotton Titus C VII, fol. 198–99v.

44　Philip to Ruy Gómez de Silva, 2 February 1557, AGS Estado 515, fol. 92.

45　Ibid.

46   Soranzo to the Doge, 6 March 1557, Brown, *State Papers Venice*, vol. VI, part II, 967–68.

47   Philip to Ruy Gómez de Silva, 2 February 1557, AGS Estado 515, fol. 92.

48   Machyn, *Diary of Henry Machyn*, 128–29. Surian to the Doge, 3 April 1557, Brown, *State Papers Venice*, vol. VI, part II, 1003. Dasent, *Acts of the Privy Council*, New Series, 6:64.

49   Soriano to the Doge, 3 April 1557, Brown, *State Papers Venice*, vol. VI, part II, 1003.

50   Feuillerat (ed.), *Documents Relating to the Revels at Court*, 225.

51   Richard Smith, *Vita Illvstrissimæ ac piissimæ Dominæ Magdalenæ Montis-Acuti in Anglia Vicecomitissæ* (Rome: Iacobus Mascardus, 1609), 38–39. This little book was translated somewhat laboriously into English and published at St. Omer in 1627. That translation is now available in a reprint edited by A. C. Southern, *An Elizabethan Recusant House, comprising the Life of Lady Magdalen, Viscountess Montague (1538–1608)*, trans. by Cuthbert Fursdon (London: Sands & Co., 1954).

52   "Relazione di Giovanni Micheli," in *Relazioni dello Impero Britannico nel Secolo XVI Scritte da Veneti Ambasciatori*, 88.

53   Harbison, *Rival Ambassadors*, 322–26.

54   Soranzo to the Doge, 26 April 1557; Soriano to the Doge, 29 April, 6 May 1557, Brown, *State Papers Venice*, vol. VI, part II, 1023, 1026, and 1028.

55   The document is reprinted in Strype, *Historical Memorials*, vol. III, part II, 515–18.

56   Soriano to the Doge, 29 April 1557, Brown, *State Papers Venice*, vol. VI, part II, 1026.

57   Mendoza to the Duke of Savoy, 28 April, 1557, Tyler, *State Papers Spanish*, 13:290–91.

58   Harbison, *Rival Ambassadors*, 326. Philip to Granvelle, 14 June 1557, Tyler, *State Papers Spanish*, 13:297.

59   In 1548, The Scots Parliament had agreed that the child-queen Mary Stuart would go to France eventually to wed Francis, son of Henry II. In return Henry was to help defend the Scottish border, an obligation the French king was happy to accept. A very readable summary of these events may be found

in Antonia Fraser, *Mary Queen of Scots* (London: Weidenfeld & Nicolson, 1969), 27–35.

60 Suriano to the Doge, 6 May 1557, Brown, *State Papers Venice*, vol. VI, part II, 1028.

61 Giovanni Micheli, outgoing Venetian ambassador, estimated that Philip had spent more than a million gold ducats in England by March 1557. *"Relazione d'Inghilterra del Clarissimo Giovanni Micheli Detta in Pregadi il dí 13 Maggio 1557,"* 344 and 359.

62 Suriano to the Doge, 6 and 13 May 1557, Brown, *State Papers Venice*, vol. VI, part II, 1028, and 1085–86.

63 Soranzo to the Doge, 8, and 9 June 1557, Brown, *State Papers Venice*, vol. VI, part II, 1149, and 1151.

64 Machyn, *Diary of Henry Machyn*, 138.

65 Machyn, *Diary of Henry Machyn*, 139, and 141–42.

Chapter 11

1 Philip to Granvelle, 6 July 1557, Weiss, *Papiers d'État du Cardinal Granvelle*, Philip to Ayala, 22 July 1557; Ayala to Philip, 23 July 1557, AGS Estado 514 and 515; Tyler, *State Papers Spanish*, 13:302, and 304–06.

2 Philip to Ayala, 22 July 1557; Ayala to Philip, 23 and 25 July 1557, AGS Estado 514 and 515; Pembroke to Philip, 29 July 1557, Tyler, *State Papers Spanish*, 13:302, and 304–09.

3 Philip to Pembroke, 29 July, 4 August 1557; Eraso to Philip, c. 31 July 1557, AGS Estado 514 and 515, Tyler, *State Papers Spanish*, 13:304–09. Wentworth to Mary, 31 July 1557, Turnbull, *State Papers, Foreign, Mary*, 326.

4 Philip to Pembroke, 4 August 1557, AGS Estado 515, Tyler, *State Papers Spanish*, 13:308.

5 *"Bataille Livrée près de Saint-Quentin. Défait des Français,"* Lettenhove, *Relations Politiques*, 1:83–84. "An Account of What Happened at St. Quentin since the Camp was Set up There," AGS Estado 514, Tyler, *State Papers Spanish*, 13:313–15. C. S. L. Davies, "England and the French War," *The Mid-Tudor*

Polity, c. 1540–1560, edited by Robert Tittler and Jennifer Loach (Totowa, New Jersey: Rowman & Littlefield, 1980), 165.

6   Juan de Piñedo to Francisco de Vargas, 27 August 1557, AGS Estado 1490, Tyler, *State Papers Spanish*, 13:317.

7   Bedford to Cecil, 3 September 1557, Lettenhove, *Relations Politiques*, 1:86.

8   Suriano to the Doge, 28 August, 5 September 1557, Brown, *State Papers Venice*, vol. VI, part II, 1265–66, and 1288–89. E. M. Tenison, *Elizabethan England*, vol. I, 1553–1568 (Royal Leamington Spa, n.n., 1933), 98–105. Machyn, *Diary of Henry Machyn*, 150–51. Davies, "England and the French War," 165–66.

9   Navagero to the Doge, 12 September, 2 October 1557, Brown, *State Papers Venice*, vol. VI, part II, 1308-09, and 1336. Braudel, *The Mediterranean*, 2:941.

10 Suriano to the Doge, 3, 10, and 31 October 1557, Brown, *State Papers Venice*, vol. VI, part II, 1337, 1342, 1357–58.

11 Davies, "England and the French War," 169.

12 Edward Clinton, "The cause I was sent for to Brussels," 1558, Historical Manuscripts Commission, *Calendar of the Manuscripts of the Most Hon. The Marquis of Salisbury, K.G., &c., &c., &c., Preserved at Hatfield House, Hertfordshire* (London: Eyre and Spottiswoode, 1883), part I, 1:149–50. Hereafter, HMC, *Hatfield Manuscripts*.

13 Davies, "England and the French War," 169–79. Davies thinks blame should be distributed evenly. "The English Council, Philip and the authorities at Calais were all over-confident," 178.

14 Micheli to the Doge, 6 December, 15 December 1557, Brown, *State Papers Venice*, vol. VI, part III, 1385, and 1394–95. A good account of the events around Calais, based on archival sources and placing the blame squarely on Wentworth, may be found in "Sixteenth Century Studies: The Loss of Calais," *North British Review* (December 1866), 45:441–58.

15 Mary to Wentworth, 24 December 1557, Turnbull, *State Papers, Foreign, Mary*, 350.

16   Wentworth to Mary, 26 December, Turnbull, *State Papers, Foreign, Mary*, 351. Wentworth, Grey, and the Council at Calais to Mary, 27 December 1557, Hardwicke, *Miscellaneous State Papers, from 1501 to 1726 in Two Volumes* (London: W. Strahan and T. Cadell, 1778), 1:104–106.

17   Mary to Wentworth, 29 December 1557, Turnbull, *State Papers, Foreign, Mary*, 352.

18   Wentworth to Mary, 29 December; Mary to Wentworth and the Council at Calais, 31 December 1557, Turnbull, *State Papers, Foreign, Mary*, 352–53.

19   Grey to Mary, 31 December 1557, Turnbull, *State Papers, Foreign, Mary*, 353. Wentworth to Philip, 31 December 1557, Tyler, *State Papers Spanish*, 13:320.

20   Wentworth to Mary, Hardwicke, *Miscellaneous State Papers*, 1:109–12.

21   Philip to Wentworth, 2 January 1558, Lettenhove, *Relations Politiques*, 1:116.

22   Wentworth to Philip, 2 January 1558, Tyler, *State Papers Spanish*, 13:321.

23   Wentworth to Philip, 3 January 1558, Tyler, *State Papers Spanish*, 13:321.

24   Davies, "England and the French War," 173–74.

25   Clinton, "The cause I was sent for to Brussels," 1558, HMC, *Hatfield Manuscripts*, part I, 1:149.

26   Rutland to Mary, 3 January 1558; Rutland et al. to Mary, 6 January 1558, Turnbull, *State Papers, Foreign, Mary*, 357–58.

27   Philip to Carvajal, 7 January 1558, AGS Estado 517, Tyler, *State Papers Spanish*, 13:321. Rutland et al. to Mary, 6 January 1558, Turnbull, *State Papers, Foreign, Mary*, 357. Davies, "England and the French War," 170–77.

28   Richard Grafton, *A Chronicle at large and meere History of the affayres of Englande and Kinges of the same, deduced from the Creation of the worlde, vnto the first habitation of thys Islande: and so by contynuance vnto the first yere of the reigne of our most deere and souveigne Lady Queene Elizabeth* (London: Henry Denham, 1569), 1356. Suriano to the Doge, 20 and 22 January 1558, Brown, *State Papers Venice*, vol. VI, part II, 1432–34.

29 Dasent, *Acts of the Privy Council*, New Series, 6:238.

30 Savoy to Mary, 16 January 1558; Mary to Savoy, 18 January 1558, printed in Lettenhove, *Relations Politiques*, 1:117–18.

31 Thomas Churchyard, *A generall rehearsall of warres called Churchyardes Choise: wherein is fiue hundred seuerall seruices of land and sea as Sieges, Battailes, Skirmiches, and Encounters. A thousande Gentle mennes names, of the beste sorte of warriours. A praise and true honour of Souldiers. A proofe of perfite Nobilitie. A triall and first erection of Heraldes. A discourse of calamitie. And ioyned to the same some Tragedies & Epitaphes, as many as was necessarie for this first booke* (London: Edward White, 1579), verso of the page following fol. Ki.

32 Grey to Mary, 4 January 1557 (1558), Hardwicke, *Miscellaneous State Papers*, 1:113–14.

33 Philip to the Privy Council, 21 January 1558, AGS 811, printed in Lettenhove, *Relations Politiques*, 1:119.

34 Grafton, *Chronicle at large*, 1356. John Stow, *Annales of England, Faithfully collected out of the most authenticall Authors, Records, and other Monuments of Antiquitie, lately corrected, encreased, and continued, from the first inhabitation vntill this present yeere 1600* (London: Ralfe Newbery, 1600), 1070, is authority for the assertion that Ferrers wrote this portion of Grafton's *Chronicle*.

35 Savoy to Philip, 19 January 1558; staff report, 20 January 1558; AGS Estado 1491, Tyler, *State Papers Spanish*, 13:320.

36 Philip to Privy Council, 21 January 1558, AGS Estado 811, fols. 8, and 10; Philip to Feria, 28 January 1558, printed in Lettenhove, *Relations Politiques*, 1:121–22.

37 Feria to Philip, 15 February 1558, AGS Estado 811, fol. 27, in José Sancho Rayón and Francisco de Zabálburu, *Colección de Documentos Inéditos para la Historia de España* (Madrid: Imprenta de Miguel Ginesta, 1886), 87:15–17.

38 Strype, *Historical Memorials*, vol. III, part II, 101–106.

39 Granvelle to Feria, 7 April 1558, translated in Tyler, *State Papers Spanish*, 13:377.

40 Feria to Philip, 10 March 1558, AGS Estado 811, fol. 34, printed in Lettenhove, *Relations Politiques*, 1:153.

41 Feria to Philip, 2 February 1558, AGS Estado 811, fol. 25, *Documentos Inéditos*, 87:7.

42 Philip to Pole, 21 January 1558, printed in Lettenhove, *Relations Politiques*, 1:120. According to Suriano, Mary had waited this long in order to be sure of the pregnancy. See his letter to the Doge, 15 January 1558, Brown, *State Papers Venice*, vol. VI, part III, 1427.

43 Feria to Philip, 2 February 1558, AGS Estado 811, fol. 25, *Documentos Inéditos*, 87:6.

44 Philip to Feria, 28 January 1558, printed in Lettenhove, *Relations Politiques*, 1:120.

45 Pedro Ocaña, 25 February 1558, AGS Estado 516, fol. 69.

46 Feria to Philip, 10 March 1558, AGS Estado 811, printed in Lettenhove, *Relations Politiques*, 1:153.

47 Philip to Feria, 17 March 1558, Archivos de Medinaceli, Archivo Historico 166, subfondo 7, fol. 9.

48 Feria to Philip, 18 May 1558, AGS Estado 811, fol. 54, *Documentos Inéditos*, 87:51.

49 Feria to Philip, 1 May 1558, printed in Lettenhove, *Relations Politiques*, 1:181.

50 V. C. Medvei, "The Illness and Death of Mary Tudor," *Journal of the Royal Society of Medicine* (December 1987), 80: 766–70. Feria to Philip, 1 and 18 May 1558, printed in Lettenhove, *Relations Politiques*, 1:181, 191.

51 Renard's notes for a letter to Philip, c. March 1558, Tyler, *State Papers Spanish*, 13:372.

52 "No dudo que . . . lo terna por bien." Philip to Feria, 17 May 1558, AGS Estado 811, fol. 5, *Documentos Inéditos*, 87:6.

53 Micheli, *"Relazione d'Inghilterra,"* 331–32.

54 Jane Dormer married Feria a few months later. The information is provided by Henry Clifford, who reported Jane's recollection of the meeting with Elizabeth. See his book, *Life of Jane Dormer, Duchess of Feria* (London: Burns & Oates Ltd., 1887), 90.

55 Feria to Philip, 23 June 1558, AGS Estado 811, *Documentos Inéditos*, 87:68.

56 Mary to Philip, undated, BL Cotton Titus B II, fol. 109, draft, translated with the interlinear corrections in Prescott, *Spanish Tudor*, 492–95. In a note at the end of the manuscript Mary

says she has held the same opinion for "four and twenty years," which is the time since Elizabeth's birth.

57   Suriano to the Doge, 27 October 1558, Brown, *State Papers Venice*, vol. VI, part III, 1538. Suriano had this information from the priest who was Mary's confessor.

58   Chapuys to Charles, 19 May 1536, in Gairdner, *Letters and Papers of Henry VIII*, 10:378.

59   Micheli, "*Relazione d'Inghilterra*," 332.

60   Renard's notes for a letter to Philip, c. March 1558, Tyler, *State Papers Spanish*, 13:372.

61   Feria to Philip, 2 February 1558, AGS Estado 811, fol. 25, *Documentos Inéditos*, 87:7.

62   "The anser to the ks ma^t 1° february 1557," BL Cotton Titus B II, fols. 59–60.

63   Feria to Philip, 2 February 1558, AGS Estado 811, fol. 25, *Documentos Inéditos*, 87:7.

64   Feria to Philip, 18 May 1558, AGS Estado 811, fol. 25, *Documentos Inéditos*, 87:53.

65   Philip to Clinton, 14 May 1558, printed in Lettenhove, *Relations Politiques*, 1:187–88.

66   Philip to Feria, 27 May 1558, AGS Estado 811, fol. 56, *Documentos Inéditos*, 87:56.

67   Clinton, "The cause I was sent for to Brussels," 1558, HMC, *Hatfield Manuscripts*, part I, 1:149.

68   Micheli to the Doge, 11 June 1558, Brown, *State Papers Venice*, vol. VI, part III, 1506.

69   Suriano to the Doge, 14 and 15 July 1558, Brown, *State Papers Venice*, vol. VI, part III, 1517–19. A force of German mercenaries who had been on their way to England arrived in Flanders just in time to assist in the relief of Gravelines. Micheli to the Doge, 19 July 1558, Brown, *State Papers Venice*, vol. VI, part III, 1521–22.

70   Suriano to the Doge, 24 June 1558, Brown, *State Papers Venice*, vol. VI, part III, 1509.

71   Suriano to the Doge, 18 August 1558, Brown, *State Papers Venice*, vol. VI, part III, 1524–25.

72   Suriano to the Doge, 3 September 1558, Brown, *State Papers Venice*, vol. VI, part III, 1526–27.

73 Wotton to Mary, 26 September 1558, Lettenhove, *Relations Politiques*, 1:243.

74 Mary to Wotton, 28 September 1558, Lettenhove, *Relations Politiques*, 1:246–47.

75 Wotton et al. to the Privy Council, 29 October 1558, Lettenhove, *Relations Politiques*, 1:261–68.

76 Philip to the English commissioners, 30 October 1558, Lettenhove, *Relations Politiques*, 1:269.

77 Wotton et al. to the Privy Council, 29 October 1558, Lettenhove, *Relations Politiques*, 1:270–72.

78 Feria to Philip, 21 November 1558, AGS Estado 811, fol. 92, *Documentos Inéditos*, 87:84. Feria repeated this later in a note about things to be discussed with Philip. Feria, *"Memorial de los negocios que llevó a cargo el Obispo de Aquila de tratar con Su Majestad. (1559),"* AGS Estado 812, fol. 31, *Documentos Inéditos*, 87:131.

79 Feria to Philip, 13 or 14 November 1558, Lettenhove, *Relations Politiques*, 1:279.

80 Christophe d'Assonleville to Philip, 7 November 1558, AGS Estado 811, Lettenhove, *Relations Politiques*, 1:277.

81 Clifford, *Life of Jane Dormer*, 70.

82 Philip to Luna, 12 November 1558, AGS Estado 649, fol. 221.

Chapter 12

1 Micheli to the Doge, 28 November 1558, Brown, *State Papers Venice*, vol. VI, part III, 1560–61.

2 Philip to Feria, 28 December 1558, AGS Estado 811, fol. 103, *Documentos Inéditos*, 87:103.

3 Feria to Philip, 21 November 1558, AGS Estado 811, fol. 92, *Documentos Inéditos*, 87:83.

4 Geoffrey Parker, *Grand Strategy of Philip II* (London: Yale University Press, 1998), 148.

5 "Como un hombre sentenciado." Philip to Feria, 10 January 1558, Medinaceli, Archivo Historico 166, ramo 7, fol. 1.

6 Philip to Feria, 10 January 1558, AGS Estado 812, Lettenhove, *Relations Politiques*, 1:399–400.

7 Ibid.

8 Philip to Feria, 12 February 1558, AGS Estado 812, Lettenhove, *Relations Politiques*, 1:416–18.

9 Feria to Philip, 20 February 1558, AGS Estado 812, fol. 28, *Documentos Inéditos*, 87:124. Feria, "*Memorial de los negocios que llevó a cargo el Obispo de Aquila de tratar con Su Majestad. (1559),*" AGS Estado 812, fol. 31, *Documentos Inéditos*, 87:133–34.

10 Feria to Philip, 24 March 1559, *Documentos Inéditos*, 87:147.

11 Feria to Philip, 11 April 1559, *Documentos Inéditos*, 87:156–57.

12 "*Ella no terná hijos.*" Feria to Philip, 29 April 1559, ibid., 180.

13 George W. Bernard, *Power and Politics in Tudor England* (Aldershot: Ashgate Publishing, Ltd., 2000), 136–38. For the report of the emperor's agent in London, see Victor von Klarwill, *Queen Elizabeth and Some Foreigners* (London: John Lane the Bodley Head Ltd., 1928), 113–15.

14 Alison Weir explored the various possibilities in *Elizabeth the Queen* (London: Jonathan Cape, 1998), 47–53.

15 Historians are divided on this matter. Henry Kamen thinks most of the accusations are true. See his *Philip of Spain*, 55, 90, 166, and 203. Menéndez Pidal thinks most of them are fabrications by people who hated Philip. See his *Historia de España*, 544–57.

16 Braudel, *The Mediterranean*, 2:953.

17 Menéndez Pidal, *Historia de España*, 491–98, and 559–74.

18 Kamen, *Philip of Spain*, 203.

19 Menéndez Pidal says the miscarriage involved twin girls. *Historia de España*, 647.

20 Information about Hawkins and Drake can be found in Kelsey, *Sir Francis Drake* (New Haven: Yale University Press, 1998), chaps. 2–11; and Kelsey, *Sir John Hawkins* (New Haven: Yale University Press, 2003), chaps. 2–8.

Bibliography

Manuscript Collections

England

British Library, London
Additional Charters 15578, 15579.
Additional Manuscripts 5415A, 14291, 25079, 28597, 72387,
    72407, 76667–70.
Cotton Manuscripts Caligula E V, Galba C I, Titus B II, Titus C
    VII, Vespasian F III.
Egerton Charters 3891.
Egerton Manuscripts 994.
Harley Manuscripts 6949.
Lansdowne Manuscripts 3.
Seals CV 8, DR 118.
Sloane Manuscripts 1578, 3562.
Stowe Manuscripts 571, 1054.

Berkshire Record Office, Reading
Granvelle Papers, Vol. 2 (Microfiche 10078), Vol. 8 (Microfiche
    10090).

Warwickshire Record Office
Dormer Collection CR 895/61.

Spain

Biblioteca de Palacio Real, Madrid
Manuscripts, II–2251, II–2255, II–2285, II–2286, II–2290.

Archivo General de Indias, Seville
Indiferente General 427.
Patronato Real 275.

Archivo General de Simancas, Simancas
Contaduria Mayor de Cuentas 1184, 1344, 1468.
Estado 15, 55, 377, 508, 510, 512, 515, 516, 808, 809, 811, 812,
   842, 879, 880, 881, 1322, 1498.
Guerra Antigua 67.
Libros de Berzosa.
Patronato Real 42–13, 43–4, 55, 55–28, 55–31, 275.

Medinaceli Archives, Toledo
Archivo Historico, Fondo de Cartas Reales, Subfondo Felipe II,
   Legajo 166.

Printed Materials

Alvarez, Manuel Fernández. *La España del Emperador Carlos V (1500–
   1559; 1517–1556)*, vol. XIX of Ramón Menéndez Pidal (ed.)
   Historia de España (Madrid: Espasa-Calpe, 1966).
—— *Charles V, Elected Emperor and Hereditary Ruler* (London: Thames
   & Hudson, 1975).
Amezúa y Mayo, Agustín G. de. *Isabel de Valois, Reina de España
   (1546–1568)* (3 vols.; Madrid: Gráficas Ultra, 1949).
Anglo, Sydney. *Spectacle, Pageantry, and Tudor Policy* (Oxford:
   Clarendon Press, 1969).
*Anno Secundo et Tertio Edovardi Sexti, Actes made in the Session of this present
   parliament, holden upon prorogacion at Westminster the fourth daie of
   Nouember, in the second yere of oure moste drad souereigne Lorde Edward
   .VI. by the grace of God kyng of England, Fraunce, and also of Irelande,
   defendor of the faith, and of the churche of England and also of Ireland,*

in yearth the supreme hed: and there continued & kept to the .xiii. Daie of Marchem in the .iii. Yere of oure saied souereigne lorde (London: Richard Grafton, 1549).

Badoero, Federico. "*Relazione delle Persone, Governo e Stati di Carlo V e di Filippo II,*" *Le Relazioni degli Ambasciatori Veneti al Senato durante il Secolo Decimosesto,* edited by Eugenio Albèri (Firenze: Società Editrice Fiorentina, 1853), ser. 1, vol. 3.

The booke of the common prayer and administracion of the sacramentes, and other rites and ceremonies of the Churche: after the vse of the Churche of England (London: Edouard Whitechurche, 1549).

Beer, Barrett L. *Northumberland: The Political Career of John Dudley, Earl of Warwick and Duke of Northumberland* (Kent, Ohio: Kent State University Press, 1973).

Bernard, George W. *The King's Reformation: Henry VIII and the Remaking of the English Church* (New Haven: Yale University Press, 2005).

—— *Power and Politics in Tudor England* (Aldershot: Ashgate Publishing, Ltd., 2000).

Braudel, Fernand. *The Mediterranean and the Mediterranean World in the Age of Philip II,* trans. by Siân Reynolds (New York: Harper & Row, 1966), vol. 2.

Brewer, J. S. (ed.). *Letters and Papers, Foreign and Domestic, of the Reign of Henry VIII* (London: Her Majesty's Stationery Office, 1872), vol. IV, part II.

Brown, Rawdon. *Calendar of State Papers and Manuscripts Relating to English Affairs Existing in the Archives and Collections of Venice and in Other Libraries of Northern Italy,* vol. VI, part I, *1555–1556* part II, *1556–1557,* part III, *1557–1558* (London: Longman & Co., 1877–1884).

Busto, Bernabé de. *Introductiones grammaticas: breues e compendiosas: compuestas por el doctor Busto, maestro de los pajes de su majestad* (Segovia: n.n., 1532).

Cabrera de Córdoba, Luis. *Felipe Segundo, Rey de España* (4 vols.; Madrid: Imprenta, Esterotipia y Galvanoplastia de Aribau y Cia., 1876–1877).

Calvete de Estrella, Juan Cristóbal. *El Felicísimo viaje del muy alto y muy poderoso príncipe Don Felipe* (original, Anvers: Martin Nucio, 1552; reprint, Madrid: Sociedad de Bibliófilos Españoles, 1930).

Cattley, Stephen R. *The Acts and Monuments of John Foxe: A New and Complete Edition* (London: R. B. Seeley, 1838).

Chueca Goitia, Fernando. *"Felipe II, El Hombre," Philippus II Rex*, edited by Pedro Navascués (Barcelona: Lunwerg Editores, S.A., c. 1998).

Churchyard, Thomas. *A generall rehearsall of warres called Churchyardes Choise: wherein is fiue hundred seuerall seruices of land and sea as Sieges, Battailes, Skirmiches, and Encounters. A thousande Gentle mennes names, of the beste sorte of warriours. A praise and true honour of Souldiers. A proofe of perfite Nobilitie. A triall and first erection of Heraldes. A discourse of calamitie. And ioyned to the same some Tragedies & Epitaphes, as many as was necessarie for this first booke* (London: Edward White, 1579).

Clifford, Henry. *Life of Jane Dormer Duchess of Feria*, Transcribed from the ancient manuscript in the possession of Lord Dormer by the late Canon E[dgar] E. Estcourt and edited by the Rev. Joseph Stevenson (London: Burns & Oates Ltd., 1887).

Colmeiro, Manuel. *Cortes de los antiguos reinos de León y Castilla* (5 vols.; Madrid: Real Academia de la Historia, 1861–1903).

Corvo, Frederick Baron. *Chronicles of the House of Borgia* (New York: E. P. Dutton & Co., 1901).

Courson, Roger de. *Quatre Portraits de Femmes: Épisodes des Persécutions d'Angleterre* (Paris: Libraire de Firmin-Didot et Cie, 1895).

Coxe, William. *History of the House of Austria from the Foundation of the Monarchy by Rudolph of Hapsburg to the Death of Leopold the Second, 1218 to 1792* (4 vols.; London: Henry G. Bohn, 1847).

Cranmer, Thomas. *Sentencia definitiva in causa nullitatis matrimonii inter regem Henricum VIII. Et Annam Clivensem*, in David Wilkins, *Concilia Magnae Britanniae et Hiberniae, ab anno MCCCL. Ad annum MDXLV* (London: R. Gosling et al., 1737), vol. 3.

Cuming, G. J. *A History of Anglican Liturgy* (New York: Macmillan & Co., 1969).

Dasent, John Roche. *Acts of the Privy Council of England*, New Series, vol. 5, *A. D. 1554–1556*, vol. 6, *A. D. 1556–1558*, vol. 7, *A. D. 1558–1570* (London: Her Majesty's Stationery Office, 1892–93).

Davies, C. S. L. "England and the French War," The Mid-Tudor Polity, c. 1540–1560, edited by Robert Tittler and Jennifer Loach (Totowa, New Jersey: Rowman & Littlefield, 1980).

Devereaux, E. J. "The Publication of the English *Paraphrases* of Erasmus," *Bulletin of the John Rylands Library*, (Spring, 1969), 51:351.

—— *Renaissance English Translations of Erasmus* (Toronto: University of Toronto Press, 1983).

Diccionario Enciclopédico Hispano-Americano (Barcelona: Montaner y Simón, 1913), vol. 4.

Dickens, Arthur G. (ed.). "Robert Parkyn's Narrative of the Reformation," *Reformation Studies* (London: Hambledon Press, 1982).

Dillon, Anne. *The Construction of Martyrdom in the English Catholic Community, 1535–1603* (Aldershot: Ashgate Publishing Ltd., 2002).

Donaldson, Peter S. *Machiavelli and the Mystery of State* (New York: Cambridge University Press, 1988).

Du Wes, Giles. *An introductorie for to Lerne to rede, to pronounce, and to speake Frenche trewly, compyled for the ryghte hygh, excellent, & moste vertuous lady, the lady Mary of England, doughter to our moste souerayne lorde kyng Henry the eyghte* (London: Nicolas Bourman, [1540]).

Duffy, Eamon. *The Stripping of the Altars: Traditional Religion in England, c. 1400–c. 1580* (London: Yale University Press, 1992).

Elder, John. *The Copie of a letter sent in to Scotlande, of the arivall and landynge, and moste noble marryage of the moste Illustre Prynce Philippe, Prynce of Spaine, to the most excellente Princes Marye Quene of England, solemnisated in the Citie of Winchester: and howe he was recyued and installed at Windsore, and of his triumphyng entries in the noble Citie of London* (London: John Waylande, [1555]).

Erickson, Carolly. *Bloody Mary* (New York: St. Martins Press, 1978).

Fantazzi, Charles. "Vives, Juan Luis," *ODNB*, 56:571.

Feuillerat, Albert (ed.). *Documents Relating to the Revels at Court in the Time King Edward VI and Queen Mary (The Loseley Manuscripts)*, vol. 44 of *Materialien zur Kunde des älteren Englischen Dramas*, edited by W. Bang (London: David Nutt, 1914).

Figueroa y Melgar, Alfonso de (Duque de Tovar). "Los Suarez de Figueroa, De Feria y Zafra," *Boletín de la Real Academia de la Historia* (Enero–Abril, 1975), 172:139–68.

Firpo, Luigi (ed.). *Relazioni di Ambasciatori Veneti al Senato*, vol. 1, *Inghilterra*; vol. 3, *Germania (1557–1654)*; vol. 8. *Spagna (1497–1598)* (Torino: Bottega d'Erasmo, 1965–1981).

Foxe, John. *Actes and Monuments of These Latter and Perillous Dayes, Touching Matters of the Church, wherein Are Comprehended and Described the Great Persecutions & Horrible Troubles, That Haue Bene Wrought and Practised by the Romishe Prelates, Speciallye in this Realme of England and Scotlande, from the Yeare of Our Lorde a Thousande, unto the Tyme Nowe Present, Gathered and Collected according to the True Copies & Writinges Certificatorie as Wel of the Parties Them Selues that Suffered, as also out of the Bishops Registers, Which Were the Doers Therof* (London: Iohn Day, 1563).

Fraser, Antonia. *Mary Queen of Scots* (London: Weidenfeld & Nicolson, 1969).

Friedmann, Paul. *Les Dépêches De Giovanni Michiel, Ambassadeur de Venise en Anglterre pendant les Années de 1554 à 1557*, (Venise: Imprimerie du Commerce, 1869), 36–37.

Gachard, Louis Prosper. *Retraite et Mort de Charles V au Monastère de Yuste* (3 vols.; Brussels, 1854–1856), vol. 1.

—— and Charles Piot (eds.), *Collection des Voyages des Souverains des Pays-Bas* (Brussels: Commission Royale d'Histoire, 1876–1882).

Gairdner, James (ed.). *Letters and Papers, Foreign and Domestic, of the Reign of Henry VIII* (London: Her Majesty's Stationery Office, 1887), vol. 10.

Gayangos, Pascual de (ed.). *Calendar or Letters, Despatches, and State Papers, Relating to the Negotiations between England and Spain Preserved in the Archives at Simancas and Elsewhere, vol. 5, part 2, Henry VIII, 1536–1538* (London: Her Majesty's Stationery Office, 1888).

Grafton, Richard. *A Chronicle at large and meere History of the affayres of Englande and Kinges of the same, deduced from the Creation of the worlde, vnto the first habitation of thys Islande: and so by contynuance vnto the first yere of the reigne of our most deere and souveigne Lady Queene Elizabeth* (London: Henry Denham, 1569).

Graves, Michael A. R. *The House of Lords in the Parliaments of Edward VI and Mary I* (Cambridge: Cambridge University Press, 1981).

Great Britain, Statutes, 35 Henry VIII, chap. 1.

Great Britain, Statutes, I Mary, Sess. 3, cap. I, *Statutes of the Realm*.

Guevara, Antonio. *Epistolas Familiares,* edited by Augusto Cortina (Mexico: Buenos Aires, 1946).

Gutiérrez, Constancio. *Trento: Un Concilio para la Unión (1550-1552),* vol. 1, *Fuentes (1549–1551) (Cartas, Despachos, Nóminas, etc.)* (Madrid: Consejo Superior de Investigaciones Científicas, 1981).

Gwyn, Peter. *The King's Cardinal: The Rise and Fall of Thomas Wolsey* (London: Barrie and Jenkins, 1990).

Harbison, E. Harris. "French Intrigue at the Court of Queen Mary," *American Historical Review* (April 1940), 45:531–51.

—— *Rival Ambassadors at the Court of Queen Mary* (Princeton: Princeton University Press, 1940).

Hardwicke, Earl of (Philip Yorke). *Miscellaneous State Papers, from 1501 to 1726 in Two Volumes* (London: W. Strahan and T. Cadell, 1778), vol. 1.

Haynes, Samuel. *A Collection of State Papers Relating to Affairs of the Reigns of King Henry VIII, King Edward VI, Queen Mary, and Queen Elizabeth* (London: William Bowyer, 1740).

Hearne, Thomas. *Sylloge Epistolarum, a variis Angliae principibus scriptarum. Quibus & alia paucula sunt interspersa, e collectaneis Smithianis (una & altera dempta Epistola) descripsit,* bound as part of *Titi Livii foro-juliensis vita Henrici Quinti, regis angliae* (Oxford: Theatro Sheldoniano, 1716).

Henry the Eyght ... beganne this thyrde Session of his moste high courte of parlyament ... wherein were established these actes folowynge (London: Thomas Bertheleti, 1544).

Historical Manuscripts Commission. *Calendar of the Manuscripts of the Most Hon. The Marquis of Salisbury, K.G., &c., &c., &c., Preserved at Hatfield House, Hertfordshire* (London: Eyre and Spottiswoode, 1883), part I, vol. 1.

Hoby, Thomas. *The Travels and Life of Sir Thomas Hoby, K^t. Of Bisham Abbey, Written by Himself, 1547–1564,* edited By Edgar Powell, *Camden Miscellany* (London: Royal Historical Society, 1902), Camden Third Series.

Hoyle, R. W. "Letters of the Cliffords, Lords of Clifford and Earls of Cumberland, c.1500–c.1565," *Camden Miscellany,* XXXI, *Camden Fourth Series,* 44.

Hoyos, P. Manuel. *Historia del Colegio de San Gregorio de Valladolid* (Valladolid, 1928).

Hughes, Paul L. and James F. Larkin. *Tudor Royal Proclamations*, vol. 11, *The Later Tudors* (1553–1587) (New Haven and London: Yale University Press, 1969).

Hume, Martin A. S. "The Visit of Philip II," *English Historical Review* (April 1892), 7:253–80.

Journals of the House of Commons, from November the 8ᵗʰ 1547, in the First Year of the Reign of King Edward the Sixth to March the 2d 1628, in the Fourth Year of the Reign of King Charles the First (London: House of Commons, 1803), vol. 1.

Journals of the House of Lords, beginning anno Primo Henrici Octavi (London: House of Lords, n.d.), vol. 1.

Kamen, Henry. *Philip of Spain* (New Haven: Yale University Press, 1997).

Kaulek, Jean (ed.). *Correspondance Politique de MM. De Castillon et De Marillac, Ambassadeurs de France en Angleterre (1537–1542)* (Paris: Ancienne Librairie Germer Baillière et Cie., 1885).

Kennedy, W. P. M. "The Imperial Embassy of 1553/4 and Wyatt's Rebellion," *English Historical Review* (April 1923), 38:251–58.

Klarwill, Victor von. *Queen Elizabeth and Some Foreigners* (London: John Lane the Bodley Head Ltd., 1928).

Knighton, C. S. *Calendar of State Papers, Domestic Series: Mary I, 1553–1558* (London: Public Record Office, 1998).

Lalanne, Ludovic (ed. and comp.). *Oeuvres Complètes de Pierre de Bourdeille, Seigneur de Brantôme* (11 vols.; Paris: Jules Renouard, 1876).

Lettenhove, Kervyn de (ed.). *Relations Politiques des Pays-Bas et de l'Angleterre, sous le Règne de Philippe II*, Tome Iᵉʳ, *Depuis L'Abdication de Charles-Quint Jusqu'au Dèpart de Philippe pour L'Espagne (25 Octobre 1555–24 Août 1559)* (Brussels: F. Hayez, 1882), vol. 1.

Levine, Mortimer. "A Parliamentary title to the Crown in Tudor England," *Huntington Library Quarterly* (1962), 25:121–27.

—— *Tudor Dynastic Problems, 1460–1571*, vol. 21 of *Historical Problems: Studies and Documents*, edited by G. R. Elton (London: George Allen and Unwin, Ltd., 1973).

Llanos y Torriglia, Felix de. *María I de Inglaterra ¿La Sanguinaria? Reina de España* (Madrid: Espasa-Calpe, 1945).

Loades, David M. *Intrigue and Treason: The Tudor Court, 1547–1558* (London: Pearson, Longman, 2004).

—— *Mary Tudor: A Life* (Oxford: Basil Blackwell, 1989).

—— *The Reign of Mary Tudor* (2nd ed.; London: Longman Group, Ltd., 1991).

—— "The Personal Religion of Mary I," in Eamon Duffy and David Loades, *The Church of Mary Tudor* (Aldershot: Ashgate Publishing Ltd., 2006).

Loyseleur, Pierre and Hubert Languet. *The Apologie or Defence, of the Most Noble Prince William, by the grace of God, Prince of Orange* (Delft: n.n. 1581).

Lynch, John. *Spain under the Hapsburgs*, vol. I, *Empire and Absolutism, 1516–1598* (New York: New York University Press, 1981).

Machyn, Henry. *Diary of Henry Machyn, Citizen and Merchant-Taylor of London, from A. D. 1550 to A. D. 1563*, edited by John Gough Nichols, Camden Society, vol. 42 (London: J. B. Nichols, 1848).

MacLaurin, C. *Mere Mortals: Medico-Historical Essays, Second Series* (London: Jonathan Cape, 1925).

Madden, Frederick. *Privy Purse Expenses of the Princess Mary, Daughter of King Henry the Eighth, afterwards Queen Mary* (London: William Pickering, 1831).

Malfatti, Cesare V. *The Accession, Coronation, and Marriage of Mary Tudor, as Related in Four manuscripts of the Escorial* (Barcelona: Alianza de Artes Gráficas, 1946).

Maltby, William S. *Alba: A Biography of Fernando Alvarez de Toledo, Third Duke of Alba, 1507–1582* (Berkeley: University of California Press, 1983).

March, José M. *Niñez y juventud de Felipe II: documentos inéditos sobre su educacion civil, literaria y religiosa y su iniciacion al gobierno (1527–1547)* (Madrid: Ministerio de Asuntos Exteriores, 1941).

Mayer, Thomas F. *Reginald Pole, Prince and Prophet* (Cambridge: Cambridge University Press, 2000).

—— and Courtney B. Walters. *The Correspondence of Reginald Pole, a Calendar* (Burlington, VT: Ashgate Publishing Ltd., 2002–2008).

Medley, Dudley J. *A Student's Manual of English Constitutional History* (6th ed.; Oxford: Basil Blackwell, 1925).

Medvei, V. C. "The Illness and Death of Mary Tudor," *Journal of the Royal Society of Medicine* (December 1987), 80:766–70.

Merriman, Roger B. *The Rise of the Spanish Empire in the Old World and in the New* (4 vols.; New York: Macmillan Co., 1925).

Micheli, Giovanni. *"Relazione d'Inghilterra del Clarissimo Giovanni Micheli Detta in Pregadi il dí 13 Maggio 1557,"* in *Relazioni degli Ambasciatori Veneti al Senato,* edited by Eugenio Albèri (Firenze: Tipografia e Calcografia all'Insegna di Clio, 1840), ser. 1.

Mulcahy, Rosemarie. "Philip II, Lover of the Arts," *Philippus II Rex,* edited by Pedro Navascués (Barcelona: Lunwerg Editores, S.A., c. 1998), 34–44.

Muller, James A. (ed.) *The Letters of Stephen Gardiner* (Cambridge: Cambridge University Press, 1933).

Muñoz, Andrés. *Viaje de Felipe Segundo a Inglaterra, por Andrés Muñoz (impreso en Zaragoza en 1554) y relaciones varias relativas al mismo suceso,* edited by Pascual de Gayángos (Madrid: Sociedad de Bibliófilos Españoles, 1877).

Nadal, Santiago. *Los Cuatro Mujeres de Felipe II* (Barcelona: Ediciones Mercedes, 1945).

Nader, Helen. *Liberty in Absolutist Spain: the Habsburg Sale of Towns 1516–1700* (London: Johns Hopkins University Press, 1990).

Navarrete, Martín Fernández, Miguel Salvá, and Pedro Sainz de Baranda. *Colección de Documentos Inéditos para la Historia de España* (Madrid: Viuda de Calero, 1842–1843), vols. 1, 3.

Nichols, John G. (ed.). *Chronicle of Queen Jane and Two Years of Queen Mary and Especially of the Rebellion of Sir Thomas Wyat* (London: Camden Society, 1850).

Noreña, Carlos G. *The Life of Juan Luis Vives* (The Hague: Martinus Nijhoff, 1970).

Osborn, M. L. "Mary Tudor and the Empty Cradle," *Midwife and Health Visitor* (1974), 10:313–16.

Osnaga, Juan de Fray. *"Relación de la guerra del Almirante de Francia contra el Emperador Carlos V,"* 1544, published in P. Manuel

Hoyos, *Historia del Colegio de San Gregorio de Valladolid* (Valladolid, 1928).

Parker, Geoffrey. *Grand Strategy of Philip II* (London: Yale University Press, 1998).

—— *Philip II* (Boston: Little, Brown & Co., 1978).

Parkyn, Robert. "Robert Parkyn's Narrative of the Reformation," edited by Arthur G. Dickens, *Reformation Studies* (London: Hambledon Press, 1982).

Pfandl, Luis. *Felipe II,* trans. by José Corts Grau (2nd ed.; Madrid: Cultura Española, 1942).

Pfandl, Ludwig. *Philipp II: Gemälde eines lebens und einer zeit* (Munich: George D. W. Callwey, 1938).

Pierson, Peter. *Philip II of Spain* (London: Thames & Hudson, 1975).

Pits, John. *Relationvm historicvm de rebus Anglicis* (Paris: Rolin Thierry & Sebastian Cramoisy, 1619).

Prescott, H. F. M. *Spanish Tudor: The Life of Bloody Mary* (London: Constable & Co., Ltd., 1940).

Redworth, Glyn. "Felipe II y las soberanas de Inglaterra," Revista de la Torre de los Lujanes (1997), 33:103–12.

Redworth, Glyn. "Matters Impertinent to Women: Male and Female Monarchy under Philip and Mary," *English Historical Review* (June 1997), 112:597–613.

—— "¿Nuevo mundo u otro mundo?: conquistadores, cortesanos, libros de caballerías y el reinado de Felipe el Breve de Inglaterra," *Actas del Primer Congreso Anglo-Hispano,* Tomo III: *Historia,* eds. Richard Hitchcock and Relph Penny (Madrid: Editorial Castalia, 1994), 113–25.

—— "Philip," *Oxford Dictionary of National Biography,* 44:14–22.

—— and Fernando Checa. "The Kingdoms of Spain: The Courts of the Spanish Habsburgs, 1500–1700," *The Princely Courts of Europe: Ritual, Politics and Culture under the Ancien Régime, 1500–1700,* edited by John Adamson (London: Weidenfeld & Nicolson, n.d.), 46–48.

Relazione di Giovanni Micheli, in *Relazioni dello Impero Britannico nel Secolo XVI Scritte da Veneti Ambasciatori,* Eugenio Albèri (ed.), (Firenze: Società Editrice Fiorentina, 1852).

Revista de Archivos, Bibliotecas, y Museos, (1874), 4:104.

Ribadeneyra, Pedro de. *Vida del P. Francisco de Borja, que fue Duque de Gãdia, y despues Religioso y .III. General de la Compañia de Jesus* (Madrid: Casa de P. Madrigal, 1592).

Richards, Judith M. "Mary Tudor as 'Sole Quene'? Gendering Tudor Monarchy," *Historical Journal* (December 1997), 40:895–924.

Rodríguez-Salgado, M. J. *The Changing Face of Empire, Charles V, Philip II, and Habsburg Authority, 1551–1559* (Cambridge: Cambridge University Press, 1988).

—— and Simon Adams (eds. and trans.) "The Count of Feria's Dispatch to Philip II of 14 November 1558," *Camden Miscellany XXVIII* in *Camden Fourth Series*, 29:302–44.

Rule, John C. and John J. TePaske. *The Character of Philip II: the Problem of Moral Judgments in History* (Boston: D. C. Heath & Co., 1963).

Russell, Elizabeth. "Mary Tudor and Mr. Jorkins," *Historical Research* (October 1990), 63:263–76.

Rymer, Thomas. *Fœdera, Conventiones, Literæ et cujyscunque Generis Acta Publica inter Reges Angliæ, et alios quosvis Imperatores, Reges, Pontifices, Principes, vel Communitates, ab Ineunte Sæculo Duodecimo, viz. Ab Anno 1101 ad nostra usque Tempora, Habita aut Tractata, ex Autographis, infra Secretiores Archivorum Regiorum Thesaurias, per multa Sæcula reconditis, fideliter Exscripta* (London: J. Tonson, 1728), vol. 15.

Salvá, Miguel and Pedro Sainz de Baranda (eds.). *Colección de documentos inéditos para la historia de España* (Madrid: Viuda de Calero, 1850), XVI.

Sancho Rayón, José and Francisco de Zabálburu. *Colección de Documentos Inéditos para la Historia de España* (Madrid: Imprenta de Miguel Ginesta, 1886), vol. 87.

—— *Colección de Documentos Inéditos para la Historia de España* (Madrid: Rafael Marco y Viñas, 1890), vol. 97.

Sarpi, Paolo. *Historia del Concilio Tridentino* ([London: John Bill], 1619).

Scarisbrick, J. J. *Henry VIII* (Berkeley; University of California Press, 1968).

—— *The Reformation and the English People* (Oxford: Basil Blackwell, 1984).

Sedgwick, Henry D. *The House of Guise* (New York: Bobbs-Merrill Co., 1938).

Shagan, Ethan H. "Fetherston, Richard," *ODNB*, 19:453.

Sierra, Adolfo M. "La Neurosis de Deseo de Maria Tudor, Reina de Inglaterra," *Revista de la Asociación Medica Argentina* (30 June 1938), 590–92.

"Sixteenth Century Studies: The Loss of Calais," *North British Review* (December 1866), 45:441–58.

Smith, Richard. *Vita Illvstrissimæ ac piissimæ Dominæ Magdalenæ Montis-Acuti in Anglia Vicecomitissæ* (Rome: Iacob us Mascardus, 1609).

Soranzo, Giacomo. "*Relazione d'Inghilterra di Giacomo Soranzo, T ornato Ambasciatore da quella Corte il 19 Agosto 1554,*" in *Relazioni dello Impero Britannico nel Secolo XVI*, edited by Eugenio Albèri (Firenze: Società Editrice Fiorentina, 1852), part 2, 32.

Soranzo, Giovanni. "*Relazione di Giovanni Soranzo, 1565,*" *Le Relazioni degli Ambasciatori Veneti al Senato durante il Secolo Decimosesto*, edited by Eugenio Albèri (Firenze: Spese dell' Editore, 1861), ser. 1.

Soriano, Michele. "*Relazioni di Filippo II Re di Spagna,*" in Eugenio Albèri (ed.), *Le Relazioni degli ambasciatori veneti al Senato* (Florence: Società Editrice Fiorentina, 1853), ser. 1.

Southern, A. C. *An Elizabethan Recusant House, comprising the Life of Lady Magdalen, Viscountess Montague (1538–1608),* trans. by Cuthbert Fursdon (London: Sands & Co., 1954).

Stone, J. M. *The History of Mary I, Queen of England, as Found in the Public Records, Despatches of Ambassadors in Original Private Letters, and Other Contemporary Documents* (London: Sands & Co., 1901).

Stow, John. *Annales of England, Faithfully collected out of the most authenticall Authors, Records, and other Monuments of Antiquitie, lately corrected, encreased, and continued, from the first inhabitation vntill this present yeere 1600* (London: Ralfe Newbery, 1600).

Strickland, Agnes. *Lives of the Queens of England* (London: Henry Colburn, 1851).

Strype, John. *Historical Memorials, Ecclesiastical and Civil, of Events under the Reign of Queen Mary I*, vol. III, part I of *Ecclesiastical Memorials*

Relating Chiefly to Religion and the Reformation of it and the Emergencies of the Church of England under King Henry VIII, King Edward VI, and Queen Mary I (Oxford: Clarendon Press, 1822).

Sturtz, Edward and Virginia Murphy (eds.). *The Divorce Tracts of Henry VIII* (Angers: Moreana, 1988).

Svoboda, Elizabeth. "All the Signs of Pregnancy Except One: A Baby," *New York Times*, 5 December 2006, D1.

Taylor, Hannis. *The Origin and Growth of the English Constitution* (Boston: Houghton, Mifflin & Co., 1898), vol. 2.

Tellechea Idígoras, José Ignacio. *Fray Bartolomé Carranza: Documentos Históricos*, vol. 22 of *Archivo Documental Español* (Madrid: Real Academia de la Historia, 1966), vol. 3.

Tenison, E. M. *Elizabethan England*, vol. I, 1553–1568 (Royal Leamington Spa, nn., 1933).

Turnbull, William E. (ed.). *Calendar of State Papers, Foreign Series, of the Reign of Edward VI, 1547–1553* (London: Longman, Green, Longman, and Roberts, 1861).

Tyler, Royall (ed.). *Calendar of Letters, Despatches, and State Papers, Relating to the Negotiations between England and Spain, Preserved in the Archives at Vienna, Simancas, Besançon, and Brussels*, vol. 11, *Edward VI and Mary*, vol. 12, *Mary: January–July 1554*, vol. 13, *Mary: July 1554–November 1558* (London: His Majesty's Stationery Office, 1916, 1949, 1954).

Tytler, Patrick F. *England under the Reigns of Edward VI and Mary* (London: Richard Bentley, 1839).

Vales Failde, Javier. *La emperatriz Isabel* (Madrid: Revista de Arch., Bibl., y Museos, 1917).

Vertot, Rene A. *Ambassades de Messieurs de Noailles en Angleterre* (5 vols.; Leyden: Dessaint & Saillant, 1763), vols. 2, 3.

Vives, Juan Luis. *De institutione fœminæ Christianæ, ad Sereniss. D. Catherinã Hispanã, Angliæ Reginam, libri tres, mira eruditione, elegantia, breuitate, facilitate, plane aurei, pietateque & sanctimonia, vere Christiani, Christianæ in primis Virgini, deinde Maritæ, postremo Viduæ, nouo instituendi argumento longe vtilissimi* (Antwerp: Michael Hoochstratanus, 1523).

―――― *Introductio ad Sapientiam. Satellitium siue Symbola. Epistolæ duæ de ratione studii puerilis* (Bruges: Hubert de Crooc, 1526).

——— *A Very Fruteful and Pleasant boke callyd the instruction of a Christen woman, made fyrste in latyne, by the right famous clerk mayster Lewes Uiues, and tourned oute into Englysshe by Richard Hyrde* (London: Thomas Berth, 1541).

Vocht, Henry de. *Monumenta Humanistica Lovaniensia: Texts and Studies about Louvain Humanists in the First Half of the XVIth Century: Erasmus, Vives, Dorpius, Clenardus, Goes, Moringus* (Louvain: Libraire Universitaire, 1934).

Vocht, Henry de (ed.). *Literae Virorum Eruditorum ad Franciscum Craneveldium, 1522–1528* (Louvain: Librairie Universitaire, 1928).

Watson, Foster and William H. Woodward. *Vives and the Renascence Education of Women* (London: Edward Arnold, 1912).

Weikel, Anne. "Mary I," *Oxford Dictionary of National Biography*, 37:111–124.

Weir, Alison. *Elizabeth the Queen* (London: Jonathan Cape, 1998).

Weiss, Charles. *Papiers d'État du Cardinal de Granvelle d'après les Manuscrits de la Bibliothèque de Besançon* (9 vols.; Paris: Imprimerie Royale, 1842–52).

Williams, Penry. *The Later Tudors: England, 1547–1603* (Oxford: Clarendon Press, 1995), 123.

Woodall, Joanna. "An Exemplary Consort: Antonis Mor's Portrait of Mary Tudor," *Art History* (June 1991), 14:192–224.

Woodward, Geoffrey. *Philip II* (New York: Longman, Inc., 1993).

Wriothesley, Charles. *A Chronicle of England during the Reign of the Tudors, from A. D. 1485 to 1559*, edited by William D. Hamilton, Camden Society New Series, vol. 20 (Westminster: Camden Society, 1877).

Index